BOOKS BY ELMER WHEELER

Tested Sentences That Sell
Tested Public Speaking, Revised
Magic Words That Make People Buy
Sizzlemanship: New Tested Selling Sentences
Tested Telegrams
Tested Retail Selling

George D. Bender

1.50

2-8-30 tested sentences-22
Public speech

How to Sell Yourself to Others

HOW TO SELL YOURSELF TO OTHERS

Elmer Wheeler

Prentice-Hall, Inc.
NEW YORK

Second printing, May, 1948
Third printing, August, 1948
Fourth printing, October, 1948
Fifth printing, February, 1949

PRINTED IN THE UNITED STATES OF AMERICA

THANK YOU,

John D. Murphy for your million suggestions—

ACKNOWLEDGMENT

THE AUTHOR wishes to express his thanks to the following copyright owners for permission to quote from their works:

To Harper and Brothers, New York, for the quotation from Merriman Smith's "Thank You, Mr. President," in *How To Get Along With People;* to the Houghton Mifflin Company, Boston, for the material from *The Autobiography of Andrew Carnegie;* to The Ralston Society, Cleveland, for material from *How to Sell Your Way Through Life,* by Napoleon Hill; to Crown Publishers, New York, for the material from *Process of Persuasion,* by Clyde R. Miller.

To *The American Magazine* for the quotes from articles by Merle Crowell, October, 1916; Alfred Pittman, October, 1921; and Bruce Barton, September, 1924.

And finally, to his many friends, for their generous permission to retell their favorite stories.

FOREWORD

Sizzling Your Way through Life

EVERYBODY, AS A CHILD, has sat back and dreamed, built Castles in Spain.

Everybody has dreamed of being a doctor, a lawyer, a merchant chief, dreamed of being a nurse, a wife, a career woman in *real life.*

What has happened to our dreams?

We end up by being an accountant, a housewife or engaging in some everyday occupation.

We still have our dreams—we still make them come true, and the purpose of this book is to help you translate dreams into fact.

It will give you practical, not theoretical ways, to get along better in life—and sell yourself.

It will help you to attain the daydreams that may have blown up, or become nightmares.

There are 101 daily situations in our lives where the right word at the right time will spell success for us. Situations, where the proper technique in getting along with others will help us to attain our Castles in Spain—help us get along better, help us to be richer in life.

Elmer Wheeler

CONTENTS

WHAT DO YOU WANT FROM LIFE?

What is *success?*

I must tell you a story. It is an interesting story of why this, another book on success, got started.

Several years ago a five-year-old boy asked a question that caused me to take a year off and compile this book on how to get along with people.

Like most questions asked by children this one seemed simple enough at first; but answering it wasn't so easy, as you will shortly see.

A group of my friends were sitting around my Stone Study, in Sizzle Ranch, at Dallas, Texas, and we were discussing successful men we know.

During a lull in the conversation, this five-year-old boy, who nobody thought was listening, looked straight at me from his perch in front of the fireplace and asked:

"Mr. Sizzle, what is a successful man?" (I am often called Mr. Sizzle because of our slogan, "Don't Sell the Steak—Sell the Sizzle.")

I realized I was on the spot and suggested that in order to answer the question properly, each guest should write down on a slip of paper his opinion of what constitutes a successful person, after which we could decide who had given the best answer.

A MOST AMAZING "GAME"

There were seven of us in the Stone Study, my workshop that has a large picture window overlooking the pecan trees and our Cactus Swim Pool.

When I opened the seven slips, quite naturally there were seven different answers.

Someone wrote that *success* is attaining *happiness.*

Another wrote that the successful person makes plenty of money to provide for his family and his future.

Another said that the successful person is the one who lives in such a manner that he is respected by his fellows.

Still another said that a man could only be considered a success if his life is of service to others.

While we were still discussing what makes a successful person, this boy popped up with another inspiration.

"Why not look it up in the dictionary?" he asked, simply, as children will ask.

WHAT THE DICTIONARY SAID

It seemed like a good way to settle the matter, so I got down my New Twentieth-Century Dictionary and looked up "success."

Here is what I found:

> SUCCESS:—*satisfactory accomplishment of something attempted—the attainment of any object desired.*

At this point Gene Flack, a high-geared promotional expert, spoke up and said, "It seems to me that we have all been wrong. Success itself is merely accomplishing whatever you set out to do."

My friend John D. Murphy, the magazine writer, said, "We have all been talking about our *own* idea of what we think a person *should* accomplish—and because we all want different things from life, success doesn't mean the same to you as it does to me."

The real answer to the question, "Who is a *successful* person?" would be simply the one who gets what he starts after.

His goal might be large or small. He might want to make a million dollars, or give a good speech. A boy might want to talk his dad out of an ice-cream cone.

Some one wants to get married; another to write a book; another to build a ship; another to get a different job, or a promotion or a date with the beautiful stenographer—or break a bad habit.

The fact remains that if you get what you want, it would be success!

WHAT DO YOU WANT?

Well this started me to thinking.

What do *you* want from Life?

Success is getting what you want from life. I like that definition. It brings success down to earth.

Success is no longer some fuzzy philosophical concept, but something concrete that you could examine and analyze.

This started a secondary discussion. "What is it," asked Clyde Phillips, my friend who is president of the Southwestern Business University in Houston, "that enables some men to accomplish whatever goal they set for themselves while others fail?"

What makes some people *winners* in the game of Life, and others *losers?* That was a good question well put.

"Could it be that there are certain traits or techniques which a man could use to achieve success, regardless of his goal?" quizzed Owen Nicholls, the well-known California hotel manager.

"I think it is largely a matter of a college education," another said.

Right away then someone else quickly pointed out that some of our most successful men have had little formal education.

IT ISN'T ENTIRELY EDUCATION

How true was this last statement, when you note that Thomas Edison had only three months' schooling. Abraham Lincoln was almost wholly self-educated.

Benjamin Franklin never attended school at all. The Wright Brothers weren't scientists but bicycle mechanics by trade.

"It must be good luck," someone else spoke up. "Successful men get all the breaks. They either marry the boss's daughter or are born with a silver spoon in their mouths."

"What about your Charles Curtis, former Vice-President of

the United States," softly asked my Mexican friend, Señor G. Guajardo Davis, head of a large company in Mexico City.

Curtis, he pointed out, was born in an Indian Village and earned his keep by driving a taxi.

"Or H. G. Wells who was born in poverty and had to fight ill health continually," put in another of our group gathered in front of the fire.

Then Professor Hovey said, "A recent survey of the 143 men who are in charge of our largest corporations showed that the average starting wage of all of them was only $13.40 per week.

"Eleven of them started for less than five dollars a week. Forty-three got less than ten dollars a week. Only seven of them received more than twenty-five dollars. That doesn't seem to back up the theory that they started out with a break!!"

WHAT DOES MAKE A WINNER?

"I think we're off on the wrong track again," put in Flack. "We have agreed that success is achievement or accomplishing our goal. And since everything that comes to us in this life must come to us from or through other people, it seems to me that the *ability to get along with people* is the principal ingredient of *success!!"*

We have to sell other people on our ideas—we have to sell them on doing things for us if we ever want to get anywhere. I saw Flack's point.

Then Nicholls turned to me and said, "Elmer, you ought to know something about that. Through your consultant work with firms like Sears, Penneys, Johns Manville, Bering Cigars, American Airlines, Hotels Statler, the Hoover Company, Western Union, Cadillac and others—you've a great selling background.

"You've taught their sales staffs how to sell their products. Don't you think your 'Tested Selling Sentences' techniques could be applied to sell *people* as well as merchandise?"

Hum-m-m that set me to thinking.

People and their hopes, ambitions, dreams, and troubles are as salable as products!

Sure, I could tell people how to sell themselves as well as square clothespins, gasoline, automobiles, cigars!

PERSONAL SIZZLEMANSHIP IS BORN

Well that five-year-old boy had *really* started something. I had never thought about applying "Tested Selling" to people.

I couldn't get the idea out of my head, so I began to make notes every time I met some successful person. I asked plenty of questions on what they figured made them a success.

I listened to what hundreds of successful men I met in my speaking tours had to tell me.

Flack's hunch was correct. When I compared my notes concerning these hundreds of live, present-day successes, I found that they all had *one* thing in common—

THEY KNEW HOW TO SELL THEMSELVES TO OTHERS!

They knew how to sell themselves to their employees—to their employers—and get co-operation and loyalty.

They knew how to sell themselves to their friends, families, neighbors—everybody with whom they came in daily contact.

They *knew* how to sell their ideas.

They *knew* how to get along with people.

They *knew* how to get people to do things they wanted done.

Then I began to dig through old biographies and history books, and got John Murphy to do some of this research for me, since he likes research.

Lo and behold, I found that the successful people even back in history had known how to *sell* themselves to other people too.

They *knew*, too, how to put themselves and their ideas across!

So—backed up by this present-day observation, plus historical research—I sat down to write this book to help you get what you want from Life.

It's All in What You Do—and What You Say

THE NEW FOUR WHEELERPOINTS

WHEELERPOINT 1: *"Don't Make 'em DRINK—Make 'em THIRSTY!"*

You can lead a horse to water, but you can't *make* him drink any more than you can lead a boy to the altar and *make* him say "yes"—without the proverbial shotgun in his ribs.

How much better it is to *make* the horse *thirsty,* and make the boy *want* to say "yes," and that is why this is our fundamental philosophy throughout this book—our *main* point to get along with others and *sell* yourself.

WHEELERPOINT 2: *"Don't Sell an EMPTY Box!"*

Grab bags often prove disappointing, so put something of real value in what you have to offer to others. The more you offer others, the more they flock to your way of thinking. You won't get far offering less than you will receive, which is why this is our second way to make people like you.

WHEELERPOINT 3: *"Get in STEP with People."*

You may have them thirsty—and your bag is filled with value—but unless you get hep and get in step—you will not find a sale for yourself to your friends and others. Tune your thinking to others. Learn *their* interests, hobbies, ambitions—then *swap* them some of these things for something you want in exchange.

WHEELERPOINT 4: *"Make 'em Part of the ACT!"*

If you want people to co-operate, give them a *part* in your *show.* Let them in on the "inside." A person "left out in the cold" can't get very enthusiastic about helping you. Change the "you" and "me" to a "we."

CHAPTER 1

YOU'VE SOMETHING TO "SELL" THE WORLD—WE ARE ALL SALESMEN

Selling isn't something exclusively for "downtown," for "selling" goes into the home, among your friends, neighbors, and even your in-laws.

THE HIGH SCHOOL boy asks, "Dad, may I have the car tonight?" Whether or not he gets it depends on how well he sells the idea to dad.

Mother wants a new sewing machine; sister wants to go to Hollywood; brother needs a new bicycle; and father wants a raise from the boss.

Regardless of who you are or what you want, your success will depend upon your ability to *sell yourself to others.*

The clerk wants to sell the boss on the idea of promoting him, and the boss wants to sell his workers on the idea of their cooperation with his new plans.

The lawyer says, "Ladies and gentlemen of the jury, you are *intelligent* people." He is trying hard to sell them the idea of turning his client loose.

We are *all* "salesmen," morning, noon, and far into the night!

EVERYBODY SELLING SOMETHING

The politician says, "Let's all go to the polls and see that we have honesty and decency in government." He is trying to sell the voters on the idea of electing him to office.

Mrs. Jones is anxious to sell herself to the new neighborhood she just moved into; and Mr. Jones wants to sell the idea that he is a great fellow to the new Civic Club he joined.

The bride wants to sell her husband on the idea that he made a "good deal" when he married her.

Hubby, on the other hand, is trying to sell her the idea of keeping expenses down.

Governments depend heavily on the ability of the diplomatic service, just a high-sounding name for the "selling staff."

Mr. Molotov made himself famous as Russia's star salesman, and Jimmy Byrnes became "Man of the Year" because of the fine job he did with his sizzlemanship ability.

And if Woodrow Wilson had been a better "salesman," perhaps both Mr. Molotov and Mr. Byrnes might not have had anything to sell, and all history would have been changed.

While a sincere and good man, Wilson failed to sell the people of the United States on the League of Nations. He had a good product—his bag of value was filled—but he did not make 'em thirsty, nor did he get hep and get in step.

You see, it takes all FOUR WHEELERPOINTS to sell others!

TAKE YOUR OWN BACK YARD

You don't have to go into history books to see how salesmanship is necessary for the success of *any* undertaking.

Ask yourself this question: "Who is the best doctor in my town?"

"Who is the best lawyer?"

"Who is best in the jewelry business?"

If you are like the average person, you have no idea whatsoever concerning the real technical skill of these people.

The doctor, lawyer, jeweler had a "name" because they "sold" themselves to their communities, and since everybody talked about how good they were, you never once asked to see their diploma or report cards from school.

You just assumed they must be good.

These people sold themselves, just as you can sell yourself once you see how easily it is done.

Some little obscure law clerk may know more law than the most prominent attorney in your city. He isn't successful because he hasn't the "name."

The "obscure" can get a "name," and you'll see how!

A GOOD PRODUCT ISN'T ENOUGH

"The-build-the-better-mousetrap" idea has long been exploded. The world will *not* beat a path to your door, unless you coax it with billboards, road markers, free bus service, and fancy-riding escalators.

The world will buy a mediocre mousetrap that is properly advertised, rather than the perfect one that keeps under cover.

The college student with his head stuffed full of knowledge but with no understanding on how to sell himself and his knowledge to others, is like an automobile manufacturer with a new car and no selling plan.

Often it isn't what you know—but what you *do* about what you know.

Mozart, for example, was one of the greatest creative artists who ever lived. He had the "goods" but didn't know how to sell them. He was so poor he couldn't afford kindling wood, and his wife and he had to dance to keep warm. When he died penniless, he was buried in a box costing three dollars.

After his death, men who knew *how to sell greatness* made many fortunes from his music.

The right formula would have helped Mozart!

BUFFALO BILL'S STORY

Many a hack writer today makes more money than the immortal Edgar Allan Poe, and so did the hack writers of Poe's day make more than he did.

Jenner not only had to find smallpox vaccine, but he had to sell the public on the idea of vaccination before smallpox was stopped.

When Howe invented the sewing machine it was several years before he realized any financial returns from it. He had difficulty in selling women on the new contraption.

Jack Dempsey, with a paralyzing right hand, made no stupendous impression until Jack Kearns took him over and sold him to the American public.

Buffalo Bill was no better rifle shot nor scout than many another man of his day; but when a dime novel writer, Ned Buntline, began to sell Buffalo Bill's talent, he became famous almost overnight.

It took Tommy Dorsey plus a good publicity agent to make Frank Sinatra the hue and cry he is, and to force Sinatra to hire an accountant to figure his income tax.

It isn't what you have, but what is done about it, that counts!

NO TRICK AT ALL

It is no trick to sell yourselves to others, to make them sit up and really notice you and what you have to offer for their friendship, entertainment, fun, or profit.

Charles Schwab once said, "We are all salesmen, every day of our lives. We are selling our ideas, our plans, our energies, our enthusiasms, to those with whom we come in contact. Thus the man of genial personality is bound to accomplish more than the man without it."

"The biggest thing in education," says Dr. Albert Edward Wiggam, "in fact, in all human life, is not selling things, but *selling yourself.*"

Real salesmanship, he says, is talking someone—or a group or a nation—into doing something they don't want to do, and then making them glad they did it!

To do this you don't need a magic wand, and it isn't a question of high-pressure selling, for that has gone out with the cigar-store Indian, the derby, and gold-plated fountain pen.

Low-pressure sizzlemanship is the new thing; don't underestimate it, for it is powerful stuff.

Remember that scientists tried to bombard the atom with high-powered voltage—millions of volts—and failed! Only to find that a *slow moving* "neutron" would do the trick.

Getting along with others—*selling yourself to them*—is no trick at all as you will soon begin to see.

There's a Lot of "Sell" in a Puppy Dog's Tail

CHAPTER 2

DON'T MAKE 'EM DRINK—MAKE 'EM THIRSTY

(Wheelerpoint 1)

IT IS THE most difficult thing in the world to *make* a human being do anything.

You can make a dog jump through a hoop. You can even make a mule do what you want him to do if you're persistent enough.

With people it is different. The surest way to antagonize a person is to give him the idea that you are trying to force him to do something.

Even a small child resents being "made" to do things.

When a mother says to little Johnny, "You *must* drink your milk," he has a tendency to refuse. He may like the milk; but it's instinctive in human nature to resent being forced into anything.

We would rather deny ourselves a genuine pleasure—cut off our nose to spite our face—eat worms—than give another person the "satisfaction" that he has made us do something.

Even Hitler, with all his armed might, had plenty of trouble when he tried to force free peoples to do things.

Our own government has recognized the truth of the statement, "You can't mine coal with bayonets!"

* * *

Ralph Waldo Emerson and his son are trying to force a young calf to leave its stall. The elder Emerson pushes while the son pulls. All to no avail.

The son screams at the calf; but it doesn't budge. Then along comes a servant girl and sticks her finger into the calf's mouth, and leads him willing out of the stall.

This story, as told by Emerson, in his writings, illustrates an important bit of psychology which applies not only to calves—but to humans as well.

It is the most difficult thing in the world to make a human being do anything!

MAKE 'EM THIRSTY

Therefore, Point One to get people to do things is not to drive them to it—but make them *want* to do what you want done.

When they are hungry enough, they'll eat.

When they are thirsty enough, they'll drink.

Successful people never try to make people do things. They know it doesn't pay to try to force people. They realize that even if a person assents outwardly, he will resent it inwardly and take the first opportunity to undermine them.

They know that you can lead a horse to water, but you can't make him drink; that you can lead a boy to the altar, with a shotgun, but when he agrees it is against his will and he'll bend every effort to get out of it as soon as possible.

So *successful people* don't try to make others do things.

My grandmother would say when I put on a pout and wouldn't eat liver, "Oh, he will when he gets hungry enough!"

So put this first secret of getting along with people to use at once; make others *want* to help you!

THE ONE BIG, BIG SECRET

All techniques for selling yourself to others are evolved from this one basic philosophy—make people *want* to do things for you.

That is the big, big secret of "sizzlemanship."

Use word magic that will *arouse a desire* within the other person to *want* to "buy" what you are suggesting.

You can do this by knowing as much as possible about what the other person wants—what makes him thirsty, what makes him hungry, for things in life.

You might appeal to a *need* of the other person; or to a *daydream.* Their hopes, desires, wishes, faults, troubles, all must be appealed to.

Making people *want* is the golden thread that weaves its thoughtful way through this book.

The farmer won't buy milk so long as his own cows produce, but the day the milk pail is dumped accidentally, the housewife makes a straight line for the grocery.

She has a *need* for milk. She *wants* milk. She will buy milk!

DEVELOP YOUR "YOU-ABILITY"

When you approach a person to ask a favor, you should remember two things: First of all, if you attempt to *make* him do anything you are very foolish. You are going against all the laws of human nature.

The second thing you must remember is that the other person is a thousand times more interested in himself than he is in you.

There is nothing wrong about this.

It is nothing to be ashamed of. It just happens to be the way we are made. Of course, like any other trait it can be carried to the extreme and become an evil.

Under normal conditions philosophers say that it is very good we are made this way. It is the law of self-preservation.

Advancement of the human race has always depended upon *individual achievement*. These philosophers have pointed out that the best way a man can help other people is first to be *successful* himself.

A poor man or a weak man can't do much good for others.

It has always been the *successful* individual men who have lifted the race to higher levels of civilization.

That is the meaning of the old proverb, "Charity begins at home." If John D. Rockefeller had given all of his money to the poor when he was starting out, he couldn't have given them millions later on.

So develop "you-ability." Think *you,* not *I.*

MAKE IT A BIG "YOU," LITTLE "I"

In any legitimate "sale" both parties must get something.

The trick is simply to put the spotlight on what the *other person,* not yourself, will get.

The first thing the other fellow wants to know concerning any proposition you bring up to him is, "What do I get out of it?"

So approach him from the *you* angle instead of the *I* angle. He isn't interested in the fact that you are working your way through college.

He doesn't care whether you need one or more sales to win a trip to Atlantic City, and telling him you are behind in your rent won't make *him* thirsty.

Queen Isabella wasn't interested in proving that the earth was round. She didn't care anything about whether Columbus was a great discoverer or just a stumble-bum.

What sold her was the promise of wealth and fame Columbus offered her. *That made her mouth water.* "Here is something for *me!!*" she must have said to herself. And she was sold.

So put this good first rule to use. Magnify the *you,* and minimize the *I.*

When you are dealing with other people, let them look through *their* end of the telescope.

Let them see *how large* is what they will get!

WHAT MAKES OTHERS THIRSTY

When you are spotlighting what the other person will get if he does the things you'd like him to do, stock your mental shelves with desirable "products" to make him thirsty and hungry.

Human beings have many *needs,* but here are the four *basic* ones shared by all of us:

1. The most important human need, according to Psychologist Adler, is the need to feel *important.*
   So sell others the feeling of importance!
2. Another human need is that for *appreciation!*
   So sell others appreciation.
3. Still another human need is to be *liked* by others.
   So supply this *demand.*

4. Human beings are all as *lazy* as they *dare* be and get by.
   So save them extra steps *in life.*

Cater to the comfort and leisure of people—make life easier for them. Let them feel *important.* Give them *appreciation,* and show them how to be better *liked* by other people.

Make people thirsty with these *four basic* principles.

NO SEASONAL MARKET

When you are dealing in human nature, unlike products, there is no seasonal demand. People *want* these four basic things every day of every week of every month of every year!

People *crave* these things.

They steal, invest, murder, love, die to get these *four basic* things!

They save; they strive; they work hard; they scheme; they gamble—to get just these four things out of life.

Then along you come, and show them how they can get these things easily, at little cost, without murder or death, and these people become your best friends.

The market is *wide* open. Help yourself!

AROUSE THESE DESIRES

So when you want other people to do things for you, don't be foolish enough to try to force them.

Make them hungry—make them thirst—for these four basic things everybody in the world wants.

Arouse this desire by becoming a *trader* instead of a *beggar.*

Don't approach people in the attitude of *begging* favors. Trade them one of these four basic commodities in exchange for what you want, and they will do business with you gladly.

There are, of course, many other desires in people, such as making more money, security, imitating Mrs. Jones, love, romance, but these four basic desires will cover 85 per cent of your daily contacts in the world.

Therefore, as your first *law* in winning people over to your way of thinking, put Point One to immediate use:

> *Don't force people, but make them* want *what you have by first making them thirsty and hungry.*

When You Lead a Horse to Water, Don't Try to Make Him Drink—Make Him Thirsty

CHAPTER 3

DON'T SELL AN EMPTY BOX

(Wheelerpoint 2)

You can't sizzle with your tongue in your cheek. Something for nothing is the fool's purchase. Sincerity is the big secret *in getting others to go along with you.*

SEVERAL YEARS AGO I was attending a State Fair. I'm a sucker for carnivals, midways, and shows, because there you meet the people of America! You and you and you!

There is something about the smell of popcorn and cotton candy, and about the barker's spiel, that gets me. I especially like minstrel shows.

So this day I was sitting on the hard board they called a seat, munching popcorn between the acts, when a flashy-dressed gentleman stepped out on the stage with his arms loaded down with boxes.

"Ladees and gentmen," he said, "I have here fifty boxes of the finest candy it is possible to buy. It is delicious—nutritious—and it is packed full of vitamins, minerals, and hormones.

"Also I might add," he went on, "these boxes contain valuable prizes—cameras, electric shavers, ladies hose—now to the first fifty lucky people who raise their hands, I am going to give the privilege of buying these boxes of fine candies.

"Not for five dollars, not for two dollars," he said. "Not even one dollar. You can have this delicious candy *and the big prize* for only fifty cents—now who'll be first—thank you, sir——"

Well, he sold fifty boxes of two bit candy for twenty-five dollars. One man held up a dollar camera. A lady got a pair of cheap stockings. Another man got a fountain pen worth fifty cents. But people weren't too disappointed. They had halfway expected to be fleeced anyway!

FOOLING SOME OF THE PEOPLE SOMETIME

But this supersalesman went too far.

That is the big trouble with such dealings, they always go too far. They don't seem to know when to let well enough alone. They believe it will continue to come easy.

Self-confident over his easy success, he rushed out to the wings and immediately returned with fifty more boxes.

"Now ladees and gentmen," he went on, "I proved to you that I was as good as my word. I was a good sport. I didn't complain when that gentman over there received that expensive camera for only fifty cents.

"So I am gonna see if you are good sports, too. Tell ya what I'm gonna do. If you buy one of these boxes you do so at your *own* risk this time.

"There might be a fifty-dollar bill inside the box you get. Or there might not be anything. I'm not gonna promise, but tell you what I'm gonna do.

"I'm gonna sell these boxes for one dollar each. I am not gonna beg you to take them. In fact, I am only gonna offer them for sale for just three minutes—flat!!

"If you want one, I must ask you not to open it until we finish selling all of them. That a deal, folks?"

All of the boxes were sold *before* the three minutes were up, as the hawker knew only too well because only too well he knew human nature!

Then customers began opening them. One man grinned sheepishly. He drew a blank. Then, one by one the others began to open their boxes. *All were empty.*

The people had paid fifty dollars for fifty empty boxes!!

CAN'T FOOL 'EM ALL THE TIME, THOUGH

The slick hawker smiled genially. "Well, folks, you are good sports—remember now, I didn't promise anything."

A tall, rawboned fellow back in the tent suddenly stood up

and said slow like, "Good sport or not, mister, I'm a aimin' to have one dollar worth of yore deceiving hide!!"

About twenty other people all seemed possessed with the same idea at the same time!

The supersalesman was mobbed. The crowd got their money back, and for good measure tore up the stage furniture.

You see "selling" anything means a fair exchange, and they did not get a fair exchange.

You should never try to sell an empty box!

You should have *more* in the box, in fact, than the other person had hoped to get!

Only in this way can you continue friendships of people, socially or commercially.

"SELLING" MEANS A FAIR EXCHANGE

Step one, you saw, in getting action from others is first to make them hungry and thirsty for something you could give them; and then step two is giving them more than they bargained for.

It is unfair to eat a seven-course dinner at their home, then invite them over for a box lunch!

You won't make friends of others by always driving to the movies in their car; use yours once in awhile. Give like for like.

In fact—give them a nine-course dinner, and use your car *twice* as often as they use theirs, and then you will *surely* have a friend upon whom you can depend.

Any legitimate sale means that each person is to receive something. It is what the lawyers call the "consideration" involved.

If you go into a grocery store and buy a can of beans the grocer gets your twenty cents, and you get twenty cents' worth of beans. If the can was empty when you got home, that grocer wouldn't last long in business.

On the other hand, if your money was found to be a phony, then *you* wouldn't be in circulation long.

"Sizzlemanship," you see, isn't fleecing people.

It is *not* using friend-making technique just for the satisfaction of seeing it work, either; it is using these formulas because deep down in your heart you want to get along better with people and *sell* yourself.

Insincere use of this book, and its many rules and techniques, will not get you far in life once people tumble to the fact you are just using "magic" on them for the sake of "magic" itself.

SINCERITY THE MAGIC TOUCHSTONE

You will find many Tested Methods, many Tested "Selling" Words, and Tested Techniques, used by successful and famous people to put themselves across and to attain success.

But the biggest *success secret* of all is *sincerity!*

Without sincerity none of the methods herein given will work for you. Sincerity is the magic touchstone that makes your personality sizzle instead of fizzle.

Don't think that you can pick up a few tricks, then go out with tongue in cheek, turn on the old personality, and get what you want from life.

Keep false faces for Halloween night only.

Today you've got to have something inside your box. The day of *caveat emptor* is over.

John Wanamaker learned the magic of putting price tags on the merchandise which up until then was whatever the salesperson figured she could get from the customer.

You can't just *pretend to like people*. You *must* like them. You must develop a genuine interest in them.

You can fool some of the people some of the time, but you can't fool all of the people all of the time.

People can easily see through the fourflusher!

UNKINK YOUR PERSONALITY

Instead of using this four point formula, and all the others to follow, to trick other people, concentrate upon developing the kind of *genuine personality* that attracts others naturally.

Each and every one of you is *outstanding* in something that has a sales value. Find it. Then compound it. Give people the baker's dozen—13!

They'll return. They'll tell others. You will soon find you are in the big business of making friends.

If you find that you do not feel a genuine interest in other people, work on your own personality first. Take a tip from the automobile manufacturers. When they get out a new model, they first send it out to the testing grounds.

If there is anything wrong with the car, they don't try to fool the public about it. Instead they go to work to take the "kinks" out of the car. They keep working at it until it becomes the kind of car which will do what the advertisements say it'll do.

Do the same with your personality.

You will find that this book contains the personality traits of successful people. Measure yourself to see how you stack up with them. If you fall short, go to work and get the "kinks" out. Then you'll find yourself succeeding and getting along with people as a matter of course.

It won't be work—it will be second nature!

SUCCESS HAS ITS SYMPTOMS

It is really only when you become a "successful type" person that you can attain any great degree of success.

Several years ago Dr. Flanders Dunbar, in reporting on a study of several thousand accident victims, came out with a startling report.

In her report Dr. Dunbar said that there were "accident type" personalities.

She found that these "accident type" personalities had practically all the accidents regardless of the hazards of their environment. If they took one of these "accident types" off a job on a lathe where he had cut off a finger and put him into an office, he would find some way to have an accident there.

He'd fall off a chair, trip on a rug, burn a finger lighting a cigarette.

Since that time many other prominent doctors have confirmed Dr. Dunbar's findings. One truck driver who had three wrecks in six months was confined to his home.

Believe it or not—just as he was getting well he managed to fall on some stairs and break his arm. Mind you, not fall *down* the stairs but actually fall *up* the stairs!

Accidents seem to seek these people out, because unconsciously they fear failure or are afraid to face life, and having an accident, according to doctors, seems a convenient method of escape.

APPLY TO YOURSELF

Well, when I read this report of Dr. Dunbar, the thought at once occurred to me that the winners in the game of Life are winners largely because of the type of person they are.

They have the "success type" of personality.

Success seems to go out and seek them and chase them all over town!

It is as easy for these "success types" to become successful as it is for a lazy person to become lazy!

Some of our most famous *winners* in history were born in abject poverty, some even in slavery. Even education, at least schoolhouse education, doesn't seem to be necessary.

Physical handicaps, ill health, and repeated "temporary failures," don't seem to be able to keep success from these people.

And, if you were to ask these "success types" why they got that way, you would find, among other things, they would tell you: Give others more than you ask from them.

Don't try to trick others. Radiate personality—but do this with sincerity.

Become GENUINELY Interested in People

CHAPTER 4

GET IN STEP WITH PEOPLE

(Wheelerpoint 3)

THE OTHER DAY I was walking down a street thinking of a lecture I was to give in Shreveport at the Kiwanis Club.

A beggar started toward me. I saw him coming. I knew he would ask for the customary dime, and this upset my thinking about my speech.

When he came up close to me *we clashed!*

I muttered something about no dimes; and he grumbled something about people who do not help others.

He didn't think to get into step with me *before* hitting me up for the dime. So we were therefore going in different directions.

On another day, in another street, a man sidled up to me from the edge of the sidewalk. He got into step with me before I really knew what had happened.

When he asked for the dime, I instinctively reached in and got him one from my pocket. I didn't lose a step. He melted away toward the curb.

This beggar got into step with me!

This, therefore, is the third Wheelerpoint to be used in this simple formula of getting along with people and *selling* yourself to them.

IT WORKS MAGIC

Step one, you learned, was to make people hungry and thirsty for you, or for what you are trying to sell to them or get across to them.

If they aren't hungry, they won't eat. If they aren't thirsty for your companionship, they will go elsewhere.

Next you learned that the quickest way to make them thirsty was to show them a *full box.* That you must give something in return for something.

That people who don't get a fair exchange won't come back to see you soon.

Now this third Point fits into this formula, for even though you make them hungry, and your box is full to the brim, you won't get far unless you line up with the other person.

No matter how attractive your "package of personality," it will have no sale if you square off in front of others.

The good Mexican executive, unlike the American, will not sit facing you across the barrier of a desk. He moves beside you in two comfortable seats, part of every good Mexican business office.

He gets into step with you mentally this way.

GO ALONG WITH OTHERS

I thought about these two beggars and their different methods the other day when I was waiting at an airport for my plane to come in.

Bill Patterson, head of United Airlines, and I were watching the sleek silver ships glide in and take off. It looked so easy it was hard to believe that man had failed to learn the secret of flying for centuries.

"Isn't it wonderful," I said, "how man has *conquered* the air?"

"Don't kid yourself," said Mr. Patterson. "Man has never *conquered* the air, and never will!!"

I looked at him in amazement, but then he went on:

"The attempt to conquer the air is what kept men from flying for so long. The laws of aerodynamics are the same today as they were in Leonardo's time.

"We haven't changed them. We've merely *adjusted* ourselves to them. Every single plane that's built must be made to *conform* with these laws of the air."

I caught on: *Man didn't conquer the air—He merely changed himself.*

I never thought about it in just that way. Those two beggars—

the first didn't get his coffee because he didn't *adjust* himself. He got in my way.

The second one made no attempt to stop me or change me in any way. He changed *his* stride to *go along with others.*

THE OTHER FELLOW'S SHOES

What kept man from learning to fly for so long is the same thing that keeps a lot of people from getting what they want from other people.

They try to figure how to bring the other fellow around to them. The secret is to *adjust yourself* and tune into the other's way. If you want people to go along with *you*—you must get in step with them.

Once you put yourself into the other fellow's shoes, once you get going in the same direction as the other fellow, you can gently guide him around to your way of thinking.

But if you start off in opposite directions, it makes no matter how thirsty the other person, or how full your box, there will only be a smash up!

Before you try to sell a person *your* idea, put yourself in his shoes.

What is *he* interested in?

What does *he* want? What is *his* attitude? What is *he* thinking about?

These things are *handles.*

Once you get your thinking *in step with his* you can use one of these handles to turn his line of thought around to what interests you.

This is what Paul Leach, a reporter for the Chicago *Daily News,* did to get an exclusive interview with Herbert Hoover. Leach was a special correspondent on Hoover's special train across the country.

Many other reporters were aboard and tried vainly to get some comment out of Hoover on national affairs, politics and so forth. Leach also tried plying Hoover with lead questions about politics.

Finally Leach asked Hoover a question about *some mines* they were passing, and Hoover opened up. This ex-mining engineer talked on for more than an hour, and Leach got a good story—but *not until* he had got in step with Hoover's own thinking.

MAGIC OF ASKING QUESTIONS

Big corporations pay large fees to companies that take "polls" and send out questionnaires to find out what their customers are thinking.

They want to know if women, for example, want frying pans that are large or small; square or round; with metal or wooden handles; black or red.

This is so the manufacturer then can get into step with the housewife, and make the things *she* wants, not what the designer thinks she should have.

This pays off.

For when producers get their products in step with the customer's desires and thinking—the products *sell* fast!

You can use this same technique of asking questions to sell yourself or your ideas to others.

Florence Ziegfeld used to stand out in the lobby of the theater as the crowds were leaving, just to overhear their reactions to his plays—this way he kept in step with the public.

Back when automobiles were hard to sell in the depression one of the larger manufacturers drilled all his distributors on the importance of asking leading questions.

Before starting a sales talk, the salesman would ask, "What do *you* like best about this car?"

The customer gave him his cue—his handle—so that the salesman could then point out the things the *customer* wanted to see and hear.*

* Read Elmer Wheeler's *Tested Sentences That Sell* and *Sizzlemanship* for detailed material on how and when to ask questions that get the answers you want.

This is the method that John Patterson used to put over the National Cash Register Company (also H. W. Hoover of the Hoover Company)—each starting with a shoe string—each ending with one of the largest businesses in their fields.

Patterson instructed his salesmen, "Don't be in too big a hurry to make a sale. Ask the customer questions. Find out all you can about *his* needs!"

This is what his salesmen did. They asked all sorts of questions. This pleased their potential customers, because it showed they were interested in their problems.

Then when they knew *which direction* the other fellow was traveling, when they knew what his problems were, they showed him the very type of machine that could help him most.

"TRAVEL AT OWN RISK"

George Little, President of General Features Corporation, famous for his "Showmanship in Business" lecture, used this method one time to settle an insurance claim. His car had suffered a broken windshield by a flying stone on a stretch of road that was being repaired.

The insurance adjuster had turned down his claim on the grounds of gross negligence. The road signs had said: *Travel at your own risk.*

This claims adjuster had a reputation for being tough. But when Little called on him in his office he noticed an etching of two bird dogs on point behind the adjuster's desk.

So instead of flying into him with a lot of tough talk, George asked a question, "Are you a bird hunter?"

The claims adjuster saw him looking at the etching and smiled. "I used to be. Can't get away much any more."

"I have a couple of pointers myself," George said, "which some of my friends tell me I should trade off for setters. What is your opinion?"

The claims adjuster was strictly a pointer man. He spent half an hour explaining why pointers were superior to setters. Long before that he and Little were laughing and talking like old friends.

Then suddenly the adjuster said, "By the way, you're the man with the broken windshield, aren't you? I've been thinking about that case. I believe we can take care of it for you."

Moral: Ask leading questions that get *yourself* into step with others.

FIND WHAT THEY WANT

Remember the story of the two street beggars, the one with the coffee and the one without it. Resolve right now to get in step with others before you try to persuade them to your way of thinking.

Take a lesson from the Wright Brothers and attempt to *adjust* yourself instead of bringing outside conditions around to your way.

Find out what goes on inside the other person's head.

Find out what *he* wants most.

Find out what others are interested in from life, or what they may be interested in *you* for.

Then start making them thirst, fill up the box, and get into step with them.

Once you get going in the same direction, just nudge them slightly and they will change their course to your course.

Asking questions is the *magic formula* for finding your *handle,* so that you can steer the other person down *his* line of thinking.

Socrates was one of the most famous persuaders in all history. He sold his ideas so well that we still study them in school today.

His big secret? This—the "Socratic method of asking questions"!!

"If there is any one secret of success," said Henry Ford, "it is the ability to get the other person's point of view and see things from *his angle* as well as from your own."

Voltaire would say, "Judge a man by his questions rather than by his answers." A principle which John D. Rockefeller knew so well. In any business deal he invariably "broke the ice" by asking questions.

So, summed up: make them hungry and thirsty for what you have to offer; wrap your "personality package" in a *full box;* don't skimp. Then, *ask leading questions so that you can* get into step *with others.*

Work WITH People—Not ON Them

CHAPTER 5

MAKE 'EM PART OF THE ACT

(Wheelerpoint 4)

THE NEW PREACHER wanted to build a new church. He wasn't the first pastor at the church to make the suggestion.

It had been tried many times before, but old Deacon Humphreys had always managed to defeat it. The deacon, you see, had a little money and the influence that went with it.

"What's good enough for my daddy is good enough for me," was the way he always killed the idea when a preacher had the courage to bring it up.

Because everybody knew they couldn't build the church without the deacon, they never pressed the subject but let it drop even though they, too, realized the bad condition of their house of worship.

You can, therefore, understand my complete surprise when I met Deacon Humphreys on the street one day and he asked for a donation for the "new church."

"I thought you were opposed to building a new church?" I asked.

"This new preacher is different," he said. "He's got better ideas —my ideas—on building a real church of the Lord.

"Furthermore," the deacon went on, "he appointed *me* Chairman of the Building Committee—and said he was counting *on me* alone to put it over!"

I wrote out a check for the deacon, and he was off grinning to collect from others, "Yes sire-e-e-e—he is a countin' on *me* to build the new church!"

THE PREACHER'S PHILOSOPHY

Ah, ha, I smelled the rat. I saw through the deacon's own thinking now. I sure wanted to meet that preacher who had done such a selling job on the deacon. Evidently, he knew something about *making people thirsty.*

"I first learned that trick of influencing human behavior when I was a kid in school," the parson told me.

"I'm afraid," he went on, "that I must have been a little stinker. I threw spit balls, dipped the girls' pig tails in ink wells, and became something of a celebrity with the other kids.

"They could always count on me to rout any new teacher. Three times I was threatened with expulsion from school, but my father had good connections on the Board of Education and they always took me back.

"All sorts of punishment were tried—and it only made me worse. Then one year a new teacher came to our schoolhouse. She was smart. Somebody must have warned her about me for the very first day she asked me to stay after school.

" 'Mark,' she said, 'I've heard that the boys in this class don't behave very well. So I am going to appoint you as Chief Monitor to help keep order!!' "

Well it was obvious to me why that new teacher accomplished what all the others had failed to do. She knew she couldn't whip 'em—so she made 'em a part of the act!

This, therefore, becomes the fourth and final Wheelerpoint to get along with people and *sell* yourself.

For if you make them thirst, give them a full box, one that isn't empty, and get into step with them, yet still can't win—then there is only one thing to do.

Retreat just a little. Join up with the other.

A BIG SECRET IN FAMOUS PEOPLE

The engineer tries to pull the long line of freight cars. His wheels just spin. Then he puts the engine in reverse. He can't whip the "sitcheashon," so he joins up with the trouble.

He backs all the cars up so they are tight, no slack—then he starts forward again, and lo, the recalcitrant cars start moving off just as nice as pie.

This is the principle of many famous men, and those perhaps

not so famous as infamous. Adolph Hitler said, "I don't want *followers*—I want *members!*"

Give the devil his due, for any time a comical-looking little paper hanger can sell himself to 80 million people, he knows a little bit about how to get along with people and *sell* himself, even though we don't approve of what he was selling.

Abraham Lincoln used this same method. It has been said that he filled his cabinet with his political enemies. These men caused Lincoln a lot of trouble.

They didn't always agree with him. But he recognized them as strong men and he knew he needed their support to win the war. He couldn't have secured their support with them on the outside—so he brought them inside.

He "jined" up with them—at least momentarily.

He made them members on *his* team, and they carried the ball along *for* him, not "agin" him!

Franklin Roosevelt used this same technique when he appointed Stimson, a prominent Republican, as Secretary of War. Stimson was an able man. More than that, Roosevelt "jined" his political enemies by giving them star positions on *his* team.

Moral: If you can't whip 'em, then jine 'em!

THE INSURANCE STORY

First you make them thirsty. Show them a box that is not empty; then get into step with their wishes—if it still doesn't get you across, then you make them a part of the act.

You bow your head to the winds, until the winds die down, then you start all over again.

Having enemies under your own roof is a good place for them. For you can watch them, and perhaps win them over, for you like people when you know them.

A few years ago a big life insurance company put on a novel advertising campaign in a large Eastern city. Instead of having professional copywriters write their ads, they asked a dozen different prominent businessmen to write a short essay on the importance of life insurance.

These ads didn't cause many newspaper readers to buy life insurance, but several hundreds of dollars' worth was sold to the big shots who had been asked to write the ads.

When they became a part of the insurance show, they sold themselves. In thinking up ideas why other people should buy insurance—they found they liked their own ideas—and so sold themselves.

When I was a kid living in a small town, we didn't have a picture show. Once a year a man with a motion-picture camera would come to town and make movies of all the kids. Then, when he showed the movies in the schoolhouse, every single family in town would attend. He had made the whole town a part of his show.

You see we fear and hate things and people we seldom see. Once we get into that "foreign" land, we find the people are really nice after all. We had just built up a bogy man against them.

So when you join up with a cause you do not approve of, often you find it isn't so bad after all.

When you go out to see that neighbor who is causing you trouble, talk things over with him. Often you come away saying, "He isn't bad when you know him."

Many a person has said of someone, "Oh, he is all right, once you get to know him." You see, you hated the unknown.

WILLIAM WRIGLEY'S SECRET

William Wrigley soon became known as the best soap salesman in his firm, when he was just starting out. He consistently sold "tough accounts" where other salesmen had tried and failed.

One of the methods he used was getting the other fellow to team up with him.

There was one old codger who wouldn't even talk to the soap salesmen, for he didn't want their soap and *that* was final!

So when Wrigley called on him he didn't give him a chance

to brush him off. "I didn't come here to sell you any soap," he said right off the bat.

"W-what's that—" the old fellow asked. "Then what in tarnation do you want then?"

"Well," said Wrigley, "I'm new on this job and I know you know as much about selling soap as anybody in these parts. I'd like to get you to tell me the best way to sell these other merchants."

The tough customer had never bought any soap from the other salesmen, but, by gosh, he sure bought it from this new, young feller, but only after spending a half hour explaining just how to go about selling soap to the other merchants.

Wrigley, you see, enlisted the *help* of his antagonist!!

LET'S YOU AND ME DO IT

Human beings have been compared to sheep in many parables and proverbs. People do like to belong to a "group" or a herd. We are more likely to co-operate with some in *our* group than outside of it.

"He's our kind of people," we say about someone we like. "He doesn't belong!!" we say of one who is on the outside of our particular group.

Moreover, we are more enthusiastic about the outcome of any venture when we are a member instead of an onlooker. The Army found out during the war that soldiers fought better and morale was higher when every man in the field, from general to private, knew the plan of battle.

In this way every man became a participant in an important undertaking. The private wasn't just lying in mud and dodging bullets—he was a part of a team—and he knew *what* he was doing and *why*.

It made him feel important.

Statler of Hotels Statler always said never give an order without explaining *why* you want it done. Never tell a bell hop to go to the tenth floor and close windows.

He will do it grudgingly. Tell him there is a rainstorm on the way, and he will run up to make sure nothing gets wet.

Join them by *telling them your plans and ideas*. Join them by *Learning their plans and ideas*.

You can join—both ways!

"WE," A WONDERFUL WORD

When we say *we* everybody is then automatically included in our thinking. Everybody gets on the team.

Clyde R. Miller, President of the Institute for Propaganda Analysis, calls this the "—together device."

"History is largely the record of the successes and the failures of the Together Device," he says in his *The Process of Persuasion*.*

"The record is seen in the spread of various religions," he goes on, "the rise and fall of feudalism; the Reformation; the rise of capitalism, fascism, communism; the scientific concept; public health movements such as those to fight paralysis and tuberculosis."

The great *persuaders* and salesmen of history knew how to say, or imply, the little word *we* with the big results it gives.

Franklin D. Roosevelt used *we* to perfection. His "My friends" was more than a salutation. It made you feel that he was on *your* side in his fireside chats.

Lincoln knew how to say *we*. His Gettysburg Address is full of *we's*. For example:

> Fourscore and seven years ago *our* Fathers brought forth on this continent a new nation. . . . now *we* are engaged in a great civil war. . . . *We* are met on a great battlefield of that war. *We* have come to dedicate a portion of that field. . . . it is altogether fitting and proper that *we* should do this. . . . the world will little note nor long remember what *we* say here. . . ."

* Quoted by permission. Clyde Raymond Miller, *Process of Persuasion* (New York: Crown, 1946).

Altogether he uses the word *we* ten times; *our* twice; *us* twice. Not once did he use the word *I*.

Imagine, all this *we* and *our* and *us* in a speech that took just four minutes.

I once clocked 13 *I*'s in the first three minutes of another president's speech when he spoke in Oklahoma City. *He lost the election!*

"YOU" GETS YOU PLACES

You is the most powerful word in your language. *We* is the next most powerful. *I* the smallest and weakest.

You and *we* together can go places!

You and *we* together become more powerful than either one by itself.

A friend of mine recently told me how he won a promotion. He had been passed up a couple of times for a job he thought he deserved; so instead of arguing with the boss why *I* should have the job, he went to ask his advice, similar to the way Wrigley sold the soap.

"I would like your advice," he told the boss. "I'll be glad to help," replied the boss. Both were on mutual ground now.

"Well, I feel that I am not getting ahead as fast as I should. Of course, I recognize that there is no vacancy at present. If you were in my shoes, what would you do?"

This time he got the boss on his team. He got a promotion shortly after that.

The idea is do not approach people as an "outsider." Approach them from the *we* and *you* angle. Give them a part to play on *your* team. Use *we* and *our* and *us* and *you* to get them on your side.

The word *co-operation* you know means *operating together*. So if you want people to co-operate, "jine 'em." Give them a job to do.

Summed up, this four-point formula is most simple. You make them thirsty for you or what you have; you show them a full box, not an empty one; you get into step with their thinking.

In most cases that is all you must do. They will be hungry enough to eat, thirsty enough to drink.

They see your display and it looks good to them, for they at once sense that you aren't trying to sell them an empty box. That you are giving like for like.

In fact—giving them *more* than they planned.

Furthermore, you are in step with their wishes, likes, demands, dreams, Castles in Spain, their needs.

You are going along *with* them, not on top of them.

Thus they buy—but often, it is necessary to wean them along farther, and if so, you use this fourth and last Wheelerpoint.

When you see them not buying you as fast as you figured, then don't force them. Join up with them. That is what General Forrest did when he said, "If you can't whip 'em, jine 'em."

Once you are on their team, you can nudge them your way. Once they are on *your* team, they will plug for you.

So remember this formula:

1. *Don't Make 'em Drink—Make 'em Thirsty.*
2. *Don't Sell an* Empty *Box.*
3. *Get in* Step *with People.*
4. *Make 'em Part of the Act.*

SUGGEST—Don't Shove

CHAPTER 6

WHAT'S THE OTHER FELLOW'S ANGLE?

A Short Short Story Number 1

DURING WORLD WAR I a German staff officer summoned Herbert Hoover and indignantly threatened to cut off all food shipments for the Belgian relief.

The American newspapers had printed lies about the Germans, according to this staff officer, and said his people were being "held up as beasts and ogres."

Hoover knew he could not argue with this man by showing him how badly the foodstuffs were needed by the Belgians. If he had chosen to argue on this point, he would have failed.

He had to think of something that would strike closer home—some good personal reason why the Germans should allow the food to continue.

"Think what it will do to *your reputation* if you withhold food from these starving people," Hoover said in a quiet, soft-spoken manner.

"Then the *whole world* will say that the German officers are heartless brutes!"

The food shipments went through!

THE NEWSPAPER PHOTOGRAPHER

A newspaper photographer I know had a system for getting pictures of big shots who were camera shy.

When a big businessman refuses to allow his picture to be taken, this smart photographer doesn't tell him that he will lose his job if he doesn't get the picture.

He doesn't weep that he is behind in his rent—needs a new suit—has a starving wife and ten kids—to gain the sympathy of the big shot. This wouldn't be using the other person's angle.

These are all personal angles—of interest only to the photographer. They do not touch the other person.

So my photographer friend on the *Times Union* of Rochester, New York, merely says:

"That's okay, sir. I think we have one in our files of you at some bathing beach with a blonde!"

Then he gets the picture!

Moral: "You-ability" will get you farther in life with other people than "I-ability." What *you* will receive isn't half so important to others as *what* will happen to them!

"YOU" Are More Important Than "I"

CHAPTER 7

MARCO POLO HAD A DIFFICULT TASK—BUT WON THIS WAY

If you would win a man to your cause, said Abraham Lincoln, *you must first convince him that you are his sincere friend.*

In school you no doubt read the marvelous adventures of Marco Polo, the merchant from Venice who opened the first trade routes from China to Europe.

But if you want to learn a valuable lesson in the art of winning people and getting what you want from life, you will do well to go back and read the story of Marco Polo again.

He was one of history's *greatest* salesmen.

He was a master in the art of getting people to do what he wanted done—yet he did this so easily and naturally that no one suspected they were being "influenced."

People actually *wanted* to do things for him. They considered it a favor to be allowed to give him things.

How did Marco Polo do this? Well, by the simple knack of making people like him.

HE LIKED TO "MIX"

Marco Polo's father, Nicolo, and his uncle, Maffeo, were experienced businessmen. For years they had been prosperous merchants in the city of Venice. They knew how to judge material—what to buy—and how much they could afford to pay for it.

Nicolo Polo was a little worried about his son Marco. Marco, you see, didn't seem to take much interest in business trends, facts, and figures. Marco Polo just liked people.

He liked to go out and mix and mingle with the crowds. He liked to ride up and down the canals of Venice in a gondola and serenade the beautiful girls who waved to him from their balconies. He was carefree and gay, and wherever he went he made people laugh and forget their troubles.

Yet Marco Polo did have a head on his shoulders. His father knew this. "The boy will either be a famous businessman or a famous poet," he would often remark.

So when Nicolo and Maffeo were ready to make their second business trip to China they decided to take Marco Polo along.

A SIX-YEAR JOURNEY

They had made one trip to the "land of the great unknown" and had seen the possibilities it held for a European trader who could do business with Kublai Khan.

China was a land of great riches—of priceless pieces of art—fine fabrics, and all sorts of the other "wonders" which would bring a fancy price back in Venice.

Nicolo and Maffeo had only been partly successful in selling themselves to Kublai Khan. They hoped Marco Polo would turn out to be a good trader, if they could get him away from Venice and get his mind on business.

It took the Polos six years to make the trip from Venice to the kingdom of Kublai Khan. And all the way his father and his uncle were drilling young Marco on how to drive a bargain, how to win an argument and how to do business with the great Khan.

But when they arrived what happened?

MARCO HAS A PLAN

Did Marco call a business conference and try to convince the Khan why he should trade with them?

No!

Marco Polo was still more interested in people than in statistics.

Instead of trying to "convert" the Khan to European ways of thinking, he was more interested in learning from the Khan the oriental way of life.

He made friends with Kublai Khan.

He was such an interesting fellow to have around that the Khan fixed him up with a spare room in the palace and had him move in with him.

Weeks went by and Marco Polo didn't even mention business. Instead he admired the women in the Khan's harem, drank the Khan's wine, and swapped funny stories and jokes.

Nicolo and Maffeo were getting fidgety. Why didn't he get down to business? Why didn't he get busy and work some of the latest thirteenth-century psychological tricks on Khan? The "boy" was a failure. He was getting nowhere.

But Marco had a plan.

A LESSON FOR BUSINESSMEN

Soon, however, they changed their minds. The Khan had taken Marco Polo to his heart. He began to heap expensive gifts upon him.

He made him a member of his Imperial Council. He appointed him his personal representative when Marco wanted to visit other parts of China and learn more of the ways of this strange land.

He even tried to make him a Prince and give him a kingdom of his own.

When the Polos returned to Europe, they were laden down with diamonds, amethysts, fine damasks, and all sorts of other precious treasures that the Khan had given them—*because he wanted to.*

You see, Marco had made the Khan hungry and thirsty to do something for the Polos.

Marco's box of companionship was always full for the Khan; and he got into *step* with the Khan and made him part of the "act."

Marco Polo, therefore, proved to be the best businessman by not being a businessman!

TIMES CHANGE—PEOPLE DON'T

In this fast-moving age, of course, we cannot afford to take up weeks and months of time lolling around spinning jokes and being genial.

Conditions have changed since Marco Polo's day, and if we attempted to move in on some businessman just to have a jolly time for a few weeks we would soon find the "Welcome" sign taken down and one saying, "This way out," put up in its place.

While conditions change, though, *people haven't!*

We still like to do things for the people we like.

When I am out on one of my lecture tours and I see a new book on the care and culture of miniature trees, right away I think, "Phil would like to have that book—he's a nut on trees."

Because I like Phil, I buy the book and send it to him.

When we really like a person, we tend to minimize his mistakes and shortcomings and magnify his good points.

When we dislike a person, just the opposite is true. Nothing he does pleases us.

This was brought home to me the other day when I was telling a friend of mine about a new phonograph record I liked.

"You should hear it," I said. "Who made it?" he asked, and when I told him he said, "I don't like him. He's sissy and too skinny and I just don't like him generally."

"But he can sing," I said. "You really should hear this record."

"Listen," he said, "—even if the guy was good, I still wouldn't like him."

That isn't right. If a fellow has a good voice, we should admit it whether or not we like the way he parts his hair—but, *human nature doesn't work that way!*

SENATOR CLAGHORN IS YOU AND I

We all laugh at Senator Claghorn.

We think it is funny when he won't go to the *Yankee* Stadium. Or when he insists that Ann *Southern* is his favorite actress. He won't accept *Lincoln* pennies, and he doesn't like a compass "because it points *north* instead of *south*."

In a way we are *all* Senator Claghorns. He is funny because he is an exaggeration of one of the traits in human nature.

When we like a thing, we have a tendency to like *everything* associated with that thing.

When we dislike a thing, we tend to *dislike* everything associated with it.

If we like a man, we like his work and his ideas.

If we dislike a man, he may have the best ideas in the world and we won't like them.

OVERCOME THIS TRAIT

These ideas are not mine, nor anyone's in particular. They have been proven true by scientific tests.

A psychologist at Harvard University asked students to rate the merits of literary selections he read to them. All the selections read were written by Robert Louis Stevenson, but the students didn't know this.

Instead, they were told that various writers had written the different selections.

When the very same selections were attributed to some author that the students *liked* they thought they were good—"fine," "excellent," they said.

Yet when the selections were accredited to some author they *didn't like,* they rated them very *low* in literary ability.

Other colleges have made similar tests, and with similar results.

Take Time to Make Friends Before Trying to Make Customers

CHAPTER 8

DON'T HIDE UNDER A BUSHEL BASKET—EXPOSE YOURSELF!

Take your "talents" off the back shelves and do as the successful retailers—put them in the show window for all *to see!*

FRED HEITKAMP, vice president of American Type Founders, told me one day as we sat around Sizzle Ranch, relaxing like the two Doberman pinscher dogs at our feet, "Here is the story of Jim."

Then he told me:

"Jim had been passed up for the promotion we had in mind. Jim was a good worker. He knew his job, and naturally he was resentful.

"What really hurt Jim was the fact they didn't even *consider* him. They never even *thought* about him in our plant, when a promotion came up."

Then Heitkamp went on to tell how he spoke to the man, asking him if he "advertised" himself to his boss.

"How in the world can an individual advertise himself?" said Jim to Heitkamp.

True—Jim could not hang a sign around his neck saying, "I'm a great guy!"

But Jim could have used a little secret I picked up in dealing with some of the most successful people in America during the past seventeen years.

LOW PRESSURE PERSONAL ADS

You cannot hang a sign around your neck. It would get you a name for being conceited, a braggart.

But there are other better ways—more effective than this high-pressure method—that have been used by successful people.

Boasting and bragging won't do it. Acting the part of a pseudo "big shot" won't do it.

You must attract attention to *yourself* if you want to get ahead, and that is why Jim was like so many "good men" who fail to get ahead.

The boss simply doesn't think about them when the time comes. For they have *nothing* on which to fix themselves in his mind, to make them stand out over other prospects for promotion.

A regiment of soldiers passing down the street looks like a blob of khaki. It is difficult to pick out any single individual, unless, of course, somebody is out of step, for there is too much "sameness."

It is the same in the business world. There are thousands and thousands of workers who punch the clock at eighty-thirty—work till five—and leave.

They fit into a common pattern.

How can you possibly pick the genius out of the mob? The answer is that you can't—unless *he steps forward of his own accord*—unless he makes himself *different* from the *average.*

HOW TO ATTRACT ATTENTION

To attract attention *you must be different.* If one sailor dressed in a white middy were marching with the soldiers, he would stand out like a sore thumb.

To attract attention you must, somehow, be different from the mob—but different in a nice way, not like the soldier who has deliberately gone out of step so he will be noticed in the news reels. He'll be *noticed* by his sergeant, too!

Leo Spinelli, a newsboy in Pittsburgh, doubled his sales of papers when he came to work dressed in top hat and tails. He was different from other newsboys.

John Gudel, co-owner and producer of "People Are Funny" radio show, had a lot of trouble getting advertising agencies interested in his show. Then he heard of a Chicago ad agency whose sponsor was dropping one of their biggest shows on short notice.

This left the agency on the spot. It also left them in the market for a new radio show.

Gudel took a piece of wrapping paper, wrote across it—"I have an answer to your problem!" Signed his name and address. "I knew they would get hundreds of long letters," he said, "and I figured my only chance was to be different."

Two days later Gudel received a wire from the agency, "What Is It?" He sold them "People Are Funny."

Then there is the yarn of the shoeshine boy who had a monopoly in his town because of his ingenious sign, "One Shoe Shined *Free*—the other 10 cents!"

Or that old one about the red-haired boy in line for a job who slipped out and had a telegram sent to the personnel interviewer which read, "DON'T HIRE ANYBODY UNTIL YOU SEE THE RED-HEADED BOY AT END OF LINE."

CHARLES SCHWAB'S METHOD

There are, of course, better ways to attract attention without resorting to the bizarre.

One of the *best ways* is to do such an *outstandingly good job* that the boss is compelled to take notice. Don't laugh now and say he won't notice. He will.

This is the method used by Charles Schwab. When given a job to do, he wasn't satisfied in doing just enough to get by. He put everything he had into it. He went all out. He ignored the clock and worked long after closing hours.

He wasn't a clock watcher!

"All successful employers are stalking men who will do the unusual, men who think, men who attract attention by performing more than is expected of them," Schwab said.

"These men," explains Schwab, "have no difficulty in making their worth felt. They stand out above their fellows until their superiors cannot fail to notice them."

My good friend Nate Greenleaf, president of O'Cedar of Canada, told me how one of his employees was always down to work ahead of him, and there when he left. "I just couldn't help noticing this fellow," said Greenleaf, "and today—well, he has a good job in O'Cedar!"

THE CLERK AT ARMOUR'S

Charles H. MacDowell was just a clerk in the Armour Company; but he knew how to step out from the herd. He later became president of the company. How did MacDowell attract attention to himself?

Mr. Armour asked his secretary to make him up a secret telegraphic code for use on a trip he was about to make to Europe. The secretary was a man who didn't believe in doing more than he was paid to do—so he passed the job on to MacDowell.

MacDowell didn't just make up a code. He prepared a small booklet that could be carried in Mr. Armour's pocket. He had the booklet neatly bound and printed.

When the secretary handed the booklet to Armour, he asked, "Who did this?" He asked for MacDowell to be sent in. "Why did you do it this way?" he asked. "I thought it would be easier for you," MacDowell answered.

MacDowell received his first promotion—and gained the attention of the president of the company—by doing a little bit better job than was required.

He didn't try to sell an empty box to Armour!

CARNEGIE, THE TELEGRAPH OPERATOR

Another thing that makes a man stand out from the crowd is the ability to use his head—to know when to take the initiative and act on his *own* account.

Andrew Carnegie was a telegraph operator on the Pennsylvania Railroad. One morning a wreck occurred on the line and his boss, Thomas Scott, was late for work. What was Carnegie to do?

He had no authority to issue orders, to clear the traffic jam which was holding up passenger trains.

If he did issue orders, he would probably be fired—maybe even imprisoned if anything went wrong. The *average* workman would have done nothing—would have said, "That is not my job—why stick my neck out?"

Not Carnegie—for he wasn't average!

Not with the purpose of self-advertisement, he began to send out orders *himself* and signed them Thomas Scott. By the time Scott got to work the lines were all clear.

From then on Carnegie was "made."

The president of the lines sent for him to work in his office. Carnegie, in writing about the chance he took, which might have gotten him fired and criminally prosecuted as well, said:

"The battle for success is more than half won by the young man who is brought personally into contact with high officials; and the aim of every boy should be to do something *beyond* the sphere of his routine duties—something which attracts the attention of those over him."

When it is necessary to violate rules—to take personal command—just *make sure* such action is called for. Use sound judgment. Be sure you know what you are doing—then when you make up your mind, *get to it and come through all out!*

Indeed, at these moments don't hide under a bushel basket!

THE STORY OF THE AMBASSADOR

Joseph P. Kennedy, ex-Ambassador to Great Britain, knew the value of stepping forward—of using original means to make himself one step ahead of the crowd.

When he got out of Harvard, he decided he wanted a job with the famous bank, Hayden, Stone & Company, in New York; but when he went to see Galen Stone about a job, he couldn't get past his secretary.

Mr. Stone wasn't interested, it seems, in interviewing any applicants just now. Besides, he was in a hurry to wind up his business and catch a train for Boston.

Kennedy left the office after finding which train Galen Stone was to ride. That evening when Mr. Stone unfolded his newspaper on the train he found Joseph P. Kennedy sitting across the aisle from him.

Kennedy introduced himself, told him of his unsuccessful attempt to see him at the office, and asked for a job. Stone recognized ingenuity when he saw it. Kennedy got his job.

Kennedy didn't hide under a bushel basket, either!

JANITOR TO PRESIDENT

Maybe you've got a little job. Maybe you figure there is no way to make your *own* job shine. Do you think you could do such an outstanding job of sweeping out a railway station as to make yourself stand out?

Charles Markham did!

E. F. Gerald, an auditor for the Illinois Central Railroad is sitting in a private car on a siding at Deming. Markham comes out with a broom and goes to work—sweeping the station platform; but *what* a sweeper.

He gets every nook and cranny. "He didn't miss any dirt or waste any licks. He handled it like a brisk piece of engineering," thought Gerald to himself.

Gerald calls Mr. Pratt, assistant general superintendent, and points to the way Markham is sweeping the platform. "I said I believed the fellow would bear watching. Well, we did watch him. We had him tried out on some work at the station office and by and by as a result of it all, he was given his first station agency." *

Markham later became president of the Illinois Central!

As Lucius Boomer, chairman of the board of the Waldorf Astoria told me a long time ago:

"If only young men realized that management is always on the lookout for men with the abilities of leadership, men who can be promoted to responsible positions. We are always in the market

* Quotations from Alfred Pittman, *American Magazine,* October, 1921.

for a man who can bring us in more business or develop newer and better ways of doing a hotel job."

And as Howard Dugan, vice president of Hotels Statler, said, "But such men are hard to find. Maybe we have such men in our company now; but unless they step forward, we cannot see the nugget that might be buried beneath a block of stone and earth."

So don't wait to be sought out—*step forward* and give some little glimmer of the gold underneath you!

999 TIMES IN 1,000

When promotions are handed out 999 times out of a thousand, the boss picks the man who "impresses" him favorably—meaning his personality—rather than by taking a calculating machine and computing his percentage of hits and misses, or figuring out his efficiency quotient.

Douglas Lurton, editor of *Your Life* Magazine, in his fine book, *Make the Most of Your Life,** cites numerous surveys of hundreds of companies which bring out the fact that *personality factors* are most important in getting a raise or a promotion.

The American Institute of Banking made a survey which showed that 23 per cent lost out on promotions because they did not have the ability, while 77 per cent missed the boat because of personality deficiencies.

Ability is always taken for granted by the big boss.

You *must* have that. But if you have all the ability in the world, but keep it under cover, you are like the merchant who keeps his stock in the back room, out of sight and so out of the customer's mind.

The boss hasn't X-ray vision.

He can't look inside your head and see how many brains you have. He can only judge you by *how* you *impress* him—and you *can* impress him fastest by *expressing* yourself.

* Douglas Lurton, *Make the Most of Your Life* (New York: Whittlesey House, 1945).

Use your head to express yourself. A person who can think will be an unusual attraction just by *thinking*.

The big slogan of the International Business Machines company, the one you see in offices everywhere in America, is just the one little, tiny word: *T-h-i-n-k!*

Use your brawn to attract attention by doing more and better work; but remember to make it a "slow moving sizzle." The braggart, the blowhard, the boaster sell themselves, maybe, but not the brass hats!

So:

Don't hang your talents behind an iron curtain;
don't hide behind a bushel basket.

Use Showmanship—But Don't Just Be a "Show Off"

CHAPTER 9

WILL ROGERS' SECRET

A magic way to win more friendships that no one can resist; even hardened criminals can be won over this way.

"I NEVER MET a man I did not like," said Will Rogers.

Many people thought this was just another funny Rogers' remark, but one time when I met him with Amon Carter, of Fort Worth, I asked him, "Surely you can't like everybody?"

I knew he must meet bores, cheats, fourflushers just like the rest of us do. How can he possibly like even them?

Will was famous as a funnyman; but he was also a wise philosopher and he could be most serious when he wanted.

"Of course I don't approve of all the things that people do," he said, "but there is some goodness and some cussedness in all of us."

He continued, "If you know a man well enough you can always find something good in him and you can always find something interesting about him. *It is just a matter of what you are looking for!*"

GOSSIPS, NARROW-MINDED, TOO?

"But what about the narrow-minded people? What about gossips? The people who do petty, mean little things? Do you like them, too?" I persisted.

"I once read somewhere," he said, "where someone asked Abe Lincoln that same question—why he refused to get mad at the people who abused him, ridiculed him and tried to discredit him.

"Lincoln replied that people's actions spring from their character and that many factors beyond their control went into making up their character—where they were born, the people they had associated with, and a lot of other things.

" 'Therefore,' said Lincoln, 'you shouldn't become angry with a person who blocks your path any more than you would with a tree which the wind blew across the road.' "

Will Rogers had no more reason for hating a person who happened to have been unfortunate enough to have acquired a habit of gossip than he did for hating a person who was foolish enough to neglect his teeth.

He didn't like gossip. Few people do; and he didn't like pettiness. He looked upon them as *foolish* behavior rather than *evil* behavior.

I am convinced that Will Rogers really did like every man he ever met.

EVERYBODY LIKED WILL

There is an interesting thing about liking people, and that is they in turn like you.

If you must start a rumor about somebody start it by saying, "I sure like that person."

This gets back to them and they say, "Well, I always liked him, too."

Another funny thing about gossip is that if they tell you things about others, you can just bet they will tell others things about you.

While there is always a temptation to listen to gossip, just remember while you are on the listening end this time with this gossiper, the next time *you* will be on the receiving end when the gossiper gets elsewhere.

Beware of the Gossip!

Avoid the company of the gossip. Don't give him a *chance* to be with you, find something out about you, then carry that story into another circle.

I am convinced that this trait of his character was largely responsible for Will Rogers being the most universally liked person I have ever heard about.

Will Rogers liked everybody *and everybody liked* Will Rogers!

THE REASON FOR THIS

The biggest compliment you can pay a human being is to like him!

Ever consider *that?*

It does something to us inside to know that someone likes us.

It makes us feel good. It inflates our ego. It makes us feel *important*—and it touches our heart. Instinctively we like a person who likes us.

So if you *must* gossip, gossip about how nice people are. The "gossip carriers" in every circle will soon carry that back to the other person and you've made a friend.

You can *use* "gossip carriers" this way. Let them carry good things—not bad things. Be careful that they can't *twist* things you say.

And, if you want to *stop* a gossip dead, use Walter Winchell's pet method: "If you don't stop telling lies about me, sir, I will start telling the *truth* about you!"

This usually frightens the gossip!

THE "WINNING PERSONALITY"

Whenever you see a man who has a "winning personality"—a person whom people instinctively "take to"—you can put it down that person has a genuine interest in other people.

Everybody liked my grandpop because he put his arms around you, "mentally," while you talked. He leaned forward physically *and* mentally. He was genuinely interested.

He was a *good listener* first, and good talker second!

The secret of people's liking a "winning personality" is that he, first, likes them.

Mark Twain was such a person. Theodore Roosevelt was another. They knew that this trait was the quickest way to make people like you—like them.

When you like people you are not appealing to their intellect. You are appealing to a deep-rooted *instinct.*

Animals are also responsive to this instinctive reflex.

Every sportsman knows that dogs and horses can *tell* when they meet a person who likes dogs and horses, and who doesn't.

Remember that old one, "Love me, love my dog!" A lot of truth in that old saying.

When you approach Sizzle Ranch, my Doberman pinschers soon sense who is friendly, who is not, though once they did miss a process server!!

DOOR TO DOOR SALESMEN

Wally Powell, director of sales education for The Hoover Company, has often told me in our fireside chats that all dogs liked him because he liked them.

When salesmen reported that they had been chased away from a certain house by a so-called bad dog, Wally would go out and have no trouble at all.

When I asked him his secret, he said, "I like dogs."

Wally Powell used his power over dogs to make sales. Once inside a home he would quickly look for a pet—cat, dog, or canary.

If it was a cat or a dog, he would ask the name. Then play with the animal, and the woman, seeing how nicely the man got along with her pet, would listen to him.

If a canary, he would ask if the canary sang. Naturally all women like to make their canaries sing, and this was a good "sale opener" for the man with the vacuum cleaner.

So many people take pride in *not* liking dogs. It is a mistake. A dog tells his master a *lot* about you, so better start liking dogs.

Pretending won't do. The dog "sees through" pretension. Albert Payson Terhune, the great dog writer, told us that.

You must *sincerely* like dogs, or other animals. Pretending to be a horse lover might cause the horse to show others that you are just pretending. He may toss you.

Pretending to like a dog is dangerous. He might prove to his master you are pretending, by biting you.

Be sincere. Like or dislike. But do it sincerely. Not behind people's, or animals', backs!

THE MILD-MANNERED SUNDAY SCHOOL TEACHER

Even hardened criminals can be influenced by the same sort of magic used by Will Rogers.

Late Monday night, December 4, 1944, twenty-five desperate convicts in the Federal Penitentiary at Atlanta, Georgia, mutinied. They captured four guards and held them as hostages, barricading themselves in their five story "isolation building," armed with clubs and razors.

Seventy-eight other inmates of the block were also held as captives, some of them perhaps willingly. The men quartered in this building were the pen's toughest customers. They were considered so incorrigible they were kept separated from the other 1900 prisoners and ate, slept, and worked in this one building.

All available guns were trained on the building. Warden Sanford dared not move in on the desperadoes, for fear of causing the deaths of the four guards being held as hostages. Heat and water were cut off in the building. The men inside had no food.

By Wednesday afternoon they had shown no signs of weakening. Instead they issued an ultimatum to the warden that unless they were served food by 5 P.M., they would toss two German spies, fellow inmates, off the roof of the building.

MORGAN BLAKE'S SELLING JOB

The mutineers asked that they be allowed to talk with Morgan Blake, an editorial writer on the staff of the Atlanta *Journal*. Blake had conducted religious services inside the pen a number of times.

These men had also heard his regular Sunday morning broadcast over radio station WSB, teaching the Agoga Bible Class from the Baptist Tabernacle.

More than twenty years before, Blake had determined to help

down-and-outers every way he could. When he preached to the convicts in the penitentiary he didn't make them feel that he looked down upon them or despised them.

"I'd be in the same place you are, but for the Grace of God," he told them, paraphrasing Doctor Johnson. "Don't think you are no good just because you've made mistakes."

This was something new to these convicts. Here was a man who didn't despise them. He seemed actually to like them and want to help them.

So these convicts asked to talk to Blake; and they refused to negotiate with anyone else.

It was decided to call in Blake.

BLAKE ARRIVES

James V. Bennett of Washington, Director of the Federal Bureau of Prisons, and Warden Sanford conferred hurriedly and decided to send for Blake.

The mild-mannered, fifty-five-year-old editorial writer and Sunday School teacher had just returned from his mother's funeral but he went immediately to the penitentiary. Unarmed, he went to the very building.

He broke the ice by reminding them of the fine record the inmates had earned during the war by earning some $4,900,000 for the Federal Government and $959,000,000 for themselves in turning out tents, knapsacks, and other essential articles for the armed services.

"I told them at the very start that the men of the Federal Prison of Atlanta had earned the admiration of the entire nation for their magnificent contribution to the war effort.

"I hoped fervently they would not continue their rebellion which would be a black mark on the institution and cause heartaches to the vast majority of the men behind the bars there."

The men listened, stony faced. Then one of the prisoners said, "Why don't you come inside, Mr. Blake. It is more comfortable in here and we promise we won't harm a hair of your head."

Blake's eyes twinkled characteristically. "Thank you for the invitation," he said, "but I can assure you I am quite comfortable out here!"

The men looked at Blake shivering in the freezing cold outside, his face purple, and they began to laugh.

"We both laughed at that," said Blake, "and the tension was relieved."

THE MEN GIVE UP

The men told Blake they had been treated unfairly at the prison and agreed to surrender to him if he would take up their grievances for them and write an article, under his own name, in the paper, outlining their grievances.

The men claimed they had insufficient medical treatment; that there had been no religious services conducted in their building for the past six months; that they had lower wages than other inmates.

They told how they were unjustly quartered with Nazi *saboteurs* and had to listen to them brag on Hitler; that they were denied the privilege of communicating with the outside world, and did not receive proper recreational activities or exercise.

Blake published these grievances and carried five copies of the Atlanta *Journal* to the pen the next day. When he showed the front page story to the prisoners they surrendered themselves to Blake and turned over to him the keys of their building.

One unarmed, one-hundred-twenty-pound Sunday School teacher marched 101 mutinous criminals to Warden Sanford! A mild-mannered, stooped, soft-spoken man *who liked people,* even criminals!

A man who saw some good in everybody accomplished what guns, force, threats had failed to do.

Hunger, cold, fear of severe punishment failed to influence these men; they were influenced by the words of a man who could see something good—even in hardened criminals.

In Washington, Francis Biddle, the then Attorney General, praised Blake's work and gave him full credit for rescuing the four guards and putting down the mutiny.

"Blake is really the man who solved this thing," he said.

So you see, as Will Rogers said, people *like* people who like them, and will do things for people who will do things in return.

Animals even respond to this instinct in humans; hardened criminals will react—anybody, even the gossip down the street—will be forced to react if you meet her gossip with nice remarks.

Summed up, we might give this as the rule to practice:

> *The easiest way to make people like you right off the bat is to develop a* genuine *and* sincere *interest in people.*

"Likes" Seem to Attract "Likes"

CHAPTER 10

THE SECRET OF THE HYPNOTIST'S MYSTERIOUS "POWER"

"Many a treasure besides Ali Baba's is unlocked with a verbal key." There is a knack in asking the questions that get the answers you *want.*

I'LL NEVER FORGET my first encounter with that mysterious force which has been called "The most powerful influence in the world," the power of suggestion.

One day while I was lecturing at Harvard University's business division, a psychology professor came in with three bottles. He asked could he use my class for a short test.

"Students," he said, "I want to test the air currents in this room. I am going to uncork a bottle of violet perfume. As soon as you smell it, please raise your hand."

He uncorked the bottle and soon hands were raised all over the room.

I even smelled it myself. Then the professor showed us that he had uncorked a bottle of plain water!

The suggestion that we would smell the perfume made us actually *smell it!*

This was especially true after the first few hands went up, and if you want to try this experiment, you'll be amazed yourself. Cock your head to one side as if listening intently and ask, "Do you hear a bee in this room?"

If there are enough people present, several will "hear" the imaginary bee.

THE RED-HOT-POKER STUNT

I once attended an initiation where a student was blindfolded and told that he was to be branded on the stomach with a red-hot iron. A poker was placed in a heater.

All the members of the group kept talking about—"get it red hot"—"it won't hurt much"—"don't hold it on him"—"just a light touch."

The poker was removed from the stove. The student's mid-section was bared. The boy with the poker pressed it against a piece of beefsteak held near the student's stomach which gave a sizzling sound and smell.

At the same time the poker was pressed against the beefsteak, an ordinary piece of ice was placed against the bare skin of the student's stomach. He gave a terrified yelp. He was burned—and *he knew it.*

He could smell the flesh burning. He could *hear* it sizzling. Afterward he told me that the pain was as intense as if he had actually been branded by the poker.

That is the *power of suggestion.*

That is why you call suggestion the most powerful force in the world.

About 99 per cent of our own beliefs and habits are the result —not of having thought the matter out for ourselves—but suggestion from others!

We adopt the manners, the speech, voice, accent, of those who live around us—all due to suggestion!

THE HYPNOTIST'S SECRET

If you've ever wondered what "strange hypnotic power" the stage hypnotist possesses, there isn't any, as my friend, John D. Murphy, writer on psychology, has often told me.

"There is no such thing as a person possessing 'hypnotic power' over another," he explains. "It is all a matter of suggestion—and the real power is in the *subject,* not in the *operator.*"

"Hypnotism itself," he says, "is nothing more or less than a state of *heightened susceptibility* to suggestion. The operator uses words which suggest sleep, relaxation, and mental passivity. With these suggestions he gradually builds up a degree of suggestibility in the subject to the point where he will believe anything—however bizarre—the operator tells him.

"The same force that you see displayed in the case of the hypnotized person *operates continually upon people in ordinary wakeful consciousness*—although usually at a lower level."

As an illustration of how far wakeful suggestion can be carried, Murphy told me of the experiments of Dr. W. R. Wells of Syracuse University.

Dr. Wells has succeeded in duplicating every one of the hypnotist's stunts—anesthesia—amnesia—inability to rise from a chair, etc.—in his students by using suggestion with the student wide awake.

No mention is ever made of putting the subject to sleep. He merely is told to relax, and Dr. Wells repeats his suggestions over and over in a confident tone of voice.

Suggestion, you see, is not a mystical something given only to a few. Anybody can with practice cultivate this ability as you will shortly see.

IN EVERYDAY LIFE

Now I am not suggesting that you go out in life and try to hypnotize people, especially those who owe you money. This would not be advisable, and fortunately is not necessary.

People react to suggestion in many forms in everyday life.

The salesperson holds up a toothbrush to the customer who has just purchased a mouth wash and says, "This new type brush cleans *between* the teeth." A sale is made by suggestion.

You see you just cannot help using suggestion in dealing with others; but what you can help is whether you use suggestion to create a favorable impression or one not favorable.

"I suggest this type paint," says the Sherwin Williams salesman, "because it will make your room seem larger!"

"I suggest a two-door car, sir," says the salesman, "because your children cannot reach the handle and open it while you are driving!"

Both are good *sound* suggestions that prove profitable to the hearer—and the speaker, alike.

Later you will see how you can use the *tone of voice*—clothes you wear, mannerisms, to suggest competence, *success*, and ability to others.

WORDS THAT "SUGGEST"

In his autobiography Andrew Carnegie tells how his brother used words to suggest what he wanted the other fellow to accept.

Colonel Piper, a partner in one of the Carnegie enterprises, was complaining to Thomas Carnegie about a contract with another Carnegie enterprise in which Colonel Piper was not a partner.

"The prices were *net* and nothing had been said about net when the bargain was made. He [Colonel Piper] wanted to know just what the word net meant.

" 'Well Colonel,' my brother said, 'it means that nothing more is to be added.'

" 'All right, Thomas,' said the Colonel, entirely satisfied.

"There is much in the way one puts things. 'Nothing to be *deducted*' might have caused a dispute."

Remember you can "suggest," but seldom can "shove" others.

"I didn't make myself quite clear," gets better reaction than, "You didn't make *yourself* clear."

A fellow during gasoline rationing was asked why he needed more stamps, and his humble, honest reply was, "To haul my wife to work!"

He got 'em!

"ONE YEAR TO PAY"

During World War II a wholesale drug concern made application to the rationing board for additional gasoline coupons for a "drug salesman." The request was denied. "Salesmen" could not get extra gas as too many salesmen found out.

Another application was filled out but this time somebody used word magic; for they asked for the coupons for a "medical supplies representative." The application was approved.

"Only one-fifth down," sounds less than 20 per cent down.

"It costs five hundred and thirty-two cents," sounds less than to say it costs "five *dollars* and thirty-two *cents*."

$2.98 is only two cents less than three dollars, but tests have shown that many people who will pay $2.98 won't pay an even three dollars.

But—if the price is $2.60, many people think you *raised* it from $2.50.

"Fifty-two weeks to pay" suggests a longer time than "one year to pay."

"It costs only two dimes a day," makes more sales than to say, "The total cost will be $79.50." The Hoover Company proved this one.

In short, pick your words so that they will put the *spotlight* on the *roses* and leave the thorns in the shadow!

NOT "IF" BUT "WHICH"

Those of you who have read our business psychology books* will find our fourth Wheelerpoint in them is: "Don't Ask If—Ask Which"; always give the other person a choice between *something* and *something,* not between *something* and *nothing.*

How true this is socially as well as commercially!

"You'll have trouble with this if you don't keep it at this degree," is bad sizzlemanship. Much better to say, "You will get *great pleasure* if you keep it at this degree!"

I scream at the instructions being issued by manufacturers that start out with: WARNING—DANGER—BE SURE. You frighten the user.

The vacuum cleaner company changed a red dot from "danger" signal to "time-to-empty" signal and sales jumped.

A husband changed "my house" and "my car" to "our house" and "our car," and got along better with his wife!

Never say to others, "Will you do this?" Instead say, "*When* you do this . . ."

When we instructed the Walgreen Drug soda clerks to say,

* Elmer Wheeler, *Tested Sentences That Sell* (New York: Prentice-Hall, Inc., 1938), *Sizzlemanship* (New York: Prentice-Hall, Inc., 1940).

"One or two eggs in your malt?" we sold many more than when they formerly said, "Want an egg in the malt today?"

This same principle works in human relationships!

MANY "WHICH" USES

Never ask someone you want to "date," "May I see you tonight?" but "What time may I see you, seven or eight?"

Never say to the boy friend, or hubby, "Are we going out tonight?" Instead say, "Where are we going tonight, dear, to the movies or dancing!"

Of course he'll quickly figure which is the cheaper—but ladies, you'll go somewhere instead of sitting home holding hands.

Always give sweethearts or husband, ladies, a *choice* between something *you* want and something else *you* want, and let the old boy figure out which *he* wants!

You can't lose on that word magic!

I never like signs that say SANITARY BARBER SHOP. I wonder why they had to use the word "sanitary." Weren't barber shops always sanitary?

Use this psychology: Accentuate the positive, and eliminate the negative!

"Is that all?" is poor suggestion in a retail store. "What else?" suggests the other person may want something more.

Avoid these negatives in handling people:

> "I suppose you think I am crazy, but . . ."
> "I guess you think I have nerve, but . . ."
> "Doesn't my hair look a fright?"
> "I hope I haven't bored you . . ."
> "You probably won't want to see me again . . ."
> "I doubt if this will interest you, but . . ."
> "You wouldn't want to go out, would you . . . ?"

Instead, be a little hypnotist with words. Ask the questions that are positive—that get the answers *you* want—ask leading questions like a good lawyer.

MONEY ORDER RECEIPT

533 S. 200 West * Portland, IN 47371

Account #: **7000** **3/22/2013**

Check #: **9035004431**

Amount: **$75.00** Fee: **$0.89**

Pay To The
Order Of: ______________________________

Memo: ______________________________

SERVICE CHARGE: If the money order is not used or cashed (presented for payment) within (6) months of purchase date there will be a non-refundable administrative service charge, where permitted by law. The administrative service charge will be deducted from the face value shown on the money order. The administrative service charge shall be a monthly charge equal to 1 1/2% of the face value shown on the money order for each month retroactive to the beginning of such (6) months period, or if lower, the maximum amount permitted by law. The administrative charge assessed at the end of the six (6) months period shall be applied retroactive to the date of purchase.

LIMITED RECOURSE: This Money Order will not be paid if it has been forged, altered, is a copy or stolen and in that event recourse shall be had only against the Endorser. This means that persons accepting this Money Order should accept it only from those known to them and against whom they have effective recourse. If the need arises to trace this money order, contact 3T, Inc. at 877-343-9900. There is an administrative service charge to trace money order. Charges may vary.

Thank You For Shopping With Us!

"The more you think about my ideas, the more you will agree," is a sound way to win someone over to your side.

Use words which *take for granted* that your listener *does* want to do what you suggest.

Adroit suggestions can often change a "no" into a "yes," if you use words that prohibit a "no" in the start.

But be *sincere* in the use of this word magic. Using it just to gain things won't win you lasting friends.

Be sure your box isn't empty when you use a "which," "when," "where," "what," or "how."

Give value received.

A good "which" well placed will make the other person hungry and thirsty to come over to your way of thinking.

Make your "which" get into step with the other person. Give them a choice between something they won't want, and something they *do* want.

You may not want to be a hypnotist—but a little suggestion is a *powerful* instrument in the hands of the right person.

So practice this good "lawyer rule":

> *Always give others a choice between* something *and* something, *not between* something *and* nothing!

Use TAKE-FOR-GRANTED Words

CHAPTER 11

TRY THIS MAGIC FORMULA

A Short Short Story Number 2

In 1934 Maytor H. McKinley was thirty-two years old and out of a job, which was typical of this depression era.

Finally he got a job with Utter-McKinley Mortuaries in Los Angeles, and within a year had doubled the company's business and had bought one-third interest in the business.

A few years later he bought out the *entire* business!

Today his business is one of the seven largest of its kind in the United States, which perhaps means the world.

Now if you are wondering what magic wand Maytor McKinley waved over his business, it was the same kind of magic that my good friend J. C. Penney advocates.

It is the *golden rule* in any business: treating others as you would like to be treated!

McKinley's company creed is: *To serve every family as if they were our own. . . . To treat every woman as if she were our own mother or sister. . . . Every man as if he were our father or brother.*

That is the kind of genuine fellowship and courtesy that can never fail to get you ahead in business, social life, in community life, or any other situation involving human relations.

PRACTICE THIS CREED

If you are a salesperson in a retail store trying to treat your customers as you would like to be treated, you will *succeed* over somebody right next to you who is merely "working for a few dollars a week."

Be as considerate of each woman as if she were your own mother—each man as if he were your own father—and watch sales records go sky high for you as they did for Maytor McKinley during the great depression years.

If you have just moved into a new neighborhood, try treating your neighbors as you would like to be treated.

If you have people working under you try treating them as you would like your boss to treat you.

And don't forget the children. When you are tempted to scold, stop and ask yourself, "How would I like to have some giant standing over me saying *'I'll tear you up if you do that one more time'?*"

Remember the schoolteacher who made the bully "Chief Monitor"; the mother who told her noneating child that Popeye eats *his* spinach!

Use word magic!

WHAT WE CALL "MANNERS"

"The only true source of politeness is consideration—that vigilant moral sense which never loses sight of the rights, the claims, and the *sensibilities* of others. This is the one quality, over all others, necessary to make a gentleman" are the wise words of William Gilmore Simms.

What we call "manners" are but the surface advertisements of the consideration we have for others in our hearts.

Advertise to others that you have an interest in them with your *smile,* with your *words,* with your warm friendly *handclasp.*

But don't try to counterfeit smiles, words, handclasps.

Don't "sweet talk" people if you don't mean it.

"Nothing except what flows from the heart can render even external manners truly pleasing," says the great Hugh Blair.

On the other hand if you do have genuine regard for other people, it is cruel and stupid not to show it.

It is so easy to accomplish with a friendly smile, word, and handclasp!

Moral:

> *We cannot always oblige, but we can always speak obligingly.*—VOLTAIRE

Concentrate on What You Can Do FOR People—Not What You Can Do Them For

CHAPTER 12

HOW TO KEEP FROM LOSING FRIENDS

Take the case of Weber and Fields—or of the "two Governors." The method of Rockefeller, Disraeli, and Lincoln. A small chapter—but with lots of meat in it. Note: *read it three times!*

YOU COULD WRITE a whole book on this chapter title alone, but that is not the purpose of this book.

You will continually find, in every chapter, methods, ideas, and ways to keep from losing friends.

It is my purpose in this chapter to point out how some 12 or 13 famous personalities in history, from Abbott and Costello of the present to Disraeli of the past, made friends by *not* losing friends.

Take the story of Rockefeller as reported by Bruce Barton in *American Magazine* of September, 1924. Here is the substance of the story:

An angry man strode into the office of a young business executive. The name on the door was John D. Rockefeller.

The angry man walked over to the young man behind the desk and proceeded in no uncertain tone of voice to "tell him off." He shouted, "I hate you—and I am going to tell you why."

For a quarter of an hour the angry man did tell off Rockefeller. Never once did Rockefeller interfere. Never once did he reply. He listened courteously, calmly.

When the angry man finished his speech, he waited for Rockefeller to blast. When it failed to come he was flustered, ill at ease. He twisted his hat awkwardly in his hands, and left.

Rockefeller had demonstrated a trait which was to make him famous—and successful. He knew a trait *not* to lose a friend. He *held* his tongue!

THE GOSSIPMONGER

A gossipmonger rushed in to tell Abraham Lincoln that Stanton had called him a fool. He waited for Lincoln to "blow up." This would be something to tell the boys.

The gossip was disappointed, however, for Lincoln remained unperturbed.

All that Lincoln said was, "Stanton is usually right!"

The gossipmonger sulked out of the office. He had failed to "bait" the great Lincoln, who knew how *not* to lose the respect of associates by compounding their insults.

Try this psychology yourself sometime. When a gossip tattles to you about something, say, "Maybe Joe is right," or, "Mary seldom is wrong."

When *that* gets back to Joe and Mary, you have *not* lost a friend—you have gained one.

DISRAELI AND GLADSTONE

Disraeli and Gladstone were bitter political opponents; but when Gladstone attacked Disraeli in Parliament, Disraeli would heap coals of fire on his head by completely ignoring the remarks.

You see that old saying about sticks and stones breaking bones where words never will, isn't always true.

Words not only can hurt you—but they can ruin you—that is, the words *you speak* to others or about others.

"Guarding the tongue" is a virtue that has been advocated by wise men from the psalmists to our present-day psychologists; but all too often it is a warning we fail to heed in time.

Yet the failure to control the tongue is responsible for many failures in business, marriage, and friendship.

In business it is very poor strategy to "get mad." Big business executives know this. They would make themselves vulnerable by getting mad.

Remember: *Whom the gods would destroy, they first make mad.*

Lose your tongue—lose a friend!

WORDS SPOKEN IN HASTE

In the first place, losing your temper gives the other fellow the advantage.

Any good counselor at law knows this strategy. Make 'em angry, and they fall apart.

You are apt to throw away some advantage in seconds, by getting angry, that you cannot recoup in years; for once you've said those words they are gone.

Remember? You can't erase the spoken word!

* * *

Last week the newspapers in my city of Dallas carried a story about a man and a woman who celebrated their fiftieth wedding anniversary the week before.

One week later—they sued for divorce!

Fifty years of getting along together—then bingo!—a few unthinking words, and it is all over.

* * *

Weber and Fields were the closest of friends for years. They were like brothers. Then one day a silly argument. Hard words were spoken.

Words spoken in haste that later were regretted.

The friendship which had been built up during the years was dissolved in a moment, and the great vaudeville team continued to entertain—but, behind the funny jokes was a stage tragedy.

* * *

Today no one ever heard of the fellow who "told off" John D. Rockefeller—but the whole world knows John D.

That, in itself, should be a small reason, not to lose your words and lose your identity in Life.

ANOTHER "BROTHERLY" FEUD

Al Schacht and Nic Altrock were "closer than brothers" for many years. Their comic baseball act made millions laugh; but this famous friendship which endured both hardship and prosperity—good years and bad years—ended in a feud.

The friendship required years to build; the feud only the interval that elapses from the time a word is spoken until it reaches the ear.

Then there was Abbott and Costello; but they "made up." Also Laurel and Hardy—but they made up.

Years building the friendship—minutes closing it out!

It happens every day. People who have been lifelong friends suddenly come to the parting of the ways.

A thoughtless word or two is spoken. Perhaps any other time it would be passed off; but the other person is in no mood to pass it off.

He *retaliates!*

Things are said which cannot be recalled—the friendship blows up, one that required years to build.

It is not how many friends you've won in life that counts, but how many you have left!

That is the acid test. For it is easy to make them, harder to hold them!

WORDS LIKE DYNAMITE

Words can be like dynamite. A little sets them off. Words are mighty useful when they do good; mighty harmful when they do wrong.

We should use them to smooth out the rocky road of life—to level the mountains of unhappiness, but never to blast a friendship.

Emerson wrote, "No man has a prosperity so high or firm, but that two or three words can dishearten it; and there is no calamity which right words will not begin to redress."

We are all tempted to make "jibes" at our friends. Something they say gives us the opening, and the perfect retort! The *riposte magnificent* pops into our minds.

We can't resist the temptation, so let it slide off our witty tongue—the other fellow looks small, and we are made smart!

We become the *hero*—he becomes the stooge, and of course a friendship melts.

THE "LAST WORD" PLAGUE

A man's wife tells him, "You're making a fool of yourself." Right back he slams with, "Why not? What is fair for the goose is fair for the gander!"

A lawyer gets a job!

It is great stuff to read about smart "come backs." The movies are filled with them in their bedroom farces; but don't *you* use them or you will lose a friend!

People don't mind laughing *with* you, but when they are the goat of the laugh, the brunt of the retort beautiful, their laugh is rather sickly.

A moment's *satisfaction* is not worth a *lifetime* friendship! !

As Douglas Jerrold put it, "The last word is the most dangerous of infernal machines; and husband and wife should no more fight to get it than they would struggle for the possession of a lighted bomb-shell!"

Avoid the "last word!" Let the other fellow have it if he is foolish enough to take it.

"GOSSIPS" ARE CRIMINALS

The high-caste Hindu takes an oath not to use words *idly!*

To sit around a cocktail lounge, a bridge table, or over the back fence and just talk for talk's sake, is prohibited by the Hindu.

He knows the harm of talking idly!

That is also a good oath for you, and me, and others to take.

You wouldn't think of putting poison in your neighbor's coffee; yet we say such poison as, "I saw Jim out with Mary"—and we start a pony express of rumor.

Thoughtlessly someone says, "I think you are a fool!" and then reaches out to retrieve the words before they strike someone's eardrum, brain, heart, soul!

It is too late. Words in flight cannot be shot down like planes.

Time was when gossips were prosecuted the same as common criminals. In 1644 Betsy Tucker of Virginia was sentenced to the ducking pool because of the indiscriminate tongue lashing she gave her poor husband.

Today, we are supposed to be too civilized to duck gossips!

The purse robber is punished; but the reputation robber goes free.

WATCH POISON WORDS

"It is with a word as with an arrow—once let it loose, and it does not return," said Able-el-Kader.

F. W. Robertson said, "You may tame the wild beast; the conflagration of the forest will cease when the dry wood are consumed; but you cannot arrest the progress of that cruel word which you uttered carelessly yesterday or this morning."

"Poison words" have been used for centuries. If they are used as a label for something that really is poison, they serve a useful purpose.

They arouse our emotions to reject that which should be rejected. Sometimes, though, the labels are false. It is best to look inside your bottle of words before giving somebody a "taste."

If you listen for poison words you'll hear them every day over the radio, read them in newspapers, or in advertising warning you of body odor, bad breath, fallen arches, and a thousand and one "bugaboos."

During the fight for the governorship of Georgia, poison words were flung hit and miss.

Herman Talmadge called Arnall a "dictator"; a Talmadge aid

called Arnall a "hog who didn't know when to leave the trough."

Arnall, on the other hand, called the State Troopers, sent to keep order, not "patrolmen" but "storm troopers."

When Talmadge changed the locks on the governor's office, Arnall accused him of executing a "pincer's movement."

Words that were cute, clever, smart—but *lost* friendships!

A GOOD FORMULA

To keep from *losing* friends remember this formula:

1. You wouldn't poison your friend's coffee with arsenic, so don't poison his mind with arsenic words.
2. You wouldn't steal your neighbor's automobile, so don't steal his reputation with idle words.
3. Before you uncork some "language," don't just look at the label, but what is *inside* the bottle!

Robert Butler of Walter Butler Shipbuilders, Inc., at Superior, Wisconsin, was a genius at getting co-operation from employees during the war and they broke many shipbuilding records.

How? One thing Butler would not tolerate was idle talk, rumors, petty gossip. His motto is a good one. In fact, I've framed it myself:

If you can't write it and sign it—DON'T SAY IT.

Don't Be a Modern Word Borgia

CHAPTER 13

PEOPLE LIKE TO HEAR "WEDDING BELLS" AND NOT "FUNERAL CHIMES"

Why words move people. How a Frenchman was talked to death and the experiment of Pavlov.

OFF HAND A DOG, a bone and a bell would seem to have little to do with word magic, how to make people like you!

Yet it was with a dog, a bone, and a bell that the famous Russian physiologist, Pavlov, first discovered the psychological "laws" by which certain words derive their "magic."

You may remember reading in school how Pavlov, around the turn of the century, rang a bell each day before presenting food to a dog. He had previously operated upon the salivary glands in the dog's mouth so the amount of saliva secreted could be caught in a test tube and measured.

Ordinarily, a dog "waters at the mouth" only at the actual sight, or smell, of food.

After repeated trials of ringing the bell just a few seconds before presenting food to the dog, Pavlov found that he could leave off the food altogether.

All he needed to do was to ring the bell—and immediately the dog's salivary glands began to secrete saliva.

Pavlov called this a "conditioned reflex." He had conditioned the dog to salivate at the sound of the bell.

I have trained my Doberman pinscher dogs to respond to the "inaudible whistle" this same way. This is the whistle tuned so that only the dog hears it—you can't.

I blow it vigorously while they eat. After a few days, I can blow it any time and they respond. It saves me a lot of yelling and hollering.

This was the simple principle of Pavlov, modernized and put to a practical purpose.

Pavlov thought only reflexes could be conditioned; but since his classic experiment other researchers have found that practically any response can be so conditioned!

OTHER SIMILAR EXPERIMENTS

In 1945 another Russian scientist was honored by Stalin for "conditioning" a dog's heart to beat faster.

He did this by ringing a bell just before administering a shot of adrenalin, a powerful heart stimulant. After several weeks he could leave off the adrenalin, and the ringing of the bell was sufficient to make the dog's heart palpitate.

Dr. Florence Mateer conditioned children to open their mouths each time their arms were touched. She merely touched the arm a second before candy was offered.

After this was repeated a sufficient number of times, she could touch the child's arm and his mouth would fly open.

Psychologist Cason conditioned the human pupillary reflex!

He rang a bell and *immediately* shone a bright light into the subject's eyes!

After about four hundred repetitions, the sound of the bell caused the pupil of the eye to contract!

You can "condition" your friends this way. If you gossip, find fault, and otherwise cause trouble, whenever you make your appearance in a room, they instinctively react against you much as in these experiments.

Foolish? No—not at all!

You cross a street when you see a bore coming your way; you freeze up when somebody you hate enters a room.

Instinctively we have "conditioned" others around us to act in a certain manner when we are present.

Strange? No—we pour an immediate drink when a drinker comes in; we talk style when a "clothes horse" walks in; we slump into our chairs when the "bore" in our circle comes dashing in.

Our friends, you see, have become *conditioned* by our own actions!

Think now—how have I unintentionally "conditioned" someone around me? Maybe that is *why* I always seem to start a line of gossip when I come in, a line of chatter, a low dud!

Think—*How have I "conditioned" people around me??????*

YOUR "OWN" SIGNALS

It really doesn't make much difference what sort of signal you use to set up a conditioned response. Almost any conceivable stimulus can be used as a substitute for Pavlov's bell.

The important thing is that *two* stimuli shall be presented *together* for a sufficient time.

A lover of gossip—the town's notorious gossip! Whenever you see *both* together in a corner you react, "Boy, somebody is being torn apart!"

After you see the two gossiping so often together, then just *one* of them will set up your thoughts that gossip must be in the offing.

For after the two stimuli are together, then just one by itself will invoke the other.

The subconscious mind, which cannot reason inductively, accepts the fact that the ringing of the bell means "food is coming"; that the swish of the gossip's arrival means gossip will be brewed!

BACK-YARD SCIENCE

For all practical purposes "conditioning" and "hypnosis" are very closely akin; they both achieve their results by planting a suggestion in the subconscious mind of the subject.

In the case of hypnosis the operator puts the subject's conscious mind to sleep, then gives the suggestion in so many words.

In the case of gossip, the gossiper puts the subject's reasoning to sleep, then gives the rumor in so many words.

First you expose the subject to *two acts* or *two ideas* until their subconscious accepts the fact that the first act means the second will soon follow.

In comes old Mrs. Endler, wagging her tongue; a few minutes

later in comes Mrs. Smithy. The two gossip. It seems they always do it when together—so you just know when you see Mrs. Endler that soon Mrs. Smithy will follow as eleven always follows ten.

The well-known troublemaker arrives. You always have seen him and his wife arguing when together—so when one arrives, you soon feel the other will arrive—then *trouble!*

The poor cook serves her usually poor meal. When you see it, you just know indigestion will follow this time as it has all the other times.

The clothes "horse" moves into the party, and you just *know* the subject, as on twenty other occasions, will turn to a discussion on clothing.

This, truly, is bringing science into your very back yard, to your front parlor, poker game, bridge party, sewing circle.

Science, you see, can help you make friends and keep friends, if you understand a little about it.

I am sure friend Pavlov never dreamed how his "experiment" could be turned around to show people how to get along better and *sell* themselves by a clear understanding of that scientific term, "conditioning."

POPULARIZING SCIENCE

In the conditioned response the subject is exposed to *two acts* or *two ideas,* until the subconscious, as I said, accepts the fact that the first act means the second is to follow.

"You are a fool," says hubby, and the dog runs into the other room, for instinctively he knows *that* "sound" always prompts wifie to toss the nearest book or frying pan at him.

If you hear a fire alarm you run out of the building, whether there is a fire or not. It might be a false alarm; but you "act" just as if there were a fire.

Somebody tells you some gossip. Later you see that gossiper talking to somebody else, and you feel maybe *you* now are being talked about.

If Mrs. Jones always cuts up after two drinks, then when you see her take that second drink, instinctively you feel she is about ready for her usual cutting up.

A train whistle sets us thinking about our last trip; the sound of the whistle plus our last trip, made this possible in our mind.

Every air-line stewardess knows that once a certain food, plus a bumpy voyage, makes you sick, the same combination is apt to do it all over again.

One provokes the other—in science, in your everyday life.

Understand "conditioning" and you will make more friends, make them like you longer.

SCIENCE "IN REVERSE"

From the above Pavlov experiment you learn one important thing, that you can control the feelings and thoughts that people have when you enter a room, by conditioning them beforehand.

If you, plus a gathering, make for smiles, fun, humor, jokes, gaiety, then the party isn't complete to others until you arrive, for they know the *two of you together* makes for good time.

However, if you plus a party, plus a drink, makes for gossip, trouble, bickering, ill-humor, bad jokes, then your friends may take either you by yourself or the party by itself—but *never* the both of you together.

See how a knowledge of science helps?

Now the reverse: You can control your effect upon others by this same reasoning. For example:

Hubby knows that whenever he appears at dinner in suspenders plus a beard, wifie gets mad.

Now if he wants to get wifie mad, then he *deliberately appears* that way, but if he wants to keep peace, then he doesn't.

Wifie knows hubby doesn't like cigarette smoking while he is eating, so the smart wife *won't* smoke unless her desire to smoke is greater than her desire to hold hubby's good will.

Smart people, therefore, *learn* what annoys others and then avoid doing it.

This is science in the "reverse."

"SETTING OFF" OTHERS

Taking this a little further, we find that Mrs. Brown and Mrs. Black never get along together. They always fight; so a good hostess never invites both together, but separately, to her parties.

This is tactful.

Now hubby has peculiarities. He doesn't mind if his shirts are not ironed on time, but he sure hates to go into a bathroom and find his wife's stockings hanging there.

The smart housewife, therefore, puts her stockings elsewhere. She avoids trouble.

The unsmart housewife gets the shirts ironed *on time,* but thoughtlessly always puts her stockings in the bathroom to dry.

We only have so much time a day. We can use this time for things the other person appreciates, and so win him; or we use it for things he doesn't appreciate, and so cause trouble.

Now if you really want to get along with others, learn those things that "set 'em off" from those they don't seem to mind.

One person is "set off" by run-down heels; this doesn't bother another person, but that other person is "set off" by a mate who giggles after the first drink.

"I hate her when she shows off," says hubby, and the good wife, naturally, won't set him off by showing off.

She says, "I can't stand his yellow striped shirt—it sets me off," so hubby is smart. He wears it only when he plays poker with the boys, and wifie can't get annoyed by it.

Learn how *not* to "set off" the other person.

MORE ON SCIENCE

Andrew Salter, prominent New York psychologist, tells in his book, *What Is Hypnosis?* (Richard R. Smith), how C. V. Hudgins actually created a "magic word" in his laboratory.

Hudgins went one step further in conditioning the human pupillary reflex than did Cason.

Instead of ringing a bell just before he shone a light on the subject's eyes, *he merely pronounced the word "contract."*

After some forty training periods Hudgins found that he could leave off the light altogether!

All he had to do was to say the word "contract" and the subject's *pupil contracted just as if light had been shone into the eye.*

This was a marvelous thing. Hudgins had manufactured a "magic word of power."

The conditioned subject had *no choice* in the matter.

It made not the least bit of difference whether he "believed it" or used his "will power" against Hudgins. When Hudgins said, "CONTRACT!!" that subject's eyes automatically contracted.

Thus is the power of "word magic."

ALL WORDS ARE "BELLS"

Virtually all the words in our language, or at least all of the "dynamic words," are "bells." They set off an *emotional* or a *physical* reaction within the range of your voice.

This is because words, which are only vocal sounds, have become *associated* in our minds with the actual things which they symbolize.

Edmund Jacobson found that even the "idea" was sufficient to evoke a physical response. With a sensitive instrument with which he could test the degree of muscular relaxation in students, he waited until a subject's arm muscles were perfectly relaxed.

Then he asked the subject to merely "think about" striking two blows with a hammer. Immediately his sensitive electrical instrument which indicated muscular tension, showed two sharp jumps—indicating that the arm muscles had contracted slightly just "thinking about" striking two blows.

When you "talk about" a sizzling steak, people's mouths begin to water.

When they see one in a restaurant moving across the room on a tray, first they *see* it, then *hear* it, then *smell* it—then *want* it!

The *sound* of the sizzling steak has "conditioned" their salivary glands—even their stomach begins to rumble for the food!

You can use this idea in many ways in your own contact with people!

DYNAMIC VERSUS DEAD WORDS

Simple words like "if," "and," "but," etc., do not evoke any particular response in people. They are not dynamic. They have no emotional appeal like the word "whiff" for coffee!

With the help of a very sensitive thermometer psychologists found that by pronouncing the word "hot" and asking the subject to think of a spot on his forehead, the skin temperature in that area was raised!

The word "cold" lowered the skin temperature!

We do not need a psychological laboratory, however, to see the dynamic effect of words such as "lemon," "dry cotton."

Some words tingle our spine, others cause our hearts to "go into our mouths"; other words raise our desires, hopes, and ambitions.

These are the words to use if you want others to like you a little better.

HOW A FRENCHMAN DIED!

The story is told of a French criminal who was sentenced to die. A group of doctors and psychologists asked the authorities if they might conduct an experiment on the doomed man.

Permission was granted and they cut a hole in the cell wall and had the prisoner extend his arm through the opening. Then the doctors made a small pin prick on the prisoner's arm—all the while talking of the "incision" they were about to make.

Then they let warm water trickle down his arm to simulate the flow of blood, all the while they kept up a running conversation.

"How pale he looks. . . . His pulse is growing weaker. . . . He can't last much longer. . . . He hasn't much blood left. . . ."

Under this barrage of words the man's pulse did begin to grow weaker.

Finally it stopped altogether. His heart stopped beating. The Frenchman had actually been "talked to death."

Let this be a moral to *you:* Don't talk *your friends* "to death," or into being enemies!

WATCH YOUR WORDS

Knowing this great power that words have on people, resolve right now to use words to build *up* people—to make them feel better—make them feel important, big, happy!

Tell them how well they look—and they'll actually *feel* better.

Speak about cheerful things and you will ring the "cheer bells" and not the "funeral chimes" inside them.

Don't be a perpetual Prophet of Doom, always bewailing the depression, hard times, sickness, trouble!

Don't tell them how bad you feel—you wish you were dead—for maybe, like the Frenchman, it will effect your nerves, blood stream, and heart!

If you do, people will *associate* you with a feeling of unpleasantness whenever you are around.

People have enough troubles of their own without your reminding them by talking about yours. What people want is *escape* from their troubles, which is why they go to the movies so much, especially on dull, gray days and lonesome nights.

Summed up:

> *Talk "wedding bells," not "funeral chimes," and watch people flock around you!*

A helping word to one in trouble is often like a switch on a railroad track—but ONE INCH between wreck and smooth rolling prosperity.—Beecher

CHAPTER 14

HOW ONE MAN BECAME THE PERSONAL ADVISOR TO TWO PRESIDENTS

A Short Short Story Number 3

WITHIN THIRTY MINUTES he became such a hit with FDR that he was invited to make a 25,000-mile trip with the famous President.

Later he made a hit with President Truman!

It was during the 1944 presidential campaign that Roosevelt met George Allen in Detroit.

They talked for about thirty minutes and Roosevelt liked him so well he *insisted* that he accompany him on the 25,000-mile campaign trip as his *personal* companion.

Most people would get tired of the same fellow on such a long trip, but Allen knew how not to wear out his welcome.

When Roosevelt went back to Washington, he carried Allen with him and appointed him head of the RFC.

While Congressmen and other government big shots tried vainly to work up some scheme to get the President's ear, Roosevelt would often pick up his phone in the evening and *ask* George Allen to drop over for a chat.

Congressmen might study Allen's method!

TRUMAN LIKED ALLEN

When Truman succeeded Roosevelt in the White House, Allen remained as the new President's confidant and companion.

Now that is interesting, because perhaps you do "click" with one person, but when his successor comes on, he usually brings "his own" retinue.

How did Allen do this?

Naturally he made many enemies. The very fact that two

Presidents went out of their way to be nice to him would certainly arouse jealousy and envy.

Allen was called by the newspapers a superficial, empty-headed playboy.

Yet he was a successful businessman before he met either of the two Presidents who liked him.

He already had a personal fortune made in business and is today on the board of directors of several of our biggest corporations.

Whether or not the criticism was just, made little difference, for the fellow certainly knew how to gain friends—and how to *hold* them afterward.

ALLEN'S METHODS

Actually, Allen's ability to gain friendship with two popular Presidents was based on putting into practice the *very same principles* of this book.

Allen first had "you-ability."

He knew how to make it a great big *you* and a very small *I* when talking with others. He knew how to make the other fellow feel superior.

He gave others credit—took *none* for himself.

He made Presidents hungry and thirsty for him; he filled his box, and didn't show up empty-handed when they phoned for him.

He played a very good role, and it wasn't the *hero role*. He let others take the due credit.

"I tell jokes on myself," says Allen, and you can just hear Jack Benny saying the same thing.

"I pretend I'm about the dumbest man in the world. I found out that when a man is always boasting how good he is, people get bored and avoid him."

Words of wisdom!

"But," went on Allen, "when you tell how bad you are, how you bungle things, then people like you!!"

ANOTHER ALLEN SECRET

When Allen tells a joke, as I said, it is always on himself.

One that he likes to tell happens to be true. Allen was on Cumberland University's football team in 1916 when Georgia Tech defeated Cumberland 222 to 0.

According to Allen, a sports writer credited him with making the most outstanding play of the afternoon for Cumberland ". . . losing only six yards on the play!"

See the point? Tell 'em on yourself. Be the stooge—not the Major Hoople!

Another secret of George Allen's great popularity is his *optimism!*

He knows how to use words that "ring cheerful bells" and not "funeral chimes." He knows how to make people feel *good* when he is around.

That is why their reaction when he appears is one of good humor, and not depression or silly gossip.

"The President hears 'feuding' all day long. Officials are feuding with each other—Congress is feuding with the President."

When a newspaper reporter asked George Allen why the President would invite him to the White House after dinner for an informal chat while other Capitol big shots had to wait in line, George Allen revealed perhaps the big secret of his success, what we have been waiting to hear.

All that he replied was:

"I'm not mad at anybody!!!"

If You're Smart You Won't Try to Appear SMART

CHAPTER 15

HOW TO BECOME "POPULAR" WITH A BASIC RULE

Popularity isn't any one rule or two, but here is a Basic Rule that goes a long way toward bringing people Success.

HAVE YOU EVER wondered why people laugh when someone slips on a banana peel and falls?

The question may seem to be far removed from the subject of "popularity," but in analyzing the situation you will see that it isn't too far removed.

How to attain popularity is a great subject of interest to all of us. Young people, especially, rate popularity as very high.

The schoolboy says, "Is she popular?" The schoolgirl asks, "Is he popular?"

Everybody wants to be popular—or to be seen with popular people.

The "fundamentals" of being popular boil themselves down to being the type of person others like to be around, perhaps because they play cards, tell good stories, play golf, the piano, or do card tricks.

But "popularity" does not entirely depend upon the number of things you can or can't do.

A little puppy, you see, is popular yet all he does is wag his tail!

YOU CAN LEARN POPULARITY

In order to be popular it is necessary to practice and practice, read and reread such books as this. It can't be learned overnight. It is often gained from one little line buried in such a book as this. You didn't see it, in fact, until the third reading.

However, there are certain basic rules and laws of human

psychology that, once learned, go a long way toward making you popular. If it took one book—one reading—everybody would be popular. Only the diggers for the nuggets gain the riches.

There is a deep-seated desire in all of us to be a "complete person." We want to be normal in every respect, on a par with our associates.

That is why when we slip on a banana peel we feel "inferior"; why it makes others feel "superior," and they laugh.

Somehow or other we like to magnify our shortcomings, with the result that the seeds are planted for an inferiority complex.

The small child is made aware of his faults, his weaknesses, and soon he grows up fearful of what the world will think of him.

Yet, a pat on his back might have gained him confidence, and led him on to ultimate popularity.

WE PUT ON "PARTY MANNERS"

We like to put on "party manners" as a camouflage of our faults, to keep others from detecting our supposed inferior points. We strut, use long cigarette holders, flood a party with "ourselves."

It has been said that "misery loves company," which is why we love to talk about our aches and pains and troubles to others, and to hear about their troubles in return.

This is why, also, that we often can't stand the *success* of our friends; their downfall inflates our ego, and we rush to their rescue.

But their *success* sets up an *envy* deep inside us.

When we see a dignified person fall, we laugh not because the situation is basically humorous, but because we unconsciously get relief in seeing him part with his dignity.

This is a *perverse trait* in human nature.

Troubles of others make us feel more comfortable; this should not be, but it is nevertheless true.

Basically it means that we realize that this other person isn't perfect either; and we derive some consolation from this fact!

A "SECRET" OF POPULARITY

The art of making people want us around is not too complicated. It often is nothing more than getting down "off your high horse," and "acting human."

Don't try to show other people how perfect you are. They will see your good points without your pointing them out to them continually.

Attempting to convince people you are "learned," is just an inferiority complex at work trying to rectify itself.

Nobody likes the "perfect person." No one feels at home with perfection. No one wants to live with a "Craig's Wife."

People may like to read about the perfect person, but to have one always around, nix!

This doesn't mean you must always "run yourself down" to be thought popular; but it is refreshing to meet people who will readily admit the fish they caught wasn't the biggest in the sea.

A person who is not ashamed to say, "I honestly don't know."

The basic rule therefore is: *Don't be a* know all!

BE A GOOD LISTENER "FIRST"

Listen to people as they tell about *their* exploits, and you stay quiet about yours.

Don't always put in your "dime's worth" of information to let others know *you* know how almighty you are.

You may be able to stagger others with your brilliant repartee, but that is not George Allen's way of winning the friendship of two Presidents. Remember?

No one likes the superman; but just plain old Bill and good old Mary.

Laugh at yourself. Mark Twain was a popular man. In telling of a fight he described it this way, "Placing my nose firmly between *his* teeth, I threw him heavily to the ground on top of *me!*"

He made himself popular by being the underdog, not the superman.

You, too, can use this same basic law to help you on your own road to popularity.

JOAN DAVIS MAKES A MILLION

The movie star Joan Davis made over a million dollars in one year as radio's most-liked female star, because she was not a "smarty pants" with fast, crisp answers.

But—the reverse!

She is invariably the "butt" of all the jokes and gags. She would wisecrack, "Mother Nature gifted me with this face and she gifted me with this figure. There is just one thing I wanna know—where's the exchange department??"

People laugh at her.

Joan doesn't mind this. It makes her money. It makes her very popular. People love to sympathize with the "poor dear."

She has another trick that makes her popular. She loves to "burn down" someone who is stuck-up, some pompous character; and how we love to see dignity crumble!

It inflates our ego!

TALK ABOUT "OTHERS"

It is not advisable in real life to go around belittling yourself and running yourself down, for this will become boresome.

On the other hand, it is far worse to go around pinning roses on your lapel and patting yourself constantly on the back. This will also get mighty boresome.

The best way is to talk modestly about yourself. Then lead others into talking about *themselves,* and they will leave you and remark, "What a conversationalist!"

Someone wisely said, "If you speak well of yourself, others will think you are boasting; and if you speak ill of yourself, they will believe it—so just don't talk about yourself!"

A young chap came to me the other day. He had made a mess of a new job. "What shall I do?" he asked, and "How can I cover up?"

"Admit your mistakes," I advised, and he returned to the boss and said, "I sure made a mess of my job."

The boss, prepared to ball out the new man and perhaps fire him, sat back. He looked perplexed, then told the young man, "Admitting mistakes is good—I like that!"

The admission saved the day and the job. If the young man had tried to cover up and pretend—no job. So he broke down and admitted his mistakes, that he wasn't the perfect employee, and this won over the boss used to others who overly bragged on their work.

ADMIT YOUR MISTAKES

"I guess I was speeding," admits the speeder, and the cop, ready for more alibis, sits back in amazement, so amazed, in fact, he lets the speeder off for admitting his guilt rather than putting up a lot of worn out "excuses."

One of the most unpopular people is the one who is "always right." Even when they're proved wrong—they won't admit it. They are dead set on convincing you that they are perfect.

All really big people know that it is no disgrace to make a mistake now and then. "The man who has not made mistakes is either a fool or a coward," said James J. Hill, the railroad magnate.

It is only the little person who is afraid to admit he is wrong.

Lincoln was famous for admitting when he had been wrong. Once General Grant disobeyed his specific orders—but won the battle.

Lincoln sat down and wrote Grant a letter—not to rake him over the coals for insubordination—but to admit that the general had been right and he had been wrong.

You can "go far" on your mistakes!

DART GETS A JOB

When United Drug Co. was considering Justin Dart for its president several years ago, a certain faction which was opposed to Dart drew up a list of "mistakes" that the youthful drug magnate had made while at Walgreen's.

At the conference these mistakes were read out to Dart and he was asked if they were true. He didn't attempt to defend himself or to deny them.

Instead he smiled and said, "Gentlemen, that list doesn't begin to give *all* the mistakes I've made!"

The directors laughed with him. The meeting broke up. Dart got the job.

Laugh at yourself once in a while, and put people at ease. Don't be the perfect person. Let others be the hero—you be the stooge.

This has been proved time and time again. *It is basic!* It is the best way to disarm an antagonistic person.

Get down off your high horse. Sit among your friends. *Be human. Be normal.*

If you try to inflate yourself and puff yourself up, people will be tempted to take pot shots at you and prick your balloon.

Like watching the man fall on the banana peel, they will get a kick out of seeing your balloon pricked!

So don't give them a chance.

How?

By not being a know it all—*the perfect person!*

He Goes Farthest Who Treads Softly

WHEELERGRAMS FOR GETTING ALONG WITH PEOPLE

Criticism curdles the milk of human kindness.
Don't talk "past" people—look 'em in the eye.
Work "with" people—not "on" them.
"P" added to "luck" spells "Pluck"!
"Now" spelled backwards is "Won"!
When you try "to get even" you *lower* yourself.
Grudges are always inflated.

* * *

Just enuff to "get by" is not enuff to "get ahead."
Resolve to be good—but good for *something*—not *nothing*.
Don't send a good-will message "collect."
Talk ten seconds—listen twenty minutes!
Excel others—and lose their friendships.
Beware of *detour* signs on people's faces.

CHAPTER 16

TRY THIS SIMPLE FORMULA TO OVERCOME SHYNESS, TIMIDITY, SELF-CONSCIOUSNESS

Spanish Proverb: *You may believe any good of a grateful man.*
Arabic Proverb: *Consideration may take the place of experience.*

THE OTHER DAY I was giving a lecture before a Chamber of Commerce in a town I better not mention. The secretary told me that he had made speeches occasionally himself, and would like me to give him a few pointers.

Next morning I went by his office and gave him a copy of our book, *Tested Public Speaking*—revised;* for good measure I took along some of our published booklets on selling and getting along with people.

I wasn't trying to sell the books. I wanted to give them to him free of cost or obligation.

The night before he had asked my advice on how to speak—which was a compliment. Since I am only human, he had made me feel important by asking my advice.

He made me feel good by praising me. He made me *want* to do something for him. In fact he had just about "sold" himself to me; but by withholding two little words he fizzled.

In fact—he spoiled my whole day.

UNINTENTIONAL NEGLECT

I walked three blocks out of my way to take him the books; but when I entered his office he was too busy to see me. His secretary told him, "Mr. Wheeler is here with some books he promised you."

* Elmer Wheeler, *Tested Public Speaking* (New York: Prentice-Hall, Inc., 1947).

"Oh, yes," he said through the interoffice phone, "tell him I am busy now, but to leave the books with you."

Well, sir, this man's ingratitude "burned me up." All day I kept thinking about it. How true it is that often you are "king for a day" only—the day you meet the people and give the speech.

They fight duels to see who will be on the reception committee at the airport or depot; then, only too often, they flip coins to see who loses and must take the speaker to the departure point.

Now this man made a lifelong enemy of me, all because he was too stingy—too selfish to use two little words, "Thank you."

TWO LITTLE WORDS

I remember another man several years ago and how differently he had acted. It was around Christmastime. This old fellow lived alone.

I hadn't intended to buy him a present—but while out shopping I happened to see a record album of selections from Shakespeare's *Hamlet.*

Well this friend of mine was a nut on Shakespeare. He could quote most of his plays by heart, and he carried a small book of Shakespeare's selections in his pocket.

So I thought to myself, "I know how proud he would be to have this album, so I am going to buy it for him."

Knowing he *would appreciate it* prompted my purchase.

When I handed him the album on Christmas Day, all he said was simply,

"Thank you—thank you."

Just two little words, but how he said them. Not once, but *twice.* Tears seemed to roll down his cheeks—and I noted a faint tremble on his lips as he repeated, "—thank you."

If you have ever wondered if it is more blessed to give than to receive, let me tell you that it is.

It makes you feel much better to give someone something provided they *genuinely* appreciate it.

That old friend was not verbose in his thanks. He didn't give me a lot of insincere pats on the back with what a great fellow I was, and a lot of palaver lacking in truth.

His simple "thank you" was my best Christmas present from him. For it made me feel good inside—and awfully important to think I could bring such *happiness* to another human being.

When I left him my step was lighter. I felt better than I had in years—all because of two little words.

EVERYONE LIKES APPRECIATION

Appreciation makes people feel more important than most anything else you can give them.

Everybody likes to be appreciated—wifie for a good dinner; hubby for a good business deal; brother by his boss; sister by her music teacher; neighbor by his neighbor.

Appreciation is the *oil* that keeps the machine of human relations running smoothly.

People crave it so passionately and it is so easy to give, that it is really cruel to withhold it from others.

I'm no different from anyone else. I like *appreciation.*

I'll go out of my way to do things for people that I know will *genuinely appreciate* it; and I'll go out of my way to eat in a restaurant where everybody says "thank you" for my patronage, hostess, waiter, cashier!

Epicurus says: *"Gratitude is a virtue that has profit annexed to it."*

That is very true. Gratitude is one of the most profitable commodities a merchant can carry in his stock.

"Thank you's" build a business. They make friends.

PRACTICE APPRECIATION

If you are looking for something to make life brighter for you —to get along better with people—to make people *glad to help you, try this formula for fourteen days:*

Appreciate what people do for you!

After fourteen days of showing your appreciation for things people do for you, then it will become a habit.

Then for fourteen more days—and fourteen more and more and more days, you will find your friends giving more of their friendships!

For you will be surprised at the end of fourteen days—surprised to find that you are less self-conscious, less shy, with more poise, and ease with people.

You may think a miracle has happened; but it is really no miracle but sound psychology and here is why:

The painfully self-conscious person has his attention centered upon himself. Self-consciousness is really a form of selfishness.

It has a little bit of conceit and vanity mixed up in it.

When the self-conscious person enters a room full of people his thoughts are not centered upon how he can make the other people enjoy themselves more, but, "What are they thinking of *me?*"

With self-conscious people it is always, *"Me—me—me—!"*

This is really a form of conceit, for the other people in the room are a lot more interested in themselves than they are in you.

The person who is timid—shy—self-conscious has an exaggerated opinion of the importance of every move he makes. He is conscious of every move he makes with his hands, every word he utters, all because his thoughts are self-centered.

When we start to *appreciate,* it forces us to think of the other fellow.

It turns our consciousness *outward* from a narrow little consciousness of self to the broader, larger consciousness of others.

To *appreciate* we are *forced* to turn our attention to what the other fellow has done. It compels us to recognize *his* importance.

It makes *him* the center of the stage instead of *us,* and this change of attention and interest is all that is necessary to cure the self-conscious person.

DON'T WAIT TO APPRECIATE

Don't wait until someone does something *big* for you to show your appreciation.

Start looking for things you can appreciate in people. This not only helps you get along better—it improves your personality.

Don't wait until *after* someone has done some favor to show your appreciation. You can oil the gears of human relations in *advance* by tacking the three little words, "if you please," onto the requests you make.

If people feel they must do something all the time before you show appreciation, or reciprocate, then the wallop is gone out of any appreciation you show.

If it is a case of, "Whose turn is it to buy the dinner?" then the oil of appreciation has gummed up. No one is appreciated for it was just a "deal" and it was your turn to do something.

Be ahead of people. Give them two dinners to their one. Be *up* on them at all times. Make appreciation come from your heart, not your pocketbook.

DON'T BE A HUMAN JUKE BOX

I am reprinting later on in this book our very successful booklet, *Take a Minute to Say "Thank You!"* * but I cannot resist right now passing on a good suggestion: Say "thank you."

Once upon a time a smart young efficiency "expert" took the bell off the cash register and substituted a "thank you" sign and a phonograph record.

The idea was that if the cashier forgot to say "thank you" the machine did it for her.

It was a big flop; for folks wanted to get their "thank you's" in the good old-fashioned way, in the flesh.

"Thank you" must be *custom tailored* just for you!!

A "thank you" that comes from the sound box and lips of a mechanical juke box, doesn't touch the "heart."

* (New York: Prentice-Hall, Inc., 1946.)

Real *appreciation* must come *from the heart* if it is to reach the other person's heart!

It may come through your lips, your eyebrows, your smile, your handshake, your pat on the back, the bouquet of flowers you sent, but it cannot be *mechanical.*

Appreciation that comes from "an empty box," is no appreciation at all but perhaps a "duty" you must perform, like phoning up next day and thanking somebody for a dinner.

So if you want to get over shyness, self-consciousness, even an inferiority complex, begin to show *appreciation.*

Because:

1. *It is the easiest way known to get along with people.*
2. *It makes people* glad *to do things for you.*
3. *It is a* sure-fire *formula to overcome timidity and to become* popular *with people.*

George M. Cohan won fame by ending every act saying, "My mother thanks you, my father thanks you, my sister thanks you, and I thank you!!"

CHAPTER 17

YOU CAN'T ERASE THE SPOKEN WORD

A Short Short Story Number 4*

WORDS ARE LIKE sunbeams, someone sagely said, for the more you concentrate them the deeper they burn.

How true this is.

How true, too, the fact that you cannot erase the spoken word; once it is spoken it is on its merry way.

On the way to make a friend or to tear down another's reputation.

Words on the loose!

How they can damage, chew up, tear apart, rip a reputation; how they can inspire, lift up, elevate!

Simple spoken words, uttered on the spur of the moment, from lips that are too thin or too full.

You cannot erase them once they are spoken.

They leap at people, penetrate their hearts, pierce their brain, leave a good thought or bury a bad one.

So often they are spoken carelessly.

Thoughtlessly, someone says, "I think you are a fool!" and then reaches out to retrieve the words before they strike the eardrum, and register in the heart of the sensitive soul.

It is too late. Words in flight cannot be shot down like planes in flight.

Be a good listener first; a good talker second, and you won't "wish I hadn't said that."

Think twice; then speak once, and you won't always be "shooting my old mouth off."

Remember you can't learn when your mouth is working. You learn when it is closed, and your ears are working.

Before you say it—write it, for then if you don't like the way it looks, you can erase it on paper.

* Article by Elmer Wheeler, *Kiwanis* Magazine, November, 1946.

These are the simple remedies for quick-spoken folks; for people who regard their words carelessly, thoughtlessly.

How cruel, though, are many words spoken in haste; when pointed directly at someone, aimed to splatter a heart or ruin a soul.

"You're wrong," or "You don't understand what I mean," someone shouts, and another person feels he is regarded as pretty dumb.

"I didn't make myself quite clear," would have been a better way to put it.

It is all in *how* you say *what* you say.

Watch your words and your words will watch out for you.

Think twice; speak once. Listen more than you talk.

Remember, *you can't erase the spoken word!*

CHAPTER 18

HOW TO LICK THAT "TIRED FEELING"

People like "peppy" people—people who make them feel "alive." You'll create a better impression if you have "zing!"

ONE OF THE MOST boresome things in the world is a person who is perpetually "too tired."

The "tired" person can be counted on to put the damper on the most spirited party; for they manage to take the fun out of any gathering.

They are depressing.

The "tired" personality fizzles. People soon become weary themselves, and avoid the perpetually tired person.

The tired person cannot generate enthusiasm.

If you are always tired, stop and take stock of yourself. It may be that you are pushing yourself too fast. You may need more sleep.

Get a doctor to suggest a vitality diet so that you can again put "sell" into your contacts with other people.

But likely as not your *tiredness* is *mental* rather than physical.

Scientific tests have shown that in 90 per cent of chronic fatigue cases the problem is not one of lack of energy, but failure to release the available supply.

That "tired feeling" can often be licked once you learn the secret of *releasing* energy.

WANT TO PROVE IT?

Most of the time when you are so sure that you are "completely exhausted," the chances are you are just plain bored.

You have an abundance of energy in reserve but have "closed the gate," so that your utilization of this reserve is cut off.

Want to prove it?

Then sometime when you are "all tired out" call up a friend

and make plans to engage in whatever activity that gives you the most pleasure.

If it is fishing, tennis, hunting, dancing, or whatever, as soon as you become engrossed in doing something that you enjoy, you will find that you have plenty of energy and that your tired feeling has mysteriously disappeared.

Joy is one of the most powerful spiritual *tonics* known, and the joy of doing something that we thoroughly like opens channels for energy to flow into us.

A friend of mine is one of those men who hates to get up in the morning. To see him cling to the pillow and watch the expression on his face, you'd think he was experiencing physical torture!!

Yet, I have been with him when a friend came in at 6 A.M. and suggested going bird hunting—and have seen him actually *leap* out of his bed in one jump.

This was something that gave him joy!

ENTHUSIASM RELEASES ENERGY

I have watched people grunting and grumbling down the street from a day of shopping, only to go into "double time" when somebody suggested going for a swim, a movie, a cocktail.

Enthusiasm releases energy.

Several years ago tests with students at Georgia Tech, in Atlanta, Georgia, showed that what we ordinarily call fatigue is mostly boredom.

Students were kept awake for several days. Even with no sleep for three or four days these students kept up a high energy level, *BUT only as long as their interest was kept alive.*

When their activities became uninteresting, they at once became "tired."

The Harvard Fatigue Laboratory made similar tests, and concluded that in 90 per cent of the cases, fatigue is nothing more than *mental boredom.*

William James stated that we all have great stores of energy within us of which we are not aware simply because we allow boredom to hypnotize us into thinking we are tired, long before we reach so-called "second wind."

SECOND, THIRD, FOURTH "WINDS"

If we would press on we would discover not only the "second wind," but the "third and fourth winds," said James.

We simply do not realize the power and the energy inherent in the human *spirit*. James advised that if we would ignore the first feelings of lassitude and press on through with our work, we should discover deeper levels of energy more powerful than the first.

Have you ever noticed how tired workers seemed filled with new life at the sound of the noonday whistle?

When I was a boy I used to plow with an old mule that, to all appearances, was half-dead with exhaustion. I often felt that passers-by must have thought me terribly cruel to work such a decrepit creature.

Late in the afternoon, however, when the day's work was done and we started home, this tired-out old animal became a veritable bolt of lightning!

When she was "headed for oats," she would run every step of the way!

Much the same thing happens with people who are convinced they are always tired.

Let 'em head for something they *want*, then watch their speed!

MY "BOY" PAT

Down on my Sizzle Ranch outside of Dallas I have a hired hand named Pat.

It is amusing to watch him work in the yard, with a slow movement that would never tire him out.

His pace is slow as he moves across the lawn, but he gets there, even though he is slow.

In fact even when the barn was on fire, he wouldn't run into the house to tell us. He merely shouted, "Hey, hey!"

Finally we decided to see what Pat was yelling about. Part of the barn was burning! After we put it out, we asked Pat why he didn't run to the house.

"No need," he replied. "I just yelled."

When we asked him why he hollered "hey" instead of "fire," his simple reply was, "Couldn't think of the word!"

That's my boy Pat—slow moving—not needing to hurry; but ring that dinner bell and watch Pat move from the barn to the kitchen dinner table!

He is "conditioned" to run then. It is a *joy* for him to eat, and not too much of a joy to work around the yard.

His fatigue leaves him at the sound of the dinner bell, although once when we rang twice and we asked him why he didn't come in the first time, he replied:

"I didn't hear the bell the *first* time!"

THE BIG "TRICK"

The big trick in handling my boy Pat is to make whatever he is doing a joy—a game—for then it brings out the second, third, and fourth wind.

Much the same thing happens with people who are convinced they are always tired. The truth of the matter is most likely that they do not like their work and the unconscious mind lowers the fatigue threshold.

They become conscious of feelings of "tiredness" long before there is any actual fatigue in the muscles. This is merely the body's method of rebelling against *disagreeable* work.

The trick is to make the work *agreeable* or *enjoyable!*

There are examples of all sorts to testify to the deeper levels of energy within the human spirit. It is a well-known fact among military men that tired, listless troops who have been for days with little food and sleep, will spring into action like fresh troops under the mental excitement of battle.

You have doubtless seen examples yourself of men who tapped energies within them that they never suspected existed before.

An uncle of mine once carried his piano—his most cherished

possession—out of the house and down a small flight of steps all by himself when the house caught on fire, although he was not known as a strong man.

It was a *joy* to save the piano!

WE HAVE ENERGY

Nearly all of us have ten times more energy than we shall ever use.

The problem is not so much how to create or store up more energy as how to utilize what we have—how to release it and make it available for use.

Enthusiasm, *joy,* and interest in what we are doing are the *great energizers.*

Boredom, negative thinking, unwholesome emotions, and mental conflicts are the great enervators or devitalizers.

During the war many writers commented on the almost superhuman energy displayed by Roosevelt and Churchill in working all hours of the day and night.

It is also well-known that these men had an all-consuming enthusiasm for the task at hand which released their energy for work.

Edison slept very little, as everyone knows. Some people say just four hours a night; Napoleon got along on very little sleep, for like Edison he could call upon his energies.

The secret? *They got a kick out of what they were doing!*

ANGER, IRRITATION, FEAR, ETC.

While boredom makes us think we are tired when we aren't, negative emotions such as anger, resentment, jealousy, irritation, fear, envy, throw the glands out of kilter and use up energy at a terrific rate.

Constant indulgence in such emotional outbursts is the one thing that can bring on genuine fatigue and deplete even the vast storehouse of energy that we carry in reserve.

As Dubois said, "an emotion tires the organism more than the most intense physical or intellectual work!"

Unresolved mental conflicts are almost as bad as emotional "benders" or "nights out."

Here precious energy is used up in the constant fight going on *inside* a person—energy that could be more profitably employed in some constructive work.

Such people should find some method of resolving the mental conflict, and call an armistice in the fight of opposing ideas and desires that is going on inside them.

Get rid of your "gremlins" inside you!!

ANOTHER FATIGUE CAUSE

Another cause of fatigue which is often thought of as physical but in reality is mental in origin, is general muscular "tenseness."

That is keeping the muscles *continually* at work!

The tenseness in the muscles is physical enough, but the underlying cause will nearly always be found to be anxiety or some unsettled "tense" mental state which is reflected *in* the muscles.

So, if you are perpetually tired, resolve to do something that will release new energy.

Find something in which you can become genuinely interested. Develop a *hobby* that you really would enjoy.

I know a person who always arrived late for work, until one day he developed a real interest in golf. That pepped him up, and now he gets to work on time.

Another person was worried about his lack of energy at the end of the day, until he told me he suddenly developed an enthusiasm for working down in the cellar machine shop.

He now finds his day at the office wasn't as tiring as he thought, and it was a wise doctor friend of mine, Dr. Frank Copeland, who suggested the machine shop instead of pills.

Often looking forward to a hobby at the end of the day actually makes the work seem less tiring.

Try a hobby!

THE ARMY PSYCHIATRISTS

You can also adopt a trick learned by the Army Psychiatrists during the war and make your job more *interesting* and so *less* tiring.

This method worked wonders in bringing new life to troops in isolated regions whose morale had dropped to a low level.

The soldiers couldn't feel their job fitted into any scheme of things—it was merely "routine" stuff.

Then the officers began to *show* the men in a series of lectures what relation their own seemingly small job had in the over-all strategy of war!

This made their jobs become *interesting*. Fatigue went down, morale up!

NO JOB UNIMPORTANT

You can use this same technique in your home, or your business. Make cleaning the yard a joy for the child; make the job of some employee interesting.

Use a little ingenuity—and this is possible.

Let others learn the purpose, the aims, the future of their daily tasks, and watch their fatigue go down.

Let them see what really happens when the small "waves" they set up with their supposedly insignificant job really get rolling.

During the war the defense plants would show pictures of the *completed* airplane, in actual use in Europe, to people whose jobs perhaps were merely inserting a small wire or rivet.

Of course this doesn't mean you can ignore the rules of *health*.

On the contrary their observance is necessary to energy.

The correct amount of sleep, vitalizing foods and exercise—these are the *raw materials* of your energy to get along with people and sell yourself to them.

They are the fuel which runs the human machine; but if these things are the "fuel," then "joy" is the spark that ignites the fuel and releases its latent energy for use.

So perhaps that "tired feeling" you experience is just mental; perhaps all you need is *joy* in doing something, *joy* in meeting people to gain pep that makes for friends.

The trouble with most "wet blankets" is they have lost the *spark* to get up their energies.

Don't be a Gloomy Gus–radiate enthusiasm, pep, joy, and watch people crowd around *you* in a room! You make them feel good. They catch some of your *pep*.

Remember that old proverb:

> *A merry heart doeth good like a medicine, but a broken spirit drieth the bones!*

"PEP" Spelled Forward or Backward Is Still "PEP"

CHAPTER 19

TAKE A MINUTE TO SAY "THANK YOU"

A SMILE and a good "thank you" warm me up faster than a thousand other things can do.

Whenever I see that sign at cashier counters, "If We Don't Say THANK YOU You Don't Have to Pay Your Check," I always try to catch the salesperson off guard.

Deliberately I'll rush him, but he will always take a minute to say "thank you."

Often I stand seemingly reading a magazine, and when I feel he is daydreaming, I quickly hand him the correct change and run for the door, but he always manages to holler after me, "Thank you—!"

I have gone even so far as to engage the salesperson in a long conversation, then suddenly hand over a twenty-dollar bill for a dime check, hoping this would cause so much annoyance the "thank you" would be forgotten.

But I have never yet, in my entire life received my check free!

IT'S SOUND PSYCHOLOGY

This cashier-counter psychology is sound. There is something to saying "thank you" by tradespeople especially. It builds business. It makes friends. It increases tips. It makes *you* feel like a *king!*

It has never made a single enemy!

Whenever a waitress smiles and says "thank you" I just have to dig deeper into my pocket for an extra coin. I'm a sucker for a pleasant "thank you."

Whenever a cab driver leaps out and opens the door and says, "Thank you," I feel positively *regal* and tip him a little extra in grand style.

Whenever a service man for my radio, the laundry man, the milk man, plumber or grocery delivery boy takes a minute to say "thank you," I go around telling people to trade with him.

I'm a fall guy for a "thank you"!

IT PAYS BIG RESULTS

It takes so little effort to say "thank you" that I sit and wonder just why more people don't say it.

People in the Latin countries always take a minute to say "thank you."

You stop someone on the street, as I often do on my lecture tours, and ask them a favor such as which way to the Hotel Reforma, and after they have told you they will always tip their hat politely and say, *"Muchas gracias, señor."*

Imagine, taking a minute to thank *me* for asking *them* a favor!

I always like to give Mexican boys American coins just to hear them say with a smile, *"Gracias, amigo!"*

Gosh, it inflates my ego!

DON'T VARY THE SIZE

The *size* of the "thank you" should never vary!

You should have the same size of "thank you" for everyone, for every purchase, whether it is a new Cadillac or a postage stamp!

If your "thank you" varies with each size order, and with each person, people will soon sense this. I do.

You must put a lot of sincere feeling behind it—so people will know you mean it.

There is one train porter I like who says, "Thank you," even when all he gets is a dime tip. He finds that maybe next time it will be more.

Often on my speaking tours I feel embarrassed because some big cigar and derby traveler unfolded a dollar tip when all I had left was a twenty-five-cent tip.

Instinctively I avoid that waiter, porter, service station, druggist, grocer, or tradesman who gives me a weak "dime thank you" instead of a big "dollar thank you."

I like people who take a minute to give me folding money "thank you's" in life!

SAME IN ANY LANGUAGE

The expression "thank you" means about the same thing in almost any language, for example:

Muchas gracias	*Merci beaucoup*
Danke schön	*Koszonom*
Tak skal de ha	*Bardzo dzekuje*
Bridheachas	*Tack sa mycket*
Dankbetuiging	*Grazie*

They all mean "thank you" providing the right feeling, the right tone, the right *ring* is put behind the expression.

People avoid people who mumble a mechanical "thank you."

You will get more worldly goods, more friends, and a greater kick out of life if you thank people for their smallest favors.

GOOD MANNERS WORK BOTH WAYS

Saying "thank you" to the boss, saying "thank you" to the employee, for even the smallest favor or request, gets that morale or personnel problem solved faster than demands or orders not hooked on to a "thank you."

Thanking the neighbor, thanking people in your club, thanking the newsboy—all make *them* feel better and *you too.*

It works both ways.

When you thank the shoeshine boy, you *both* feel better—and it makes your dime tip look like a quarter to *him.*

So learn the Emily Post technique of good manners, saying "thank you" to everybody around you, until you have them all over to your way of thinking.

Some "thank you's" sound like a phonograph—the same to each

person, so that a retail store often sounds like it was the aviary of a zoo, filled with talking birds and parrots.

Don't be a Johnny-One-Note, saying "thank you" first high, then low; fast, then slow—make it sound as interesting as the thing you are selling.

WATCH THE DOG

Watch him say "thank you" by merely wagging his tail—even a short stump of a tail. He beams up at you; he doesn't look at someone else when he says "thank you," but right at *you*. He looks you in the eye, and this is a good tip:

When you say "thank you!" look the other person straight in the eye!

Faces and eyes can express "thank you" just as much as the words themselves.

That beam, for example, on the cashier's face; that freckled grin on the teller's face; that light in the eye of the old railroad ticket agent!

A "thank you" not backed up by a smile is only half a "thank you!"

IT'LL MAKE YOU RICH

Spread the habit of saying "thank you" around your office, your bank, your sales room, your hotel, your restaurant, your corner store in the suburbs.

If you operate a drug, hardware, grocery, or laundry and dry cleaning store; or a suburban movie, gasoline station, or ice house, spread "thank you" around the neighborhood.

It will catch on like fire!

That's what happens to you when you take a full minute, a good sixty seconds, to thank people.

A cheerful "thank you" touches people's hearts and after all, the heart is physically located closer to the purse under the arm or the wallet in the hip pocket!

"Thank you" *properly spoken* will make you *rich!*

Try these "thank you's" today:

1. "Thank you" to the children for doing *anything*—it starts the habit early in them.
2. "Thank you" to the newsboy who hands you the morning newspaper.
3. "Thank you" to wifie when she reminds you that you forgot your handkerchief.
4. "Thank you" to hubby when he takes you out to dinner.
5. "Thank you" to the agent who sells you that travel ticket.
6. "Thank you" to the waitress when she brings you that second cup of coffee.
7. "Thank you" to the person who holds the door open for you.
8. "Thank you" to the doctor, lawyer, Indian Chief.

Make "thank you" a daily habit, just as taking vitamins or orange juice for breakfast.

Politeness may be the "old oil"; but it greases your social contacts. It lets you rub elbows with other people around you without bruising them!

So learn to take a minute out now and then to say "thank you!" It will get you places in life!

THANK YOU!

CHAPTER 20

YOU CAN'T GET ALONG WITHOUT THIS SHORT CHAPTER WITH A "LONG" LESSON

Here is a "product" you already have. Take it off the back shelf and use it. A Dutchman paid $40,-000 for it—a French lady $50,000. You can have it for nothing.

* * *

I HAVE DELIBERATELY put stars at the top of this chapter because it is one of the *most important* in this entire book.

It really should have been the first chapter, but this secret is so simple, so easy and so commonplace, I was afraid you would skip over it too hurriedly.

This is not a new secret. It is a very old one—like most all successful secrets of getting along with people.

But it works—works magic!

Don't just browse through this chapter. Read it once. Then twice.

Study it—for the four Wheelerpoints will not work without it.

When Adolph Zukor was in New York for dedication of the Paramount building, he had two full days of speeches, conferences, meetings scheduled.

In the midst of all this activity two old people appeared on the scene. They quietly asked to see Zukor. A few minutes later he came out with them, ordered his secretary to cancel all appointments, and he disappeared for two days.

When he returned Zukor told why. You see when he was a young immigrant boy, broke and hungry, this old couple took him into their home. They were kind to him—*and he never forgot it.*

JIMMY GETS TO HOLLYWOOD

It is Christmastime, 1944, in a French village of Baccarat. A GI is watching the French women standing in line to get food. One old lady is too tired and too weak to stand in line.

She is sitting outside with her bucket. The GI, James Kilpatrick of Atlanta, sees the old lady, and goes over and gives her his own food.

He finds that the old lady lives alone. While he is in Baccarat he goes often to her house to cheer her lonely hours; then his outfit pulls out for Germany and Kilpatrick hears no more from Madame Marchal.

Not until he gets home. He then learns that the old French lady has died, and because he had been kind to her she left him her entire fortune of $50,000.

A dream come true for Jimmy.

He had always wanted to sing in the movies; but he couldn't afford to take the gamble.

Now he went to Hollywood and has already appeared in several pictures.

$40,000 FOR ONE SMILE

Hans Bergen was grotesquely ugly. His neighbors in the Dutch Village of Ide would have nothing to do with him. His ugliness frightened and repulsed them, and Hans led a lonely, starved life until his death.

The surprised villagers found that Hans had left an estate worth $40,000.

Left it to a young girl, Anne Martin.

No one could understand why. She had never so much as spoken to him in his entire life; but when they read Hans' will they found out.

Anne had *smiled* at him *one time!*

"All the rest of you," the will said, "have frowned or looked away when I passed down the street. But Anne, when I met her one day, gave me a friendly smile, the only one in all my life."

CIVILITY BUYS EVERYTHING

Now I am not telling you that if you will be kind to old ladies you will inherit a fortune. I am not suggesting that if you smile at every ugly man you meet one of them will leave you $40,000 in his will.

I just wanted to tell you about these two cases where *courtesy* paid off—to show you what an important item this little courtesy is in dealing with human beings.

Anything that can make a great man cancel all appointments for two days—that will prompt a person to confer a fortune on another person—must be a *powerful* friendmaker.

Don't be suddenly courteous to people with the aim of "taking" them. That kind of courtesy is no good. It is an *empty box.*

But genuine *courtesy* that springs from the heart, cannot fail to make you richer.

If it does not bring you a rich inheritance—it will certainly enrich your life in many other better ways, for there is not a single case in history where anybody lost anything by being too courteous.

As Lady Mary Wortley Montague once said, "Civility costs nothing—and buys everything!"

WHY ARE PEOPLE RUDE?

My friend Murray Johnston of Oshawa, Ontario, has the answer to why people are rude.

"During World War I," he tells me, "I had occasion to serve under many commanders, Canadian, American, and British. I was terribly impressed with the careful courtesy that was nearly always exhibited by the British officers when you were dealing with them.

"It seemed to come naturally to them and was apparently without effort. You felt they *had time* to be courteous.

"I mentioned this to an old British officer and he said, 'My boy, always remember that rudeness is *just a cover for ignorance.'* From that time on, I was never guilty of being rude.

"So I learned," says Johnston, "that courtesy should not be kept in the cupboard for use on special guests only, but we should keep it on display always. Our mothers used to tell us that you catch more flies with sugar than vinegar and I guess the old adage still holds."

TAKE TIME FOR COURTESY

Take plenty of time to be courteous. Don't be in too big a hurry. "Life is not so short but that there is always time for courtesy," said Emerson.

It requires no great effort to be courteous.

Actually it takes fewer muscles to smile than to frown. You don't have to spend a single dollar to be courteous.

It is the little things—the trivial things that often we forget—that count up.

"In all the affairs of life, social as well as political, courtesies of a small and trivial character are the ones which strike deepest to the grateful and appreciating heart," said Henry Clay.

How well Adolph Zukor knew this—and Jimmy Kilpatrick—and the little Dutch girl!

It is *easy* to be courteous.

You don't have to memorize a lot of rules.

"Manners" change from country to country and from time to time, but real courtesy is nothing more than *genuine regard* and consideration for the feelings of others.

If you will just develop an interest in other people, you will never worry about violating the "rules" of courtesy.

You won't butt in when someone is telling a joke and say, "Oh, I've heard that old gag."

You won't correct people in such a way as to embarrass them.

You won't interrupt when they are talking to put in your own two-cents' worth.

You won't ignore people—you won't frown and yawn in their faces, because when you develop a genuine interest in other people you will be concentrating on making them feel *good.* That old fourth Wheelerpoint, remember?

J. C. PENNEY'S SECRET

"True politeness is perfect ease and freedom," said Chesterfield. "It simply consists in *treating others just as you love to be treated yourself.*"

The golden rule is the foundation stone of all genuine courtesy. Genuine courtesy means that we have consideration for the other fellow's interests—his wants, desires.

It means that we want to do unto others as we would have them do unto us.

J. C. Penney, founder of that vast chain of stores "with a million partners," whom I have been with on several speaking programs, said in an article in the *Rotarian*, "The golden rule is still golden."

He went on to say, "It is my belief that the golden rule principles are just as necessary for operating a business profitably as are trucks, typewriters, or twine."

Mr. Penney's phenomenal success in the business world is founded upon that deep spring of courtesy which makes a man want to treat others as he would be treated.

He is known as the "man with a million partners," which is certainly putting "everyone in the act," making his workers feel a part of the organization, dividing the profits with them to make them partners.

So in this short chapter you see you wouldn't go far in life if you didn't practice this doctrine of courtesy, politeness, and doing unto others as you want them to do to you.

Remember the stories of Adolph Zukor, Jimmy Kilpatrick, the little Dutch girl who smiled and did not frown—of J. C. Penney who made everybody a "partner," and the success this all brought to them.

Truly, you can't get along without this short chapter with its *long* lesson!

Leave People SMILING—Not Frowning

CHAPTER 21

AN EASY WAY TO WIN MANY FRIENDS AND GET MUCH CO-OPERATION

A "knack" used by famous people to make the other person feel "important"—to get things done for you *willingly.*

"I AM GETTING so I hate to go out with Walt any more," a friend told me the other day, "because Walt always expects to pay for the check."

Strange, you say? Not liking someone because they *always* pay the check.

The following letter appeared some time ago in an "advice to the lovelorn" column:

"My husband is a good provider. He is kind, generous, and very considerate. He is always doing things for me. I appreciate this, but he carries it too far.

"On week ends he cleans the house. He draws my bath. He brings my breakfast on Sunday morning. I know many wives would be proud of him, but there is a limit!!

"The trouble is he will *never let me do things for myself!!*"

Strange, you say? Kicking because someone is overly nice!

Then you read further, "If I try to do him a favor—he won't have it. It's all one way—one sided. How can I make my husband, dear Miss ——, understand he is robbing me of my self-respect?"

You see, he was always the Knight in Shining Armor! She wanted to play the hero once in a while!

THESE PEOPLE CRAZY?

What is wrong with these people, one who kicks because his friend always pays the check, the other because her husband is always doing things.

Are they crazy?

No—not crazy—just cheated!

Cheated and robbed—of that feeling of *importance* that everyone craves!

Doing "little things"—doing your share—conferring favors—these are *good ways* to make people like you. That is, unless *you carry things too far!*

If you never let the other person do something for you, you are not giving him a chance to "feel important," to maintain his self-respect.

When you are winning friends use both *top* English, and *reverse* English! Take the high road, then the low road.

Do things for other people—then let them have the *fun* and the *thrill* and the *enjoyment* out of doing something for you in return.

No, these two people who kicked weren't crazy, just *starved* out of the right to "play the hero role."

THAT KINGLY FEELING

In the old days kings were the only people who could confer favors. Ordinary people didn't have that *privilege.*

It was something *reserved exclusively* for the king, for it made him the hero!

It still makes a person feel like a *king* to confer favors.

It gives him a feeling of importance. He is playing "the big shot" role. He is the guy who has the *power* to give the favor.

For example, two brothers were running for office in Tennessee. One of them made it a point to kiss babies—give away fans and almanacs. People liked him for that. He "gave them something."

But the other brother was *even* smarter!

When he mounted the platform to speak he would feel in all his pockets, *look helpless,* and say, "Has anybody got a chaw of terbaccy?" He contrived to *let* people do things for *him!*

This then made *the people* feel important!

They went out bragging "how I gave him a chaw of my terbaccy." To think *they* were in a position to actually help a big politician!

So this was the brother they elected!

The first brother gave the "hero role" to himself; the second brother, the smart one, let the *people* play the hero!

KING OR SERF, WHICH?

The history books are filled with examples of famous men who became famous by "asking favors," instead of always heaping them upon an embarrassed people.

Benjamin Franklin comes to my mind—how he won over a man who was cool toward him. Now Franklin didn't write this man a love letter, or send a "peace offering."

Instead he wrote the man a note and *asked a favor*. Imagine, asking a favor of an enemy?

He asked the man if he could borrow a book from his library. Ben was a smart casting director. He cast the *other* fellow in the *superior* role.

He made the other fellow feel important by borrowing a book he *knew* the man regarded with great pride. This flattered the man's ego—to think someone *else* admired this very same book!

"He that hath once done you a kindness," wrote Franklin, "will be *more ready* to do you another, than he whom you yourself have obliged."

You've heard that old saying, "The quickest way to lose a friend is to loan him money."

There is a heap of truth in this old saying of wise people. When you loan your friend money you automatically place yourself in a *superior role* and your friend is in the inferior role, one he doesn't like to play.

He may appreciate the loan, but if you are not careful how you handle him, he will unconsciously *resent* that you have placed him in the inferior position of having to borrow from you.

Change the pace now and then. Get out your reverse English, and we will learn more of this shortly, and don't always insist upon being the one who gives the favors.

When you do this you make your friend become *king.* So let the other fellow do you a small favor now and then. Borrow something small from him, accept a cigarette, and temporarily *he* becomes *king.*

However, don't overdo this—and become a *bum!* Don't carry anything too far. Remember what Socrates once said, "Nothing in excess!"

IT WORKS MAGICALLY

"I *need* you—" are three words that make people feel important.

If you want your wife to be happy that she married you, tell her, "I need you." Just don't stop at telling her in so many words. Tell her in *actions* by letting her do little things for you now and then.

Then, of course, you'll make her feel more important by those two other friendmakers, "thank you."

No matter how good a husband may be—at the moment he convinces his wife he doesn't *need* her—the marriage is slipping.

Nothing so charms a little child as to "help mama" in the kitchen—to "help daddy" mow the lawn.

People want to feel that they are *needed.* The servant, the banker, the poor family down the street, everybody—everywhere—likes that feeling of *importance,* of being "needed."

If you want to get better co-operation out of your employees, make them feel you *need* them. Ask them small favors—not big ones they can't give—but little things.

An executive with one of the nation's largest corporations gains the good will of employees by asking small favors. He takes a stroll through the plant, stops and asks an employee for a match—to witness his signature on a paper—anything at all to let the employee feel he has done "something for the boss."

One of the country's most successful personnel directors tells each employee:

"I have a favor to ask of you. The company gave me this job because I convinced them I had good judgment in picking men. If it turns out I am wrong I won't have a job very long. I want to ask *you* to help *me* make good on my job by proving to the big boss that I was right when I hired you."

It works magically!

So use this easy way to *success*. Make people feel *important* by asking them some small favor. Let them have the fun of playing the *hero*.

How? This way:

> *Let others feel you* need them *and give them a chance to prove it.*

It Is as Blessed to RECEIVE as to GIVE

CHAPTER 22

THE POWER IN WORDS

A Short Short Story Number 5*

THERE IS NO such thing as "magic words," but there are words that "work magic."

The day of Ali Baba and his "open sesame" is over, and no pinch of smoke produces a friend.

You do have a greater power, though, the power in words; words that make people do things for you faster and with greater willingness.

For example, when you call wifie, never shout, "Bring *my* car down—I'm ready to leave."

The little lady is tired of driving *your* car, living in *your* house, eating *your* food.

Use a little "word magic" and say, "Please bring *our* car down, dear." Ah, the power in words.

Here are the *five* best words in the world to make people sit up and like you:

"I am proud of you."

Use them on the boss, on the employee, on the friend, husband, wifie, the kids. Tell them you are proud of something they did.

Watch these five little words inflate them; make them careful never to let that fine opinion of yours change.

Here are the *four* best words to gain willing information from others:

"What is your opinion?"

Stop a congressman, a banker, a prize fighter, anyone, and ask them their opinion on something; and see their eyes brighten as they cough importantly and say, "You have come to the right person—now *my* opinion is this . . ."

The *three* best words to get people to do things for you are:

". . . if you please!"

* Reprinted from *Kiwanis* Magazine.

Tag this harmless little phrase onto every request you make, every order you give to others, and watch that sprinkling of "word magic" react on others.

The *two* best words to make people glad they did something for you; two words to insure yourself of their support on something the next time, are:

"Thank you!!"

How simple these two words. How little they are used. Yet if you "Take a minute to say thank you," and it takes that long, you have purchased word insurance that the next time people will respond quicker to your wishes and orders.

The *one* greatest word you already have had, the word "our"; but did you know the smallest word in the world, the word "I"?

It is the quickest to write—the quickest to say, and the one few people ever like to hear!

If you were to ask me now for the greatest phrase ever spoken, the world's most famous combination of words, they are:

"Jesus wept!"

Two words that make you visualize the man and all of his thoughts, as no other combination of words have ever done.

Inside each of you are words that "work magic" on others. Locate these words; and you will gain new friends, new wealth, and new happiness in the power of your own words.

THE "LOST ART" OF REVERSE ENGLISH

On and off I have given you subtle hints on the great power that lies behind "reverse" English, hitting the ball so that it reverses itself and scores a point.

By this means in human relations, bending "backwards" often gets the other person to "go forward" with you!

The engineer often backs up a long train so that the cars "tighten up," and then when he goes forward he does so *without* jerks and bumps to the passengers.

So important is "reverse selling" in getting along with people and *selling* yourself, that we have three chapters on this profitable and interesting subject.

1. *When you want to talk—LISTEN!*
   This is a good rule to make people like you immediately. It leaves a nice impression with others.
2. *What can "I" offer?*
   It isn't what the other person can do for you, but what you can do for him that *sells* him on even lending you money or his favorite hunting dog.
3. *Let the other fellow argue "your" case.*
   State your case moderately and accurately, and don't go at people with a tone of positiveness and arrogance. Note the magical results.

CHAPTER 23

WHEN YOU WANT TO TALK—LISTEN

Reverse English Number 1

WE ALL WANT to make a good impression the first time we meet someone, so what do we usually do? What is normal—the human thing to do?

We want to *talk* of course!

We want to tell about all the great things *we* have done. *We* want to talk about the smart things *we* have said. We try to impress the other person with how important *we* are.

But does this create a good impression? Well, you know the answer to that one. It doesn't.

The real way to make a good impression is to put reverse English on that desire to *talk,* and do just the opposite, *listen!*

If you want a person to like you instantly—let him feel that *you* are favorably impressed *with him.*

Be a good listener first—a good talker second.

AVOIDING THE YAWNS

Consider how *you* feel when you meet someone who starts right off buzzing into your ears—talking them off your head. . . .

"I want to tell you all about my operation." . . . "Let me tell you how I told off that sourpuss clerk." . . . "Have you heard how I won the bridge tournament?" . . . "I want to tell you about my trip." . . .

Are you *impressed?* No. You start to yawn. "Here we go again," you say to yourself or under your breath to someone, and sit back to be bored.

Now what happens when you meet someone who does just the opposite? "Tell me of *your* trip," he asks, or, "How is business with *you?*"

The person who greets you with, "They tell me you ran up a

fine score the other day—tell me about it?" Or, "How's *your* operation, Mrs. Sawbones?"

Now *you are* interested. You let loose, sit back, and with a long breath start off on what seems to interest you most, *Y-O-U!* Especially, if the other person is very courteous and hides his boredom, that vacant look in his eyes, but leans toward you in utter enjoyment of your recitation.

He won't break in and interrupt you in the middle of a sentence. He won't stifle a yawn, nor let his glance wander away from you.

Instead he leans forward physically—and mentally—he "listens a little closer"—so as not to miss a single word you are saying.

You walk away later on and say to someone, "He is sure a *great conversationalist*, isn't he????"

SIX MORE MAGIC WORDS

If your friend is really good at using reverse English, he will keep the conversation going with six little magic words that make you feel wonderful.

Every time you stop to catch your breath, he will say tactfully, ". . . *and then what did you do???*"

Oh, boy—off you go again on chapters 2, 3, 8, 32 of your adventures or your operation!

You feel mighty good. How his six words have inflated your ego!

All your life you have been wanting to tell *your opinions* and people kept cutting in to tell you *their* opinions, but here at last is a person who will hear you out.

He has recognized the importance of your opinion. He is anxious to listen to you, and down in your subconscious mind here is what is happening: "This man is the first to recognize my true importance—therefore he is smarter than other people. He is intelligent. He's a darned good fellow!"

But, you say, what pleasure or profit do I get always listening? This:

1. The pleasure of pleasing people.
2. Learning something you didn't know.

Because remember, you can't learn when your mouth is open!

HOW TO CONVERSE

If you want to get a reputation as a charming conversationalist just remember those six little words, ". . . and then what did you do?" or, ". . . and then what did you say?"

They'll do more to win you popularity than all the personal exploits you could tell others about yourself.

Most people are like the playwright who spent an hour telling his dinner companion all about how he had come to write his various plays, where he got his plots, his characters. After an hour of this he turned to his companion and said:

"But enough of this. You must tell me all about yourself—tell me—what do *you* think about my plays!!!"

Something like the ham actor who said, "Let's talk about *me*, dearie."

Disraeli, the famous English statesman, started out with two strikes on him. He was a nobody, and he was so brilliant that he aroused the envy and jealousy of other politicians.

But Disraeli became accepted, not only as one of England's most brilliant statesmen, but also as one of the most charming dinner guests. His presence was in great demand in "high society."

All the blue-blooded matrons were charmed. We wonder what Disraeli's technique was and then from his personal notebook we find his little secret of getting along with people and selling himself. He wrote, "Don't talk *too much*—never argue!"

Disraeli "listened himself" into high society.

DWIGHT MORROW, "AMATEUR"

Dwight W. Morrow was called an "amateur diplomat" when Calvin Coolidge first appointed him ambassador to Mexico; but Morrow accomplished what the professionals had failed to do.

He ironed out the difference between Mexico and the States, made a lifelong friend of Mexico's President Calles.

How did Morrow accomplish this? He "listened the whole thing over" with President Calles.

He used the ". . . and then what did you do, President Calles?" technique.

Bruce Barton, in telling of his first encounter with Calles says that Morrow had breakfast with Calles. Morrow didn't even mention the many problems—the points of differences between the two countries.

He just passed his plate for more pancakes!

After breakfast he lighted a cigar, pushed back his chair and asked Calles *to tell him about Mexico!*

This *is* using reverse English!

A WIDE-OPEN MOUTH

Indeed, you can't learn when your mouth is open!

That is a good reason for putting reverse English on your desire to talk, so that you will learn, like Morrow learned about Mexico by getting Calles to do the talking.

"The average man talks too much, especially if he has a good command of language," said Elbert Gary.

Some of the most successful businessmen use the strategy of "intelligent listening," to influence people—to get what they want —and to *learn* something they didn't know.

Harold Stassen owes much of his ability to get along with people to his ability of listening.

When he was Governor of Minnesota he earned a reputation for being a "peacemaker" between capital and labor. He managed to get along with both—and to bring them together for their mutual benefit.

Stassen did this by "listening."

He was always willing to "listen out the other fellow's story." He had regular meetings once a month with labor leaders, and at these conferences Stassen not only talked—but listened.

He encouraged the other fellow to "get it off his chest" and to "tell the whole story."

And Stassen *learned* both sides of the story!

DON'T HUSH UP OTHERS

This is a strategy you will do well to use when you are dealing with someone who has a complaint. Don't try to hush them up.

Encourage them to talk. Make sure they tell it all. You won't get very far as long as they have something *unsaid* bottled up inside of them.

Insist they tell everything!!

This will clear the air of tension. It relaxes the other fellow to get it off his chest. When he is "told out" and has "told all," he will be out of ammunition and willing then to listen to *you.*

So practice this technique—and *don't hush up* the one with complaints.

If you bottle up steam it will soon explode—but if you give it an outlet, it cools off.

Don't hush up complaints!

FAMOUS "LISTENERS"

James F. Lincoln, president of the Lincoln Electric Company of Cleveland, has never had any labor trouble.

There has never been a strike in his plant, for every two weeks he calls a conference of labor and management where problems are discussed—not argued.

If the employees have any complaints, they are encouraged to speak of them. They aren't allowed to build up steam inside of them for explosion down the street some night after working hours.

At these conferences Mr. Lincoln does more *listening* than he does talking.

So—no strikes!

John D. Rockefeller was a famous "listener."

In conferences, Edward T. Bedford said, "He was always glad

to listen to anyone. He always encouraged others to talk. We seldom knew what he was thinking, but he always seemed to know what *we* were thinking."

Merle Crowell, writing in the *American Magazine* in October, 1916, said of Charles Schwab:

"Without saying a word Mr. Schwab can flatter more than any man I have ever met.

"Listening with him is an instinct as well as a rare charm," continued Crowell, "for whoever talks with him, be he day laborer or financier, faces a man who harkens gravely, attentively, eye to eye, until the speaker is quite done."

Notice, please, that Crowell says that listening was *instinctive* with Schwab, because with most of us *talking* is instinctive, not listening.

* * *

Arabic Proverb: *If I listen I have the advantage; if I speak others have it.*

Spanish Proverb: *A fish dies by an open mouth!*

* * *

When you shoot a billiard ball the *natural tendency* is for the cue ball to roll forward after striking the object ball.

Skillful billiard players overcome this natural tendency by applying "reverse English" to the bottom of the cue ball; then instead of rolling forward—it backs up!

I once saw Willie Hoppe "draw" a cue ball around the table for five cushions.

To be an expert at billiards, the player has to learn *when* to apply reverse English.

In the game of Life that *you* are playing, knowing when and how to apply "reverse selling" is just as important—if you want to be a winner, instead of a fizzler.

When you are using the Four Wheelerpoints to win friends, to get along with people, to sell yourself, remember it is *how* you use these "Tested Points" that counts.

Willie Hoppe uses the same cue ball throughout a match; but

sometimes he strokes it with "top English," sometimes with "reverse."

So if you find one of the Four Wheelerpoints isn't working as well as you figured, the chances are you are using it with too much "top English."

Try the "reverse" occasionally!

A LOOK AT HUMAN NATURE

What is the *natural tendency* in human nature? What is it that everybody wants? Why, to *push themselves* of course!

> We want to impress other people how smart *we* are.
> We want to feel important.
> We want to get all that's coming to *us*.
> We want to "shine."
> We want to be *somebody*.
> We want people to look up to us.
> We want people to love us.

It is all right, perfectly all right, to want these things, and these desires can be satisfied. You *can* be charming. You *can* get what is coming to you.

But not by going after them directly, which is the natural tendency in human nature.

The man who makes a direct frontal assault to impress us with how smart he is—only earns a reputation as a blowhard.

The matron who is determined to be charming at any cost—ends up as an "eager beaver"—and a terrible bore.

The wife who feels she is entitled to the love of her husband and *demands* that she get it—seldom gets it.

The worker who uses a club to "demand his rights" may get a small raise out of industry of a few cents an hour; but he will never rise from the role of a laborer to president of the company as did Carnegie, Schwab, and all the other "successful" men of our time who "rose from the ranks."

These people go at what they want from the wrong angle—don't *you* make similar mistakes in life.

PAID TO "LISTEN"

Intelligent listeners are so much in demand, and so rare, that people will actually pay for the privilege of talking.

In St. Petersburg, Florida, there is a lady who makes a good living charging hourly rates to "listen" while others talk of their troubles.

In Little Rock, Arkansas, there is a business known as the "Southern Listening Bureau." It advertises itself as follows:

> We offer well-trained and experienced listeners who will hear you as long as you wish to talk, and without interruptions, for a nominal fee. As our listeners listen their faces portray interest, pity, fellow feeling, understanding; where called for, they exhibit hate, hope, despair, sorrow, or joy. Lawyers, politicians, club leaders, reformers can try their speeches on us. You may talk freely about your business or domestic problems without fear of having any confidence betrayed. Just let off steam into the discreet ears of our experts—and feel better.

* * *

When Einstein was asked to give the mathematical equation for success, he replied:

"If *A* represents success in life, the formula is *A* equals X plus *Y* plus Z; *X* being work and *Y* being play."

"And what does Z stand for, Mr. Einstein?" he was asked.

"Z," he replied, "is keeping your mouth shut!"

* * *

Arabic Proverb: *When the mind becomes large—speech becomes little.*

* * *

You can improve yourself with "reverse English" by being first the good listener, *then* the clever conversationalist.

But before people will listen to you, you first must "listen them out."

When you "listen your way in" you don't have to "talk your way out."

You have two ears, one mouth. Therefore, use your ears twice as much as your mouth!

Don't try to "out talk" the other person. "Listen the whole thing over" with him, like Morrow did with Calles.

Remember:

> *When your tongue is in* high gear *your brain is in low gear, until you shift into "reverse."*

Carole Lombard's advice on how to make a hit with the boy friend was, "Be the best audience he has ever had. That means, see to it that your date does most of the talking. Keep him talking about jobs, hobbies, sports. . . . As long as he is the center of conversation he'll stay thoroughly at ease . . . and he'll like that. . . ."

CHAPTER 24

CHANGE "WHAT HAVE I GOT COMING?" TO "WHAT CAN I OFFER?"

Reverse English Number 2

WHEN WE WANT more money, such as a raise in pay, or in income, what is our natural reaction?

We start thinking how we can hit up the boss, our customers, or prospects for *more* money—how we can *make* the other fellow pay us more.

It is easy to sit back and convince ourselves that the world owes us a living. We "demand our rights." We use force—threats—to get what we want.

At least that is the *natural* human thing to do. Wanting more money is okay. The only thing I have against the "force" method of getting more is that *it does not work.*

Simple enough reason for not using force, isn't it?

Not a single one of America's successful men attained success by forcing someone to give them "their rights." No schools have ever been endowed by a man who sat down and hollered for the world to give him more.

No libraries have been founded by such men.

No monument has ever been erected to a man who became a success by *demanding* that others give him "his just due."

If there was a single solitary case in *all history* where such methods had worked—I might recommend them. But there is none!

So why consider "failure methods"?

AN ALTERNATIVE METHOD

The alternative to using *force* is, of course, to use Wheelerpoint One, "Don't Make 'em Drink—Make 'em Thirsty."

Make your boss want to give you more money. Make people

want to buy more of your goods. Make industry *want* to do something for labor—make labor *want* to do something for industry.

Most kids will quickly tell you the hickory stick did less to make them want to do good things, than just plain, old hunger, getting so hungry they stopped eating worms and came inside to fill up.

To use Wheelerpoint One, though, you've got to put the old reverse on that human desire to get what you want by crying for it. Then the point works most effectively.

You must turn that question, "What have I got coming?" inside out to "What can I offer?"

For when "What have I got coming?" is reversed, it is then rightside out and says, "What have I to offer?" Better, isn't it?

When you have something of genuine value to offer—some prize inside your box—then you'll make people hungry and thirsty—you'll make them *want* to give you more.

Try this technique to get money, or a raise.

TAKE B. C. FORBES

If you are the boss instead of the worker, this rule works for you, too. It works both ways, which is why I like it better than the heavy club method.

Your company will prosper more if you ask yourself, "How can I best help my employees to help me?" Much better than if you merely ask, "How much can I get out of these people for how little?"

B. C. Forbes is one of the most astute businessmen and one of the most brilliant scholars of economics in the world. He not only built a personal fortune by following his economic philosophy, but he has taught thousands of other people how to become successful.

He was one of the very few men with enough foresight to see the 1929 market crash *before* it happened. Those who followed his advice got out. Those who didn't—were most sorry.

B. C. Forbes says that the question that should be uppermost in your mind during any sort of business transaction is:

"What is there in it for—THE OTHER PARTY?"

If the other person gets little, there is no deal—no inclination on his part to make a deal, or stick by one he is forced into.

"Human nature has not been suddenly regenerated," he says. "Unselfishness has not routed selfishness. The new version is being adopted because *it pays.*" *

When you are tempted to concentrate on "What is there in it for me?" put the reverse English to work and concentrate on "What is there in it *for the other party?*"

A formula that will make more money for you.

INTELLIGENT SELFISHNESS

We have said in a previous chapter that all human beings are selfish. In a very learned essay Aristotle once wrote that it is not the desire to help yourself that is evil—it is only when man tries to help himself *in the wrong way* that selfishness becomes evil.

"Should a man love himself most, or someone else? People criticize those who love themselves most, and call them self-lovers, using this as an epithet of disgrace, and a bad man seems to do everything for his own sake," says Aristotle in his essay *Politics.*

". . . and the more so the better he is, and acts for his friend's sake, and sacrifices his own interest," continues Aristotle.

You see there is *intelligent* selfishness, which is all right—and much better than *stupid* selfishness.

"But," says Aristotle, "the facts clash with these arguments, and this is not surprising. For men say that one ought to love best one's friend, and a man's best friend is one who wishes well to the object of his wish for his sake, even if no one is to know of it; and these attributes are found most of all in a man's attitude toward himself."

A lot of words—heavy in Aristotle's style—but so timely for the present-day world when we simplify his teachings to—tell 'em what they will get, not what you want or expect.

* B. C. Forbes, *Finance, Business and Business of Life* (New York: Published by author, 1915).

SELFISHLY UNSELFISH

What we usually call by the name of "selfishness" is not true selfishness at all—because it is not successful—it does not aid yourself.

It is the stupid way to be selfish. It is the unsuccessful way to be selfish.

True self-help, or intelligent selfishness, consists in putting reverse English on old-fashioned selfishness, and as Forbes says you should not concentrate upon what the other fellow gets merely because it is the noble thing—or because it is your duty.

There is a much more important reason for *you. It pays off.*

When you put reverse English on old-fashioned selfishness, you will find that the *most selfish thing you can do is to be unselfish.*

A THOUSAND PROOFS!

Now if you think that sounds like an extravagant statement let me tell you about more than a thousand people who have *tested* it and found that it works.

Today, the Lincoln Electric Company of Cleveland, Ohio, is the biggest manufacturer of arc-welding equipment in the world. It does approximately half of the total arc-welding business of the United States and more than a quarter of all the arc-welding business in the world.

In 1934, James F. Lincoln inaugurated a plan that has accomplished what appears to be impossibilities. Under this plan the annual volume of business done by this firm jumped from five million a year in 1934 to 33 million in 1943.

The cost of the manufactured article to the customer was about cut in half despite the rise in cost of raw materials.

The amount of dividends paid to stockholders was increased approximately four times.

The annual average wage for Lincoln's one thousand employees jumped from a little over a thousand dollars in 1934 to better than $5,400 in 1946.

What was this magic plan that increased profits, lowered prices, raised wages?

It was simply the practice of what Mr. Lincoln calls "intelligent selfishness," and here is how it worked.

MR. LINCOLN'S THINKING

First of all Mr. Lincoln made his employees a "part of the act," the fourth Wheelerpoint.

Together they worked out a plan whereby workers would share in the profits of the business. This made them thirsty—made them *want* to work harder, *want* to produce more—*want* to figure out better and more efficient ways of doing things.

Because the more they made for the company, the more they made for themselves.

Mr. Lincoln's employees stopped concentrating on what they had coming and began to use their brains to figure out what ability—what talent, what ingenuity *they* could give to the company.

Some amazing things happened.

Ordinary "working men" came up with ideas that would do justice to an inventive genius.

There were no "slow downs." The workers realized that they would be paid upon management's "ability to pay"—and at the same time that management's "ability to pay" depended upon their ability to produce.

The workers weren't selfish in the old-fashioned way. They were "intelligently selfish."

EVERYBODY BENEFITS

When the time came to pay the workers, Mr. Lincoln wasn't selfish in the old-fashioned way either. He realized that for his business to be successful he must have men who could produce.

The surest way to make them *want* to produce was to give them an incentive.

The average wage of $5,400 per year is the highest in the industry; but when I asked Mr. Lincoln about the high wages—and the bonuses—some of which run as high as $50,000 a year—he told me:

"We do not *give* anything to our men!"

I was startled, and he continued.

"We are just about as far from that as we possibly can be. Every dollar our people get they earn.

"They earn it by making a very much better product to be sold at a very much lower price. They produce many times as much as is produced in other plants because of their development of their abilities and co-operation."

Lincoln's employees *help him* so he will be able to *help them.*

Simple, isn't it? Better than crisscross fights over how much "do we get" and here is "what we will do in return."

Everybody benefits this way!

HELPING EMPLOYEES WIN

In this way, Mr. Lincoln *helps his employees* so they will want to *help him.*

Sort of an endless chain—eight in a row, each scratching the back of the fellow in front, and getting his own back scratched from the fellow in back.

In speaking about "intelligent selfishness"—helping the other fellow to help you—Mr. Lincoln told me:

"This is what makes our plan a success. It makes all industry a success. It is the thing that makes married life a success. It is the foundation of all human progress."

You see you can't elevate yourself by pushing the other fellow *down!*

* * *

Old-fashioned selfishness is attempting to help yourself at the other's expense.

"Intelligent selfishness" is helping yourself by helping others to help you.

"Intelligent selfishness" works every time.

* * *

This is one of the secrets of Frank E. Gannett's success—from newsboy to the biggest newspaper owner in the U. S. One of Gannett's early mottoes was "Make Yourself More Useful." Although he knew he would never be a stenographer, he took courses in shorthand—"to make himself more useful." He took courses in bookkeeping for the same reason. And early in life he learned all he could about salesmanship—to "make himself more useful" later on.

* * *

What you are "worth" depends upon what you are worth to the other fellow.

When you want more—make yourself worth more.

Then you will get your "due" gladly and willingly—without having to holler for it.

If one man won't pay you—another will.

For men who are worth money aren't allowed to sit around idle.

SEWELL AVERY'S STORY

The very first year Sewell Avery was president of Montgomery Ward, he brought the company out of the "red" into the "black."

Dividends were paid to stockholders.

Yet some of the higher-ups thought Avery's salary of around $100,000 a year was too much, and an attempt was made to get control of the company away from Avery.

At a meeting of the higher-ups in the company one man spoke up and said, "Personally I'd rather pay a man $100,000 a year who can make *me* money than to pay $25,000 a year to a man who can't."

Avery kept his job.

When someone remarked to John D. Rockefeller that Judge Gary made an exorbitant salary, Rockefeller is reputed to have said, "I don't know how much he makes now; but if he'll come to work for me tomorrow I'll double it."

And when someone asked Andrew Carnegie why in the world he paid Charles Schwab around a million dollars a year, Carnegie's answer was simply:

"He's worth twice that amount!"

JUSTIN DART'S STORY

When Justin Dart was made president of United Drug Company in 1943 at a salary of $75,000 per year, he had an offer in his pocket from another concern (Ward's) offering him $150,000.

He could quit United tomorrow morning and half a dozen companies would gladly pay him more than he is getting. Why? Simply because Dart is *worth* big money to any company that hires him.

Dart is a man of ideas. He also is an exponent of "intelligent selfishness."

One of the first things he did when he went with United was to inaugurate his "opportunity-unlimited" plan whereby 10,000 independent druggists would be able to compete on equal footing with superstores of Dart's *own* chain!

To some, this might appear as dangerous business.

Not to Dart. A big corporation may gain a temporary advantage by forcing a small merchant out of business, he says, but in the long run such methods would be ruinous to big business itself.

Big business is possible only in a system of free enterprise.

"The continuance of our economic system depends upon every businessman's having the opportunity to succeed in his own business," Dart says, "be it a curbstone fruit stand, or a large factory."

Then he goes on to say, "If small business is crushed, big business and our system of private enterprise will crash too!"

That is sense.

It paid off, too, for Justin Dart started out in the drug business as a clerk making twenty-five dollars a week.

Had his philosophy been to "demand his rights," he would be making perhaps forty dollars per week today. He might even make seventy-five dollars.

But by concentrating upon what he had to offer—instead of what he had coming, he is now making approximately $1,500 a week and could make twice that if he chose.

Are you beginning to "catch on" to what I said earlier, that I would advocate *force* and *threats* to get a raise, money, or a better job *if* these things worked!

Since they won't work—and since the reverse *works*—this alternative method is the only one I am plugging for!

What have you to *give* others?

Study about that for awhile. If you think about it long enough —and then if you put your thoughts into action—you won't have to worry about what you have coming—*you'll get it automatically!*

When we think of successful men we invariably think of their *contributions* to the world.

It was Edison who "gave" the world the electric light—Ford "gave" us the low-priced car—De Forest "gave" us the radio.

One of Thomas J. Watson's mottoes is "SERVE—AND SELL." It is significant that Mr. Watson, whose IBM salesmen are recognized as among the best in the world, puts the "Serve" first and "Sell" second.

YOU DON'T HAVE TO BE A CROOK TO MAKE A MILLION DOLLARS

About the most stupid thing that has ever been said is the old bromide, "You have to be either crooked or lucky to make a million dollars."

All you need do is figure out something that you can *offer* other people.

Some article that will make their life more interesting, happier, easier.

The fortune you will make will depend upon the value of the thing you have to offer; and when you make yourself rich by service to others, you won't be a crook or lucky.

You'll enrich millions of others *with* you.

To make more money, remember that motto of B. C. Forbes and put reverse English on the tendency to think about what you get.

Instead, ask yourself:

> *WHAT IS THERE IN IT—FOR THE OTHER FELLOW?*

CHAPTER 25

LET THE OTHER FELLOW ARGUE "YOUR" CASE

Reverse English Number 3

AARON BURR is perhaps the best example history could offer of how *not* to sell yourself. He had brains, ability, courage. He had just about everything except the ability to get along with people.

As a young man he became a famous hero for his bravery in the Revolutionary War. General Washington appointed him to his staff, but he didn't stay long.

He was brilliant and he knew it; and he didn't hesitate to use his brilliance to "show up" Washington every chance he got. He was a man with ideas, but didn't know how to put them across.

When he approached Washington with an idea, he attempted to cram it down his throat—whole; and when Washington would disagree with him he didn't hesitate to come right out and say, "You are wrong, General—dead wrong!!"

It didn't take Washington long to get fed up on this, and he got rid of Aaron Burr.

It was the same story everywhere that Burr went. He managed to get himself elected Vice-President—found himself forced to flee the country as a fugitive a few years later. His whole life was one long series of "near successes"—followed by failure and disgrace.

One main trouble with Aaron Burr was that he didn't know how to use reverse English. When he tried to sell other people his ideas, he used too much "top English" and instead of pulling them toward him, he forced them farther away.

"FORCED FEEDING" WON'T WORK

"Forced feeding" doesn't work any better when you are dealing in ideas than it does in food. To put your ideas across you must get out Wheelerpoint one and "make 'em thirsty—make 'em hungry" for your idea.

As a contrast to Aaron Burr, who failed because he attempted to force feed people on his ideas direct, let us take a look at one of the *best* "idea salesmen" of all history.

During Wilson's administration Colonel House came to be known as the "power behind the throne." It is said that Colonel House had more influence on Wilson than any other man. He had the satisfaction of seeing President Wilson put many of his ideas into practice.

"I learned the best way to convert him to an idea," says Colonel House, "was to plant it in his mind casually, but so as to interest him in it—*so as to get him thinking about it on his own account.*" *

You can't catch trout with a bear trap!

Colonel House's technique was in *suggesting* an idea to Wilson, rather than in coming right out and attempting to drive it home. He would bring his idea out subtly—gently—like a trout fisherman casting his fly just out of reach of the trout's mouth.

If you try to hit the fish in the mouth with your fly, you'll only scare him away; but by merely placing it where he can see it, he is "made thirsty"—"made hungry"—to come take it *of his own accord!*

That is one of the best ways to get acceptances of your ideas. Place them out where people can see them—then let them come *to the idea.* Let them make up their own minds to take it.

Colonel House merely "planted" the idea in Wilson's mind. After a few days the idea would germinate—Wilson would accept then *his own idea* and adopt it.

That is one of the *real secrets of selling ideas.* Let the other person accept it as his own.

In selling ideas it is best to let the other fellow sell himself, for then he'll *stay sold!*

* Arthur D. Howden Smith, *The Real Colonel House* (New York: George H. Doran Company, 1918).

PERSUASION BY DEFAULT

Sometimes, particularly when you are dealing with a "contrary" individual, it is best to go all out on the reverse English—even so far as to appear you are taking the *opposite* stand.

Some people are *contrary* by nature. It is their nature to disagree. Say to one of these individuals, "You wouldn't say that, would you?" and he'll come right back with, ". . . and *why* wouldn't I say that!!"

Say to him, "I didn't think you'd be interested in that," and he is apt to reply, "Why wouldn't I be interested!!"

Br'er Fox in the famous Uncle Remus stories was one of these so-called contrary individuals; and Br'er Rabbit used reverse English on him when he said, "Please, Br'er Fox—whatever you do—don't throw me in dat briar patch!"

Br'er Fox proceeded, naturally, to throw him in!

Benjamin Franklin is known as one of the cleverest diplomats that ever lived, which means he was a real sizzler at selling ideas.

FRANKLIN'S SHREWD ADVICE

Franklin's advice on how to sell ideas to one of these contrary individuals is:

Let the other fellow argue YOUR CASE

"The way to convince another," said Franklin, "is to state your case moderately and accurately. Then scratch your head, or shake it a little and say that is the way it seems to you, but that of course you may be mistaken about it—which causes your listener to receive what you have to say, and as like as not, turn about and try to convince you of it."

But if you go at the other person in a *tone of positiveness* and arrogance, you only make an opponent of him.

I told a contrary salesman for automobiles the other day, "You fellows have a reputation for not giving much on trade-ins."

"What do you mean!" bellowed the salesman. "Where's the car you want to trade in?" and he gave me more than I had anticipated just to "show me" a thing or two.

Thad Childre told me recently how he used this method to sell a large insurance policy. This man was one of those contrary individuals. No matter what you said he would disagree.

So Childre called him by phone and said, "I want to come over and see you—I promise not to talk insurance—because I know you are not interested."

"What gave you that idea?" smacked the prospect.

"Well," said Thad Childre, cleverly, "can you pass a physical these days?"

Pass it—*pass it!* The fellow jumped through the phone. He showed Childre later on he could pass it, by buying a policy!

Try a little reverse sizzling on the contrary cuss!

IT'S SOUND SIZZLING

Edgar Giles, a star salesman of Cadillac, sells the large and expensive Fleetwood model this way.

He shows the customer the regular Cadillac, then tactfully walks to a Fleetwood about to be delivered. He merely rests his arm on the door as he talks.

The customer, sooner or later, says, "What's this model?"

"Oh," says Edgar, "that's the Fleetwood, but it is more money than you want to pay!"

Is that so—well now—and many a customer is thusly traded up into a nicer, higher-priced job.

Eddie Marcus, of the famous Neiman-Marcus store in Dallas, often likes to get down on the floor and sell.

His favorite trick is to show the customer what he or she asks for, then just lay down something especially good, but expensive, and when the customer picks it up and talks about it, Mr. Marcus is apt to say:

"Oh, that is something we picked up for one of our customers who likes the unusual!"

Wow!—do you think that contrary woman will permit him to

sell *that* to the other customer? Isn't *she* interested, too, in the "unusual"?

These star salesmen let customers sell themselves.

THE "DOUBLING BACK" METHOD

If you can somehow get the other person to accept your idea as his own, he is sold.

One method of doing this is planting the idea by *suggestions* as did Colonel House; but by using the proper words you can often sell the other person that *your* ideas are *his* ideas—immediately.

The idea you are trying to put across may never have entered his head before—but if you *credit* it to him—it gives him a chance to claim it *immediately!*

Here are some "doubling back" Tested Words that convince the other person he is really the one who thought of it:

1. "As you have implied . . ."
2. "You once said . . ."
3. "As you say . . ."
4. "I agree with you that . . ."
5. "I see your point . . ."
6. "A few days ago you said . . ."
7. "You are certainly right . . ."
8. "Last time you remarked . . ."

This is "lawyering," that is, putting words into people's mouths, words you know will win them over, make them see your way of thinking because they think they thought them up.

Putting words into people's mouths is a tedious business, but it can be done.

It requires tact and subtlety. If you are too crude, you are apt to have the other person say, "I never said such a thing!"

If you are careful and say something he would have *liked* to have said—is the sort who would say such a thing—it is easy for him to convince himself he thought of it first, and you are really doing that person a genuine favor.

Another very good "doubling back" phrase to introduce a new idea is "Something you said the other day impressed me, and started me to thinking. Why couldn't we . . ."

Congressman Tom Reed from California was for many years Speaker of the House of Representatives and known as one of the most powerful persuaders on Capitol Hill.

According to Clyde R. Miller, who tells the story in *The Process of Persuasion,* Tom Reed once revealed the secret of his persuasiveness to a friend.

When Reed sat in on a committee hearing, he would do a lot of listening and little or no talking. This, in itself, was good technique.

All the time he was listening, he would do a lot of thinking. He would make notes of different points. Finally, when everyone else had argued themselves out, Reed would say:

"Gentlemen, it seems to me that what has been said here can be boiled down to five points." He would hold up the five fingers —showing as well as telling them. Then on one finger at a time, he would name each point *but* add his own ideas!

When Justin Dart, president of United Drug Company, calls a conference, he *listens* while points are discussed. He weighs the evidence and they arrive at a decision.

Once the decision is made all argument ceases, for his men gladly accept back their *own* ideas.

DISCUSS—DON'T ARGUE

It is better to discuss than to argue.

Arguing gets you nowhere. Attempting to "drive home" your points only arouses antagonisms; and the more *force* you employ to put your ideas across the more *resistance* the other fellow brings up to combat your force.

Don't try to go *through* the other fellow's resistance by beating his resistance down.

Instead, go around his resistance by using discussion instead of argument.

Don't be like Aaron Burr and say, "I'll show you I am right and you are wrong."

Instead, say, "I'd like to discuss this further with you and get more of your opinions."

When a new salesman first enters the IBM sales school at Endicott, N. Y., the first thing he sees is these words, engraved in gold on the steps as he enters the building: READ, LISTEN, DISCUSS, OBSERVE, THINK. You'll notice there isn't anything said about "Talking" or "Arguing."

It is impossible to "win" an argument. Remember: "A man convinced against his will is of the same opinion still," and that old bromide about leading a horse to water but you can't make him drink.

Old—but true. Old—but aged in the woods of history!

DISCUSS THE MATTER

Indeed, yes, discuss the matter. "Agree with thine adversary quickly" (Jesus), especially on minor points.

Give in—concede on unimportant points—and then as Richard C. Borden says, "He'll give in—concede—on the major points."

Give in on the "big print," then when you get to the "fine print," the part that matters, try introducing your side with these "word handles" which turn the other person's thinking to your way:

1. "Of course, you are right, and have you considered this . . ."
2. "I thought so too, all along, until suddenly . . ."
3. "I used to say the same thing, then one day . . ."
4. "I see your point, but how about this . . ."
5. "Yes—but . . ." (the old famous magic!)
6. "I see you have thought it out, now . . ."

These *handles* make it *easy* for the other fellow to agree with you.

He "saves face"—he is given an "out."

"STEALING" HIS AMMUNITION

In preparing for a discussion of this sort it is important that you prepare yourself by anticipating what the other fellow is going to say—then beat him to the punch.

Once while debating, the opposition said, "My opponent [me], will probably tell you . . ." and then the fellow told exactly what I had planned to tell and took the ammunition I had right out of my hand.

When it came time for me to take over, I had all my ammunition drenched. It was burned out. I was "robbed."

Abraham Lincoln was famous for his "arguing both sides of a question." He didn't really argue his side at all. He *discussed* both sides—showed where his side was the better of the two.

An opposing lawyer once said of him, "He made a better statement to the jury of my case than I could have made myself."

Benjamin Franklin was also famous for *discussing* the other fellow's case, showing where his side was the more logical or preferable.

At the Constitutional Convention in 1787 Franklin was anxious that the Constitution be adopted. Listen to him as he *sold* the delegates on the idea. Nowhere is there any argument. At times he appears to be on the other side.

He starts off by saying, "I confess that I do not entirely approve of this Constitution at present; but, sir, I am not sure I shall never approve it; for having lived long, I have experienced many instances of being obliged, by better information or fuller consideration, to change opinions even on important subjects which I once thought right, but found to be otherwise.

"The older I grow, the more apt I am to doubt my own judgment of others. Most men, indeed, as well as most sects in religions, think themselves in possession of all truth.

"Steele, a Protestant, in a dedication, tells the Pope that the only difference between our two churches in their opinions of the certainty of their doctrines is that the Roman Church is infallible, and the Church of England is never in the wrong."

Franklin, you see, had admitted he doesn't approve of the Constitution *entirely*. He admits he may be wrong, and then—

"In these sentiments, sir, I agree to this Constitution, with all its faults—if they are such; because I think a general government necessary for us, and there is no form of government but what may be a blessing to the people, if well administered. . . ."

Franklin reluctantly lets himself be convinced of his own idea. He goes on to *discuss* the Constitution further—elaborate on its faults and virtues—then ends with the fine plea:

"On the whole, sir, I cannot help expressing a wish that every member of the convention who may still have objections to it would with me on this occasion doubt a little of his own infallibility, and, to make manifest our unanimity, *put his name to this instrument!*"

If you were to take this same logic, put it into your own words, for your own "cause," be it that of getting a new fur coat from hubby; a raise, a promotion; it would work magic for you.

The logic is terrific! Test it out *today* on someone, and watch them come over to your side.

DON'T TELL 'EM—ASK 'EM

Another effective method of getting around resistance is to put reverse English on your positive statements of fact and turn them into questions.

Patrick Henry could sway men as few could in history. When elected to Virginia's House of Burgesses he was a political nobody. But every single resolution he introduced passed the house.

Get out Patrick Henry's "Liberty or Death" speech and see how statements of fact can be transposed into questions so as not to arouse resistance.

Patrick Henry had perhaps the most difficult "selling" job of all time. He was attempting to "sell" the assembled delegates on the idea of declaring the colonies' independence from England.

If they try, and fail—it means certain death as traitors.

Patrick Henry's speech is full of questions:

> "Our brethren are already in the field . . . why stand we here idle?" (*Why?—well, why?*)
> "Shall we lie supinely on our backs . . . ?" (*Certainly not!*)
> "What is it that gentlemen wish? What would they have? . . ." (*I'm interested, what?*)
> "Is life so dear or peace so sweet as to be purchased at the price of chains and slavery?" (*No, NO!*)

You can just see the listeners saying the things to themselves that Patrick Henry wanted them to say, as he framed his questions so tactfully, *"chains and slavery—or fighting England?"*

And that famous sizzling "which" of all times, "We must all hang together, or we shall all hang separately."

And that master "which"—"Give me liberty or give me death!"

BRUTUS, THE SALESMAN

You would never think they sold the sizzle back in the days of Rome, because you think the sizzle is something modern and associated with steaks.

But listen to Brutus trying to sell the Roman Senate on the idea that he did right by having Caesar killed:

> "Had you rather Caesar were living, and die all slaves, than that Caesar were dead, to live all free men?" (*What a "which"!*)
> "Who is here so base that would be a bondman? If any, speak; for him have I offended." (*Would you have spoken up?*)
> "Who is here so rude that would not be a Roman? If any, speak; for him have I offended!" (*Thundering silence!!*)
> "Who is here so vile that will not love his country? If any, speak, for him have I offended!" (*Double silence!!*)

Notice how Brutus's questions strike home! Now transpose them into positive statements of fact, and see how much power they *lose!*

"Yeah, I killed Caesar—so what!!"
"He deserved being stabbed—!"
"Any good Roman would have done it—!"
"If you don't agree, you aren't a good Roman!"
"So you'd rather be slaves, huh!!"
"Too bad if I've offended you bondsmen."

Summing up this long chapter—long because it is important, and important enough to be read several times to get every morsel, I would say:

1. Forced feeding won't make people swallow ideas.
2. Never argue—try discussion instead.
3. Put your ideas into well-framed questions.

The Woodsman Uses BOTH SIDES of His Ax!

WHEELERGRAMS TO GET ALONG WITH PEOPLE

When they wind the clock, you should have left long ago.
When the cocktail shaker is empty, so is your welcome.
Excel—and lose friends.
Compliment—and win them.
The joke that flops—flops you.
Don't be a "chain talker."
Don't slap people in the face—*mentally*.

* * *

Stop—before you're *stopped*.
Let the other fellow win once in awhile.
Show intense interest in people's problems.
Mean what you say—say what you mean.
The more you *tell* the more you *sell*.
The highest art is the art of concealing bad thoughts.
The open mouth catches the most flies.

CHAPTER 26

HOW TO BE A SMART "CASTING DIRECTOR"

All the world's a stage, and all the men and women merely players. They have their exits and their entrances; and one man in his time plays many parts.—SHAKESPEARE.

HOW TRUE it is that people play many different parts, and here is a method for influencing human behavior that will work wonders for you.

All of us have a little of the saint and sinner in us.

One part is grouchy, mean, non-co-operative. Another part is cheerful, happy, easy going.

Which actor we bring out on the stage depends to a large extent in how the other person approaches us.

A man who is a "holy terror" at the office is the epitome of meekness and kindness at home. A man who is "ruthless" in dealing with men, becomes a "softie" in dealing with children.

The part we play depends usually upon the person we are dealing with at the time.

PLAYING THE ROLE

At home she is sloppy, unkempt, and untidy—but when she steps out, she is all glamour. She has two "roles."

Down at the office he is the "perfect gentleman," but at home he is the "suspenders and cuspidor" type.

Johnny is the perfect little man until his daddy gets home, and then he becomes a holy terror.

At the office Mabel is an old grouch, but when she dates the boy friend she hopes will marry her, she is the "life of the party."

Now there is a big secret for getting people to play just the role you want them to play, and that is to approach them in the attitude that *they are expected* to play the role you want. *Assume* that the other person *will* act just as you *want* him to act.

Dr. Albert Edward Wiggam, the famous columnist and psychologist, tells me, "Hardly anything is stronger in suggestion than the calm *assumption* that the other fellow is going to do what you want him to do."

While I was growing up a traveling salesman ran off with a farmer's wife. The farmer got out his shotgun, caught up with them, and shot the salesman.

This man was played up in the papers as a "dangerous" character. When the sheriff went out to arrest him he carried five deputies and stationed them with drawn guns around the house.

The farmer was then forced to live up to the role the sheriff had cast for him, and shouted movie fashion, "You'll have to come in and get me, sheriff! !"

This would never do.

THE CITY MARSHAL ARRIVES

Still typically melodramatic, the wise city marshal came on to the scene in the nick of time.

He talked the sheriff and his deputies into leaving; then he took off his gun, so the farmer could see him, and dropped it to the ground.

"John," he said, "You and me have always been like brothers. I know you ain't goin' to shoot me. I'm a coming in to talk to you."

This time the farmer had his role switched by this clever "casting director."

Before he played the part of a Class B bad man. Now he was playing a Class A role, that of "brother."

The unarmed marshal went in and brought out the farmer.

You, too, can make others play roles for you by not giving a "dog a bad name."

THE CLEVER NURSE

A friend of mine, who takes some pride in the fact that he is a blunt, plain-spoken, and hard-to-get-along-with cuss, tells of the time he had his appendix out and a smart nurse gave him a "role" to play.

"When she brought me some medicine to take I told her flatly I wouldn't take it," he said, because he didn't believe in medicines.

"But she said to me, 'I know you've got everyone around here thinking you are cranky—but I can see through your bluff. You're just a bighearted, good-natured fellow—and I won't let you play the tough guy part with me, see!' "

The tough guy melted with the words of the "casting director," and later on told me, "We got to be great friends. I've sent her a birthday present every year since."

You see she was a very clever nurse.

DON'T LIE DOWN

People seldom want to walk over you until you lie down.

Did you ever wonder why it is that some people always get the best tables in restaurants? Why head waiters treat some people as if they were kings and others as if they were beggars?

Did you ever wonder why some people always command the respect of other people in any situation?

Did you ever ask yourself, "How in the world does he get by with it?"

Well, I'll tell you. A trick of people who command respect is just that—their attitude "commands" respect.

They act as if they expected to be treated like a king, and they usually get what they ask for.

The fellow with the hangdog look, the apologetic attitude, the retiring approach, is putting everybody on notice that he doesn't expect people to pay him much attention.

By his manner and attitude he suggests to the world at large, "I'm a nobody. I know it." The world takes him at his word, and puts him into that role.

Moral: *Don't lie down!*

DAVY BANKS' TECHNIQUE

Act the part you want to be. Act as if you *expect* others to play the part along with you, the role you want most in life.

Assume by your dress, attitude, smile, words—by your exits and entrances—the role you want others to accept.

One night I went to see the famed "Celtics" basketball team in one of their exhibition matches. Davy Banks, one of the smartest basketball players of all time—and a good showman with it—demonstrated very convincingly that night just how far you can go in influencing people's behavior by acting as if they're supposed to act in a certain way.

Midway in the game Davy found himself hemmed in in the center court. He couldn't pass—he couldn't dribble.

All of a sudden he laid the ball down on the floor and stepped back a couple of steps.

He held up his arms and said, "Hold everything—wait—wait!!"

Spectators and players alike thought something terrible must be the matter, although nothing had happened. Davy motioned to the men who had been guarding him.

"You there—step back—farther back—!"

Somewhat confused, the opposing guards moved back. Davy then calmly walked over, picked up the ball, and took careful aim.

He had a clear shot at the basket, and before his opponents realized what was happening he had looped in one of his famous ceiling-scraping shots from center.

Davy was a good "casting director."

FATHER FLANAGAN'S METHOD

You have heard of the wonderful work that Father Flanagan did at Boys Town, Nebraska.

He was not only a master sizzleman—selling decency, honesty, moral courage, and good citizenship to the boys who came to him—but he was also a good "manufacturer."

The product he turned out—*men*—is the most important commodity in the world.

A few of the boys who go to Boys Town are pretty tough. Some of them have had brushes with the law. They are what we like to call "juvenile delinquents."

This is only part of the "raw material" that goes *in* the production line at Boys Town.

The products that come off the assembly line are models of good citizenship that any community would be proud to equal.

Graduates of Boys Town have distinguished themselves in the business and professional world. Their war record was something to make Father Flanagan proud.

And he never had occasion to be ashamed of a "product" that he "manufactured."

VERY GOOD "CASTING"

How did Father Flanagan manage this?

He insisted that, "There are no bad boys!" He not only said it—but *believed* it with all his heart.

That was his one secret.

Faced with this great belief that they are not bad, the boys find it impossible to play the bad-boy role.

I asked Father Flanagan how he could say there were no bad boys, and this is what he wrote me:

"People often ask me how I can say that there are no bad boys. What puzzles me is how anyone can say that any boy *is* bad.

"I realize boys sometimes make mistakes, serious mistakes; but my experience with thousands of homeless, neglected and abandoned boys has convinced me no boy really *wants* to be bad.

"The boy no less than the adult tends to live up to the opinion others have of him.

"It is wrong to blame a boy for not doing better when we have not expected anything better of him.

"Some of the boys who come to us have the idea they are pretty tough, but they find it difficult to play that role once they know something better is expected of them.

"Show a boy you are on his side, and impress upon his mind that you have faith and confidence in him, and he will not let you down."

There's the whole secret! Good "casting"!

TRY IT YOURSELF

Bad boys become good boys because someone *expects* them to.

Someone has cast the boy into a good role, and this is not a trick to outsmart the boy.

That wouldn't work, but sincere, genuine belief that all boys are good—makes all boys become good boys.

Try this method of Father Flanagan's yourself.

How do you usually regard people around you? Do you believe that all men are crooks, gossips, cheap skates, or cheats?

If you do, you'll find plenty of them in your life span.

Why not try a little experiment?

If you think the world is heartless, unkind and cruel, you may be surprised to find that you can change it.

Not by waving a magic wand on the world, but by changing *your own self*. Try this thirty days.

Change your attitude from negative to positive.

Become a human explorer and start looking for the good in people with whom you come in contact.

You will find it if you look hard enough—for deep down in everyone there is good. When you look for it, and assume in your actions that it is there, you'll be surprised to see it pop to the surface.

When you approach people in a skeptical, critical attitude they go on the defensive.

They draw back into their shells and put on the protective armor of hardness; but when you show them that you regard them as good, honest, decent people—they thaw out, and the good role comes out.

Try being a casting director. It's fun.

THE FERRYMAN'S STORY

There is an old story about a ferryboat man that illustrates that people find what they look for.

In the morning a family boarded his ferry with all their worldly goods. They were moving from Jonesville to Smithville.

"What sort of people live in Smithville?" asked the head of the family.

"What sort of people did they have in Jonesville?" asked the boatman.

"They were the rottenest bunch I ever saw—thieving—gossiping—stupid—lazy—good for nothings."

The ferryman paused a moment, looked at the man and said, "I am sorry to say you'll find just the *same sort* of people in Smithville!"

That afternoon another family boarded the busy little ferry. They, too, were going from Jonesville to Smithville, and like the preceding family they made the same normal inquiry.

"What kind did you leave behind in Jonesville?" again asked the ferryman.

"Fine, decent people—good neighbors—the salt of the earth."

"You'll find the same kind of people in Smithville," smiled the ferryman, and everybody smiled back.

Moral: *Don't give man or beast a bad name!*

IT'S UP TO YOU

If you give a boy, a man, or a dog a bad name, you will inspire him to live up to it. So don't.

"The worst part of giving a dog a bad name is not that it makes everybody suspicious of the dog, but that it makes the dog suspicious of himself," says Robert Quillen.

"I try to be what those who love me think I am," May Robson once said.

So do we all. We always try to *be* what people *think* we are.

We try to *act as we feel we are expected to act.*

When Shakespeare said we are all players, he could have gone on to say we are all casting directors; for we are continually giving those around us roles to play by our attitude—by our manner—by the way we approach people.

These things *suggest* to the other fellow how we expect him to react toward us.

So why not be a *good* casting director and give people good roles instead of bad ones?

Why not cast the other fellow in the role of hero, instead of villain?

You'll get along better with people, and you will be happier in life.

Always assume the best intentions in a person. Then you may succeed in arousing them.—ELIZABETH, late Queen of Rumania.

CHAPTER 27

A SECRET FOR DOUBLING THE POWER OF YOUR WORDS

Why the motion picture is more interesting than the phonograph, and why schools have black boards. Can you talk in pictures?

FRANCIS ROLT-WHEELER, in his book, *Thomas Alva Edison,** tells how Edison explained electricity to an English nobleman:

"If you had a dog something like a dachshund," Edison told his visitor, "only long enough to reach from Edinburgh to London, and you pulled his tail in Edinburgh, he would bark in London."

Edison then explained, "I can't tell you exactly what goes through the dog or over the wire!"

Had Edison been talking to a scientist or an electrician he could have given a technical explanation; but in order to make this man understand he used a device that salesmen have used since the Stone Age when man carved pictures on the cave, pointed to them as he grunted to a neighbor.

He talked in pictures—a favorite Edison system of persuading and clarifying.

To put your ideas across—to sell another person—you must somehow plant your own idea inside his mind. The human mind has five doorways through which outside ideas can enter.

The doorways of *sight, hearing, touch, smell,* and *taste!*

UNLOCKING THE DOORS

The Chinese have a proverb, "One picture is worth ten thousand words."

* Francis Rolt-Wheeler, *Thomas Alva Edison* (New York: The Macmillan Company, 1925).

When we want to know if someone understands us we ask, "Do you see?" We seldom say, "Do you hear?"

And when light dawns on us we say, "Oh, I *see* what you mean!"

"Seeing" and "understanding" come pretty close to being the same thing. "Theory" really means "looking." "Evidence" and "vision" come from the same root.

We read in the papers that millions are starving in India, and forget in five minutes; but we pick up a pictorial magazine and see one picture of a gaunt, starving child in front of a bombed railway station, and we are unable to forget it.

Convincing writers and eloquent speakers use many little stories to "illustrate" their facts.

We say that a person who makes himself clearly understood makes a "graphic" statement.

The greatest teachers and persuaders of history have made use of "stories" to make their listeners "see the point."

FDR, WILSON, JESUS, HITLER

Jesus taught his philosophy in terms of simple parables which his listeners could understand.

He told his message in terms of the everyday life of the people. When he spoke of the "sower going forth to sow"—or the son who wandered away from home—the guests at the wedding feasts —these were things the people could "see" in their mind's eye.

The good speaker, the good persuader, the good seller, always uses many "for examples" and "for instances" to bolster up his story.

"For example," he says, and proceeds to give you some examples to prove his point.

"For instance," he goes on, pointing to things to clarify his meaning.

FDR, Wilson, Lincoln, were all famous for using little stories, jokes, anecdotes, fables, parables to get their ideas across in fast time.

Hitler practically hypnotized a whole nation by his ability to paint verbal pictures. When he spoke he made the people "see" visions of the glory, power, and honor that would be theirs if they followed him.

When Napoleon wanted to sell his troops on the idea of sticking out the hardships of the Italian campaign, he painted them a picture of the rewards to be theirs if they fought it out: "You will return to your homes and people will point you out on the street, saying, 'He was with the army in Italy!' "

Russell Conwell made a fortune from his one essay, *Acres of Diamonds,* which was a vivid word-picture story illustrating the fact that one may find his opportunities "in his own back yard."

The smart salesman "says it with flowers." He gives them something to look at as well as listen to.

He will *drop* a square clothes pin on the counter as he says, "Look—it won't roll when dropped!"

He lights a match when he says, "This is as silent as a match—see!"

So synchronize your words with pictures!

USE TECHNICOLOR PICTURES

It is a controversy whether or not we dream in "black and white" or in "technicolor," but it is no controversy that we sell in "color pictures."

Bacon sizzling in the pan gives an entirely different mental picture to the listener than when you use the nonvisual "bacon frying."

Compare Churchill's famous and stirring "technicolor wording," "We will fight them on every beachhead, on every street" to the nonvisual black and white, "We will defend ourselves if attacked."

See the difference?

Doesn't the first immediately bring into your mind a visual picture of actual fighting—making the situation more stirring, more "real"?

Learn how to "talk in pictures." It will help get your ideas, your thinking, over faster to the other person.

Where possible put your pictures into "technicolor," so that they will register even faster on the mental machine of the listener.

You may not "be in pictures," but you surely can "talk in pictures."

SUBDUE THE SOUND TRACK

Avoid jawbreakers—words that burst your jaw, and rupture the eardrum of the listener.

It isn't the big highfalutin words that win friends and sell them your thinking, or products, but the simple, everyday words, the easy to understand, easy to *see* words.

The red bird can be seen quicker on the tree limb than the black-and-white bird or the dull sparrow.

But subdue the size of the words—add color if you want, but subdue the complexities of the syllables.

"I love you" is stronger and more sincere than, "You stir my emotional nature."

As Will Rogers once said, "I love words but I don't like strange ones. You don't understand them, and they don't understand you. Old words are like old friends—you know 'em the minute you see 'em."

Don't depend upon high-sounding words. Instead, use words that invoke pictures as well as sounds.

A PRESIDENT'S SYSTEM

Merriman Smith in his fine book, *Thank You, Mr. President,** tells how Franklin D. Roosevelt used little stories to get his ideas across in technicolor.

"He loved to tell parables," says Smith. "During the early stages of the war when inflationary trends were first showing themselves in force, he told a press conference a story. He swore it was true.

* Merriman Smith, *Thank You, Mr. President* (New York: Harper & Brothers, 1946).

"It seems a garage mechanic friend of his dropped in for a chat. Now how in the world a mechanic ever dropped in on Mr. Roosevelt was beyond explanation.

"He claimed a lot of friends in comparatively low stations of life. I regarded them as his imaginary play-mates because I doubt seriously if one of them ever existed.

"He told one of a Chinese laundryman he knew, a baseball player, a small dirt farmer, a garage man.

"This mechanic, he said, had come to him complaining about the high cost of strawberries in February. His Missus, the mechanic was alleged to have told the President, was having to pay a God-awful price for strawberries.

"The President said he lectured his mechanic friend sharply. Since when could mechanics afford strawberries out of season? Why didn't they eat something else? Why throw away their defense plant wages in such a foolish fashion?

"The President used this to prove that the price line was actually being held, but that too many people were spending their money on unnecessary luxuries.

THE STORY GOES ON

"About six months later, the inflation question came up again in a press conference. Someone wanted to know whether the President really thought the price line was being held, and how much longer it would last.

"The President declined to comment directly. He thought for a moment and added there were too many people like a master mechanic he knew.

"This man, he said, had dropped in 'to chat' and complained about the high cost of asparagus.

"And since when, the President said he told the mechanic, did he find it necessary to have asparagus, out of season, on the menu?

"I couldn't resist it. I knew it was presumptuous and bordered on the disrespectful, but I had to ask the question.

" 'Mr. President,' I said, 'Is that the same mechanic who came in a few months back to complain about the price of strawberries?'

"The press conference exploded into roars of laughter. Mr. President turned a little pink and shouted over the guffaws: 'My God, Merriman, it is true—it was the same man.'

"But he could hardly finish the sentence because he was laughing too hard himself."

Well, the idea is that a President's system was to talk in colorful pictures, although the moral might be, "Remember what you tell!!"

WORDS THAT PUNCH

Emil Ludwig said of Napoleon that the secret of his genius lay in his ability to use vivid "picture words."

"Suit the action to the word, the word to the action," said Shakespeare, which simply means *do* and *say* all at one time.

Keep the eye and the ear both busy.

Do something while you are talking so that your listener can help "see" your words.

If you can't do anything better than stick a pin on a chart, draw a diagram in the sand, hold up your fingers, point to a bucket, do *something*.

Synchronize your words with actions and gestures. Get excited and *everybody* else gets excited with you.

That is how to pack wallop in words.

Remember, words are the most *powerful instruments* in activating people—to get action from them.

Why not make them work for you, and not against you?

The More You Concentrate Words the Deeper They Burn

CHAPTER 28

HOW TO TELL JOKES TO INFLUENCE PEOPLE

Six simple points that will make you the life of the party, and not the bore. Traveling salesmen are back—but they have forgotten how to tell winning jokes that make friends and business.

THE JOKE is an instrument for influencing human behavior, and can become a *powerful* thing to "make" or "break'" you.

It is the quickest way known to "break the ice" in any situation, whether selling underwear or selling ideas or personality.

It is the easiest way to win the other fellow over to your side—*instantly!*

Here is the psychological reason:

As my good writer friend John D. Murphy says, psychologists agree that laughter is the result of a *superior adjustment* within a person.

We only laugh at what makes us *feel superior!*

By this I mean, when we see a man slip on a banana peel we feel superior—we are not slipping on the peel, therefore we *laugh!*

PAT AND MIKE

When we hear a joke about how dumb Pat and Mike were in some situation, we feel superior again. *We* would *never* have made that mistake, we say to ourselves and laugh.

The old-time medicine man used to "get in good" with his audience simply by telling a joke on a neighboring town, and that system is classic with the old vaudeville comedian who made excellent use of this psychology.

This is the art of making the folks of Jonesville feel *superior* to the residents of Smithville, and they loved it, and to show their appreciation bought the corn remedy or applauded the vaudeville show.

Whatever it is you are selling—potato peelers, ideas, or yourself—you will always make your friends, neighbors, and utter strangers like you if you make *them* feel superior.

But there is an *art to winning people* with jokes.

How rare is this art and how few people can tell stories that get across.

"Good humor is one of the best articles of dress one can wear in society," said Thackeray, and says also the sales manager of any selling organization.

This art boils down to six simple rules that anyone can put to good use.

Memorize these rules. They will help you become or remain the life of any party; they will help you sell more goods to buyers; help you win a high public office; get in solid with your neighbors.

JOKES WELL TOLD

You can make a fortune if you are an expert like the movie comedians or radio comics; they make big salaries because they make millions of people feel superior.

You can sell more underwear at the crossroads of life, or have more people attend your political rally than if free beer and hot dogs were offered.

How powerful is the joke well told; how often it is *not* well told.

Every salesman's training should include the *art of joke telling;* every course in public relations should include *how to tell funny stories;* and after-dinner bores and weak chairmen should be made to memorize these six simple rules.

Politicians should take a tip from Dwight Morrow who took Will Rogers with him when he was appointed ambassador to Mexico. Will "broke the ice," relieved the tension, and opened the way for co-operation between Morrow and Mexico's President Calles.

What the newspapers had headlined as a "tense situation" was smoothed over in a few days—not by political mumbo jumbo—but just a few well-told jokes that won Calles over.

As Bruce Barton said, in describing the event, "You can't keep men from getting on well together once they have laughed at the same funny stories."

Others have written volumes on the science of making up jokes; some have compiled thesauri of jokes, catalogued according to events.

All we want to tell you is the art of telling jokes to bring people over to your side of the "sale"—to make them like you—to buy *more* from you, and here are the six simple rules.

SIX WHEELERPOINTS

Point 1: Tell Jokes Jack Benny Style.

The real *wit* tells jokes to make *others* feel superior—only the *half-wit* tells them to make others feel small.

So never *personalize* the joke.

By this I mean, don't let the other person be the brunt of the fun.

You will embarrass the other person. He laughs—yes—but it is a mighty weak laugh, for you deflate his ego. You make him the laughing stock of your joke.

"We love a joke that hands us a pat on the back while it kicks the other fellow down the stairs," says C. L. Edson, which points out the great danger behind a joke that is misdirected.

Edson meant that the joke must be on somebody *not* present!

You may give somebody free publicity by making him the wrong end of the joke, but it isn't the kind of spotlight that helps you win him over.

So don't highlight any person or persons present; don't make someone the stooge. Make him the *hero.*

Let people laugh at *you.* They will love you for it. Jack Benny has proved this, Joan Davis, Cass Daley and others who make fortunes and fame telling funny stories—*on themselves.*

Jack Benny makes *himself* the tightwad and that elevates his audience and sells his sponsor's product!

So Point 1, to tell jokes that win and don't lose, *tell jokes Jack Benny style.*

Point 2: Don't Tell Gags that Gag!

Will Rogers once told me, "The secret of telling a joke is to tell the right joke at the right place at the right time."

If you want your jokes to "get across" use good timing.

This means "good taste," for unless your gags have good taste they may gag your listeners, perhaps the person about ready to place a good order with you.

Good taste means first of all the proper time and place.

The joke that amuses the fraternity banquet may be weak at the stag; but that applies the *other way* around, too!

When you are speaking before a formal group good taste dictates that you keep it "clean"—whether your audience is stag or mixed.

This is a mistake many jokesters make. They do not realize there is a difference in a group of men sitting around a table in a formal business conference, and the same group of men lounging in the smoking car.

One speaker, addressing a Kiwanis meeting, started off, "Well as there are no ladies present I can tell some jokes."

One of the Kiwanians expressed the sentiment of everyone present when he stood up and said, "I would like to remind you, however, that there are *gentlemen* present!"

So learn the Emily Post of proper timing.

Be sure to pick the proper *place*. The business office may be too busy. The buyer may be in too much of a hurry. Later in the evening the joke may *fit* in better.

The next element in proper timing is to fit the joke to the *situation*. By this I mean, *don't drag* in jokes just because they are funny —*make them fit the event!*

You will get your point over quicker, if you tell a joke that fits the situation; and only too little will the chairman's Pat and Mike story dragged in at the last minute fit the speaker's lecture.

Democrats like funny stories on Republicans. It makes them feel *superior*.

Kiwanians like to hear 'em on Rotarians. But be sure they are *properly timed*.

Keep the clambake joke at the clambake!

Point 3: Don't Hog *the Show!*

I like people who know when to go home from a party, without your having to wind the clock or shake the cocktail shaker with that "it's empty" look on your face.

I like the jokesmith who knows when to *stop* to give others a chance to play the big-hero role.

For if you don't know when to *stop*—somebody is apt to stop you dead right in the middle of a joke.

Give others a chance to tell their best ones; don't be so quick to rush your joke right into the laughter of the last joke.

Don't be a scene stealer!

After he has finished his story, give it a chance to spread around the circle, and enjoy a few minutes of "life" before you kill it off with your laughmaker.

Let the joke die down—naturally, not because you topped it off with a haymaker yourself, then it is all right to say quietly, "That reminds me of a story . . ."

Don't tell too many jokes—space them.

Anything that is *too much* or *too frequent* cheapens itself; so if you want your jokes to be *golden gems,* don't cheapen them by too many of them at one sitting.

Don't overdo your ability to tell a funny story.

Make 'em want more!

That is the big secret of the "paid laugh professionals," to make you applaud harder and longer for "more."

If the strip-tease dancer took off everything *at once,* her audience would walk out on her.

Learn how much to tell—how often to retell—before somebody is twice glad. Glad you dropped in—but darned glad you are leaving with your worn out repertoire of Joe Miller's.

"The secret of making one's self tiresome, is not to know when to stop," claims Voltaire, with the acumen of a modern sales manager who realizes the war is over and the traveling salesman's joke, properly told, is coming back with new products.

Tryon Edwards says, "Have something to say, *say it,* and stop when you're done," and old Cicero once claimed, "Brevity is the best recommendation of speech, whether in a senator or an orator."

Brevity is the *soul* of the joke!

Point 4: Don't Steal *the Other Fellow's Candy!*

Even if you have heard his old chestnut, never interrupt his storytelling.

Let him have his fun.

Bend forward mentally and physically, if you wish to win him, and listen to his every word.

He will "buy" more of your products or your "good will," if you enjoy *his* jokes, and in return he will enjoy and laugh at your ancient "eggs."

The best way to build an audience, is to be a good audience yourself.

Remember it isn't the joke—but *how* it is told, that most people enjoy.

Everyone has his pet way of telling a story. You might learn a new twist for yourself by first being a good listener, and then second, by being a good yarn spinner yourself.

Someone once remarked that there are only seven original jokes, and maybe this is true, so don't nudge a friend during a joke to tip him off that you have heard the one now being told.

Never sit back with a smirk on your face as if to say, "Go on and tell it. I've heard it—but that's all right." Smart-aleck listeners make few friends or "sales" for themselves.

Wives should study this rule carefully, for too often while the husband is entertaining the prospects in his home and begins to reel 'em off, she ups and says, "My God, must *I have to listen* to that old one again!!!"

You can make many friends merely by being a good listener to their jokes.

Even when he says, "Stop me if you've heard this one," don't stop him. He never expects you to! He just said that from force of habit.

Listen to every joke just as though the big boss who paid your salary, or an important client who filled your pockets with gold, was talking.

Don't treat 'em like your mother-in-law!

Point 5: Make 'em *Short!*

Long stories like long letters get boresome, and aren't welcome in today's busy life of people.

They haven't the time nor patience to listen to a long yarn, as might have been told in the palaces of mythological princes.

In today's modern business, the court jester doesn't spin long yarns.

He doesn't have to amuse to save his head, much like Scheherazade.
She saved *her* head by using her head.
She made her stories every night so entertaining, so short, always ending on such a high pitch, that the king never beheaded her as he did all the others.
Thus was originated the *Arabian Nights.*
Today is the day of the short short stories. The day of the "quickie" joke, so learn how to make them short.
Avoid such bromides as, "Stop me if you've heard this one . . ." or, "This is an old one, but . . ." Give the joke a *fair chance* to stand on its own legs.
Never apologize for having to tell jokes. Get up and tell them—and assume no one has ever heard them before, at least the *way* you spin them in true Scheherazade fashion.
If the joke is too long, people's minds wander. They get itchy to tell one themselves.
"If you would be pungent, be brief; for it is with words as sunbeams—the more they are condensed, the deeper they burn," spoke Southey.
Another good quotation, "As it is the characteristic of great wits to say much in a few words, so small wits seem to have the gift of speaking *much* and saying *nothing!*"
So say it fast. Be a modern Scheherazade!

Point 6: Twist 'em Profitably!
While laughter is a powerful instrument for winning friends, it can also be an effective weapon *against* an enemy.
You can often twist jokes around to make them profitable for you, as well as amusing to others.
There are occasions when you may need to put reverse English on these Six Points to make the other fellow come around to your way of thinking, or an enemy.
Never lose your temper when you are heckled. Instead squelch the heckler with humor.
"Wit should be used as a shield for defense rather than as a sword to wound others," said Fuller.
A heckler says to Ole Johnson, "This is the dumbest show I've ever seen." To which Ole replied, "I'm not as dumb as you are—you *paid* to get in!"

When you laugh at a person or get others laughing at him, he is whipped. His ego is deflated. He has no more fight.

Uncle Joe Cannon, when heckled about having oats in his farmer pockets, quipped back, "Not only do I have oats in my pocket but hayseed in my hair!"

My good friend, Señor G. Guajardo Davis of Mexico tells how one of his friends was squelched by an American salesman who won a business contract with a joke.

The salesman heard the Mexican say in Spanish, "I do not like this man's looks. I wouldn't buy a jumping bean from him!"

The salesman knew Spanish so replied, casually, "Well, I'm afraid there is nothing I can do about my looks, gentlemen, but I can promise you one thing—you won't have to worry about my selling you jumping beans!"

Everybody laughed. Their laughter defeated themselves. They liked the American immensely because he made a joke work in his favor. He earned their business.

Learn this reverse English method of twisting jokes around—in *your* favor!

LIFE'S RAREST GIFT

If you can tell jokes you can make fame and fortune. Radio, the movies, the magazines, all will pay you a fortune for making people laugh.

You get less money when you make them cry.

But telling a good joke is life's rarest gift, but one that you can acquire if you put your mind to it.

The joke can make friends and sales, or can lose them, all in the fraction of a second.

You must study these six pointers, memorize them, practice them, until you know when to tell the joke, how to tell it, where to tell it—and when *not* to tell it.

Dorothy Dix advises girls that the best defense against a "masher" is simply to laugh at him. A man can stand a slap in the face better than being laughed at.

So learn the many *variations* of telling jokes, their effectiveness, their numerous slight tones and hues that spell the difference between a welcome storyteller and the boring jokester.

You'll get rich in friends—and money—making people laugh because laughter makes people happy!

It is all up to you.

He must not laugh at his own wheeze; a snuffbox has no right to sneeze!—KEITH PRESTON

CHAPTER 29

HE MADE THEM PART OF THE ACT—AND MADE A MILLION DOLLARS

A Short Short Story Number 6

TODAY, GAINESVILLE, GEORGIA, is the second largest poultry center in the world.

There is more than 60 million dollars' worth of poultry grown in and around this small north-Georgia city.

The man who is largely responsible for this whole industry, which is only about eight years old, is a young fellow in his early forties named J. D. Jewell.

When I asked Mr. Jewell the secret of *his* phenomenal success he told me that back in 1927 he had operated a feed store in Gainesville.

Then he got married and wanted to make more money, so decided he needed to sell more chicken feed than he had ever sold before.

The farmers, however, wouldn't buy more feed for the logical reason they didn't need it—the chickens were getting enough!

THE SOLUTION

Now it would have been silly and bad business tactics to overload the farmers with chicken feed that would rot and never be used.

This would be leading the horse to water—and *forcing* him to take a drink by a swift kick.

Jewell had a better plan. Remember Wheelerpoint 1, "Don't make 'em drink—make 'em thirsty"? Well that is just what this chicken king did.

So he went out and located places where he could *buy* baby chicks and made a note of the prices, then took a trip throughout his feed territory and told this to the farmers.

He figured if there were more "mouths to feed" he'd sell more feed. A logical thought—when there is *no market,* go out and create one.

But it didn't work!

A SECOND SOLUTION

So he dusted off Wheelerpoint 4, "Make 'em part of the act," and bought the chickens himself, and resold them to the farmers on credit—along with twelve weeks of feed.

When the chickens reached twelve weeks, the broiler stage, he *bought* the broilers from the farmers, settled up their feed bill, and started them all over again.

The farmers caught on to the "show" in which they were "partners," part of the act. They now *wanted to raise chickens,* for it cost them nothing.

They soon found that a cash return every twelve weeks was better than selling cotton once a year in the fall.

But now Brother Jewell had broilers! So what to do with them?

A THIRD SOLUTION

You guessed it—he opened a chicken processing plant where the broilers were dressed, packed, and frozen!

He had his own hatcheries and brood hens, and by now he had fifty farmers tending his brood hens on this co-operative plan—and over 500 farmers raising fryers from the baby chicks he furnished them.

This plan turns out now better than 15,000 processed chickens *per day!*

Last year J. D. Jewell, Inc., did more than seven million dollars' worth of business all over the country!

"No man can enrich himself alone," Jewell told me. "If you want to make money you've got to *serve other people.* If you can figure some way to make the people around you more *prosperous* —you, yourself, will prosper!"

Look around YOURSELF for Trees with Dollars on Them

CHAPTER 30

THE TECHNIQUE OF TRAVELING TOGETHER TO MAKE FRIENDS—AND TO KEEP THEM

How not to pack a gripe in your grip—and to let everybody else have a good time—and return friends, not enemies!

ANOTHER ERA of traveling is here again!

After long war years of not traveling, people are getting the urge again for trips to New York and Boston and Chicago, and Mexico, Canada, Europe!

The railroads, steamships, and planes and buses, are all releasing their attractive folders, and along with Chambers of Commerce and foreign travel bureaus, they are making people itchy once more to "see the world."

While traveling broadens us, and is "the best education," it can often prove upsetting to yourself, and all too often friends who started together singing, return not speaking to each other.

This story is dedicated mainly to the "terrible traveler," the one who may be a social smoothy at home, but away from it he cultivates all the rules and regulations to make the pleasure trip *tough* on everybody.

Therefore, to make traveling together easier, to help the terrible traveler get over some of his bumps and humps, and to make friends and hold them, here are three traveling rules:

THREE TRAVELING RULES

Rule 1: Give and Take!

Remember the trip isn't just for *your own* pleasure, so don't always be the first to say selfishly, "Let's go over here" or "I want to eat now."

Instead, try, "How many vote for going here?" and, "Who would like to eat now—or later?"

Take a vote on what the *others* might like. Just because you like train trips into the hinterland, don't think others want to go. They may like to see a church, a movie, some historical sights.

When you get to a city, don't rush off to the stores, night clubs or the pyramids just because they interest you; others may want merely to "rest up" in their rooms, go on a boat excursion, or have a typical local dinner.

You can make yourself a four-star nuisance by always making others trot off to the spots that interest you, even though they don't interest others.

Give and take!

If you give in now and then, so will the rest of the party.

Give and take is a *big rule* for enjoying traveling with others.

Rule 2: Don't Always Be the Fuss-budget.

Take the "self" out of "selfishness."

You won't find, perhaps, as nice food traveling as in your home.

You may not like the beds, hotel service, and other petty discomforts found in traveling.

But accept them—don't be a fuss-budget who always finds fault with everything.

Accept this as part of the fun.

Don't be first to say, "I just can't enjoy this foreign food," or, "I simply can't go another mile—I'm worn out."

Quit fussing—enjoy yourself!

Rule 3: Don't Pack a Gripe in Your Grip!

By this I mean, don't "take a bad time with you."

Never make up your mind, in advance, that "I simply won't have a good time—I just know!"

Be cheerful about the whole thing, and you will have a better time, make more friends as you go along, and *return* with friends not enemies.

If you develop a bad disposition, you will be "taking a bad time with you."

When someone told Socrates that a certain man had not enjoyed his trip, Socrates replied, "I can very well believe it for he took himself along with him."

When you take a trip with friends, leave part of yourself at home.

Leave behind the self that is determined, *beforehand,* to gripe about everything.

As the great traveler Halliburton once remarked, "The bee, though he finds every rose has a thorn, comes back loaded with honey from his rambles—and why should not other tourists do the same!"

You can—by not packing gripes in your grip!

DON'T GO HOG WILD

Just because you are away from home, don't go hog wild.

Don't make yourself a bore by trying too desperately to be the life of the party that usually wakes up with a hang-over.

As Packe said, "There is nothing that a man can less afford to leave at home than his conscience or his good habits; for it is not to be denied that travel is, in its immediate circumstances, unfavorable to habits of self-discipline, regulation of thought, sobriety of conduct, and dignity of character."

Don't feel that you must drink everyone under the table just because you are away from home; and don't go on a big spending spree just because you feel free.

Relax and take it easy.

You'll have more fun and you won't have to wonder if you made a fool of yourself.

GETTING ALONG WITH OTHERS

There are a few simple things to do to get along with the people you come into contact with in your travels, ticket agents, hotel clerks, waiters, and others.

A good point to remember in traveling in strange cities, states, or countries, is to avoid the great American curse—*bragging!*

Don't brag!

Sure, maybe yours is the largest state; maybe you have the biggest buildings, the largest dam, the tallest mountains, the finest drinking water.

Just keep this to yourself.

Let the stranger brag about his features, and you just smile. He'll like you—and do all possible to make your trip more fun.

Maybe the food was bad, but don't be the first to yell, "Say, is this the kind of service you get here—now back in *my* home town . . . !"

Get along with people by not bragging!

COMPLIMENT—DON'T CRITICIZE

Never criticize a hotel clerk, waiter, or servant. Compliment instead. Say, "You have such lovely rooms, I wonder if you can give me one that is a little more quiet?"

Never cry out, "Say this stuff is cold!" Say, "Your food is so delicious, won't you warm it up for me—I let it get cold."

Don't beef about slow Latin service. Get into the swing. Don't shout, "Say, I've been patiently waiting here for twenty minutes —what kind of service is that??"

Slow up on trips. Enjoy yourself more. Give your nerves a rest cure. Give your stomach a tonic. Do this by eating slower—eating easier.

Don't gulp American fashion!

Canadians, Europeans, Latin Americans won't like you if you gulp down their food, and with a man-size burp jump up, leave an overtip, and strut out with a smirk of superiority on your face.

That overtip won't correct vulgarity!

GET INTO STEP

If the custom of the city or country is to eat at one o'clock, don't yelp, "Say, where I come from we eat like human beings!"

Get in step with customs.

If it is the custom of the Pullman porter to make up beds at 9 P.M., so he can finish everybody up by eleven, don't rush up with, "Hey, I never turn in till twelve!!"

Get in step with others.

If the people you are traveling with prefer their heavy meal at noon, don't ridicule them with, "Haw, that's silly—why I always eat heavy at six—like most people."

Everybody has his peculiarities—especially you.

If people take digestion or sleeping pills, don't make fun of them. If they avoid certain foods, don't overly kid them. They may be as sensitive about this as you are about that wart on your cheek.

Get in step with others—especially those in countries where customs and viewpoints are different from yours.

SHARING THE EXPENSE

Share and share alike is a good rule. No favors to anyone. Just because you didn't have the steak, don't cheapen yourself by saying, "My bill was only one dollar—here!"

It is better to divide equally, unless of course somebody really goes to town on the bill, and his share rises sharply over the average.

If you find your average bill is slightly lower than others, they will take care of you on something else.

Some people have five-cent drinks, others fifty-cent drinks. A split then is not fair. You can figure out your portion and let the bigger bill holder pay his just share.

On the other hand, if others order small items, don't you sock them with big items. Pay your just portion.

Divide gasoline and oil bills with everybody. Even share repairs, unless of course the car falls apart!

If the other person refuses to let you share these bills, then "get even" by buying a dinner now and then.

If the driver is arrested for speeding or overparking, share, since you are part of the act.

Naturally, if the driver is a really poor one and just compounds fines and car damages, you may feel justified in not sharing but next time, don't travel with him. Pick a more stable companion.

FIT INTO THE FUN

He who travels alone may travel farther and faster, as the Chinese say, but not with as much fun and pleasure as he who travels slower but with good companions.

The fun of being together with congenial people who make the trip more pleasant, who fit into things, is the *best fun of all.*

It is just as much fun seeing others enjoying themselves, as it is for you to have all the fun yourself.

Don't be afraid, for example, of being a "rubbernecker." Sightseers see more than people who think this is corny to do.

It is no disgrace to be a "visiting fireman."

See all the historical spots, else when you return somebody may say, "Did you see the floating gardens?" and you will say you didn't and feel as if you "wuz robbed."

HOW TO "SEE" CITIES

The way to "see" a new city, state, or country, and enjoy and not miss a single thing, is to get the guidebooks and know where to go and at what time.

Visit the spots that are nearest first, then go to those a little farther away from base, and so on until you are really way out beyond the beaten tourist paths.

You will quickly learn from a good travel bureau, or ticket agent, whether or not in certain spots it is better to see churches, movies, famous eating places, or the volcano.

A great traveling error is to avoid Grant's Tomb and the Statue of Liberty because you feel it is corny to go "where the tourists go."

See these famous sights. See the battlegrounds. See the famous statues. See all you can *first,* then afterward become choosy.

Get your background by *seeing America first,* then near-by countries, then the distant ones.

Be a tourist. It is fun!

WHEN YOU RETURN HOME

You can be just as boresome to friends at home, as you were to your traveling companions, or the people in the places you visited, if you keep on reciting your adventures.

Tell them once, yes. Tell them in an interesting, not a bragging way. Avoid ". . . and when that waiter saw I meant business, brother, did that furriner hop to it!"

Don't be the "Yeah, them hotels was good, but they don't come up to my own bed!"

Don't relate the faults of travel—brag on the good points.

Sure your food at home tastes good, just as good maybe as the kidney stew at the Royal York in Canada after the typical drugstore-style suppers American fashion.

And every time somebody comes over, don't hand them the picture book of the trip, and go over it picture by picture; show them your movies *once,* not every time they happen to drop in.

Otherwise, you'll wonder why people don't drop in any more.

PLANNING YOUR TRIP

Half the fun, they say, is planning the trip.

All winter long you can sit and look at the literature, and get all set for the trip.

Here are things to remember, though:

Mainly, today you *must* make reservations. No longer can you jump up some morning and say, "Well, let's start now."

Rather, tell the hotels weeks in advance when you are to be there—tell them the *exact* hour of arrival, and *when* you will leave.

Ask them for *confirmation!*

Then don't cancel out without advising them well in advance, else you may find you are on their future "banned list."

It is better to get up early and travel while it is cool, and rest up when the sun is really boiling. Besides, you will arrive at the hotel *before* the late afternoon salesman's rush.

SOME GOOD ADVICE

When traveling by auto, have many stops, for this breaks up the monotony. Don't drive too fast—you'll see more by going at a normal speed, with lots of stops.

See things as you go along.

Don't "dress down" because of car travel. Look presentable. If you are a size 48, don't wear slacks!

Be comfortable, yes, but not sloppy.

Maybe your husband is used to seeing you wrapped up all day to "make curls," so you can blossom out at night; but your companions may not like seeing the "Witch of Endor"!

Get a lot of guidebooks. They tell you the highlights of places.

Hire a guide when you arrive. They'll save time—and won't cost half as much as an expensive night club!

Stay in reputable hotels. They may seem to cost more—but they have the less-expensive rooms, too, if you want them.

Don't overeat—or overdrink.

Break yourself into a "new climate" the easy way. You don't have to rush everything up the first day, and grunt and groan the rest of the trip.

Avoid too much of *anything*—even strange water. Watch water, by the way; and fresh vegetables. Take things that are well cooked. That is always the safe bet.

It is fun to travel—educational—when you can go along the highway of travel and *enjoy* yourself.

It is not fun when you carry gripes, cause discomfort to others, and then for ten years tell people about the trip.

These few simple pointers will help you make friends—and *sell* yourself while you travel.

It's fun to travel—together!

Beware of Detour Signs on People's Faces!

CHAPTER 31

"WISE WAYS" TO GET ALONG WITH PEOPLE YOU LOVE

Henry Ford made the automobile, but do you know who "made" Henry Ford? A Tested Technique for insuring marital happiness.

THE MOST SUCCESSFUL "career woman" I ever met was never inside an office in her entire life.

She didn't know the first thing about business—that is, the business of buying and selling and entering figures in a big ledger.

She knew, though, all about the business of how *to be happy* and how to get what she wanted from Life, and as far as I know she got everything a woman could ask.

She had a fine home, expensive clothes, servants, diamonds. Plus the great satisfaction that comes from being successful—and *plus* the love and adulation of a good man.

She didn't have to worry about "equal rights." She enjoyed *special* privileges.

She had no college degrees, read few books, and never clipped out Dorothy Dix to slide under her husband's dinner plate!

She was my grandmother!

GRANDMA'S STORY

Grandma, as I said, had no degrees—other than in human relations, the ability to get along with "her man."

She had the biggest degree in her lodge, though, and among her neighbors and me, "grandma's boy."

"A lot of married women worry about whether they are happy or not," I once heard her say, "but the easiest way to be happy is to make your man happy—for a happy man makes a good, kind husband."

So grandma specialized in making a husband happy! She graduated in high circles—with more flowers during her life, and at death, than are given many a so-called "career woman."

Everybody knew Grandma Emma Strobel of Rochester, New York.

She had married a rather shy, retiring man who was a cigarmaker, and loved to travel, and turned him into an important restaurant man.

She did this by making him a *happy man.*

When he came home defeated and pessimistic, she filled him with confidence.

She made him feel *important*—she let him play the hero role, and she played the "stooge" to his feelings.

She kept insisting that Joe Strobel was a great friendmaker, and his restaurant and German garden behind it, would soon profit and he began to believe it himself—and it *did* become important and profitable.

GRANDMA'S METHODS

Grandma Strobel had subtle little ways of making "her man" feel important. People noticed how she praised him in company, "No one can carve a roast like Joe," she would say.

The way she listened to what he had to say, made other people feel Joe Strobel was a great man, and husbands nudged their wives and said quietly, "Why aren't you like *her*?"

I thought about Grandma Strobel not so long ago when I happened to meet Hank, an old friend of mine whom I had not seen for several years.

Hank had changed. He was about 25 pounds heavier. His suit was custom-tailored. He was driving a Cadillac Fleetwood. He was the very picture of what folks call "prosperity."

The last time I had seen Hank, he had been rather down at the mouth. He was barely making a living. His suits were nicely pressed—but threadbare, and his face had a strained, drawn look.

"What has happened?" I asked in amazement, and Hank laughed.

"I changed wives!" he said simply!

I pulled Hank into a coke parlor for this was something of great interest to me—how a change in wives brought this man prosperity.

"Do you remember how Helen used to nag me all the time for not making money, and continually embarrass me in front of my friends?"

I remembered only too well—and so did all his friends.

How unlike Grandma Strobel.

MANY HELENS IN LIFE

"Well," he went on, "I finally met a woman who made me feel like somebody. She gave me confidence in myself!

"She seldom nagged—and when she did, it was not in front of others, or over meals, or out in movies. She did talk to me, but not in a nagging tone of voice.

"Mostly, however, she seemed to notice only my good points. She got me to *sell* these good points, and to minimize my weak ones.

"That is why she became Wife Two—and so here I am, the very same man I was before only now I am *successful!*"

You have probably seen lots of "Helens" among your acquaintances. They seem to be motivated by what the psychologists call the "will to fail."

They seem deliberately to set out to make themselves unhappy, and to *make sure* that their husbands are unhappy and failures.

They point out that the successful husbands around their circle are "frauds" or "wife beaters" in their home. They have this defeatist complex.

They gripe because their husbands don't make more money, and yet they see that their poor guy is as ill equipped as possible to go out daily to face life.

They nag him until he can't think straight.

They destroy his self-confidence. They undermine his prestige by "making a fool of him" in public. Then they wonder why he doesn't have any urge to amount to something.

It is similar to a man buying an automobile, disconnecting all of the spark-plugs, pulling out the distributor, throwing sand into the gas tank—then complaining because the darned thing won't run.

They are the very opposite of Grandma Strobel.

WHAT MAKES MEN "TICK"

A man is a peculiar sort of animal. Somebody has said that men are just boys grown tall.

In a lot of ways men are like babies. They need a woman to look after them—to feed their ego.

A successful man must have a lot of things, but first he must have plenty of *self-confidence.*

There never has been a successful man who did not have a good opinion of himself.

Sigmund Freud was the first to point this out that a man's self-confidence is intimately tied up with women and sex.

If he's a "hit" with the ladies it makes him feel like a great guy. He's a *man.*

To keep his self-confidence he needs some woman to keep reminding him that he *is* a big hit at least with her—that he is really a wonderful hunk of man.

Maybe that is childish—but that's the way men are made.

The opinion of a woman can make or break a man. The small boy stands on his hands. He plays the harmonica with one hand. All to make some little girl think he is a great guy.

When he gets older, he will play football because he thinks he is interested in manly sports. Then he will try to get a good job and make lots of money to buy a bigger car and more expensive clothes because he thinks he is "ambitious."

But Freud says there is a different reason underneath the surface that the man doesn't know about.

Freud says that men do things for the same reason that the peacock struts—for the same reason that moose meet and paw the ground and fight during the mating season.

All to impress females with his "manhood."

FREUD HAD SOMETHING

Freud shrewdly observes that the basic motivation behind everything a man does is the desire to please women. Usually, one woman in particular.

That if there were no women on earth all business would come to an end, and men would give up all semblance of civilization and live like savages—much as when they go on hunting trips even today.

That it was the woman behind the skyscraper, the big canal, the new invention, the big bank, the theater—that caused them to be built by some man who wanted the adoration of some woman.

A gamecock is the "fightingest" thing on two legs, but did you know that a gamecock has absolutely no "fight" in him until he has tasted of romance?

Smart cockfighters turn the cock out "to walk"—turn him loose with fifteen or twenty hens and let him go his merry way for six months, then they try him out for fighting.

During this period the admiration of the hens does something to him. The way they follow him around and cluck for him when they find a worm, blows up his self-esteem and he begins to think he is a world beater.

After that he will fight any other gamecock on sight to the death—just to make a good impression on his lady friends, or perhaps, to make sure he won't have "competition."

Men are not so very different.

When his little woman gives him the idea that she considers herself mighty lucky to have him—that she thinks he is something very special—it does something to him.

He goes out into the business world to prove she is right.

When he is getting his back rubbed, his dinner served the way he wants it, newspapers, slippers—he will do a lot of fighting to make sure no one else gets his little lady and robs him of these pleasures.

Duels are fought over this kind of women!

WHY MEN LEAVE HOME

On the other hand, when he has to dry the dishes, tend the baby, mop the floor, cater to the whims and fancies of a selfish woman, he won't fight a duel for her.

The best way to destroy absolutely all self-confidence and ambition in a man is to give him the idea that she doesn't consider him much as a husband.

Once he gets the idea he is a failure as a *"man,"* he's a goner.

He is whipped before he goes to business.

Men leave home for but one reason. This instinctive urge to be important to some female is so strong that if one woman doesn't fulfill it, he goes to one who can and will.

What happens to Joe Doakes when his wife keeps nagging and fretting and running him down? He takes it for a while. All the time he is wondering.

Then suddenly he meets the "other woman." She may not be as pretty as his present wife. Often the "other woman" isn't.

She may not be as intelligent nor as well-educated. Often she isn't! That isn't her stock in trade!

But she can do *one thing.* She knows, woman fashion, how to make a man feel important. She knows how to make him feel that he is necessary to some woman, preferably herself!

So instead of laughing at him and calling him a "good for nothing loafer," she whispers in his ear, "You're wonderful, honey."

She treats him like a king. She does *little things* for him. Her eyes light up when he comes around as if he has done her a favor. She tells him what a great fellow he is.

So he up and divorces the "old battle-ax," gives her the brush off, and sets out to prove that all the good things the other woman thinks about him are true.

So he starts beating his brains out for her to buy her diamonds, sables, limousines, to keep her thinking he is wonderful.

Naturally, the first wife accuses the "blonde hussy" of stealing her man, and she sets out to down both of them.

If she had only known that the best way for a wife to be happy is to make her husband happy—first!

Most successful men are happily married men!

MRS. FORD HELPS HENRY

Henry Ford was a poor farm boy, who had but a few years of formal schooling. When he was growing up, he liked to tinker with watches.

He wanted to make things, and when he was sixteen years old he went to Detroit and became a mechanic. At night he had another job—cleaning clocks.

Between the two jobs he made all of three dollars per week!

At one time he tried to organize a watch-manufacturing business but his plans fell through. His future looked anything but promising.

When he was nineteen, he went back to his father's farm. Shortly afterward he met Clara Bryant. Ford had about given up the idea that he could ever make lots of money by inventing some useful machine; but Clara Bryant did things to him.

She made him feel that maybe he *could* amount to something.

They were married on April 11, 1888. Henry's dreams to "make something" were rekindled and he decided that a horseless carriage was what he should concentrate on.

He took wheels off old farm wagons and made homemade steam engines in the back yard—but all of them failed.

Did Mrs. Ford berate him for wasting his time? Did she tell him he was making her the laughing stock of the neighborhood? Did she tell him she couldn't understand why he wasn't as smart as that model husband, Mr. Jones, who had a splendid job in town making twenty-five dollars a week?

No—she never nagged him!

Instead, she encouraged him to keep on trying.

FORD WINS OUT

Several years later Ford saw a crude gasoline engine on display in Detroit. He went home and told Clara that he had at last found the answer to his dreams.

If he could build a small powerful gasoline engine, with the power plant carried on the car, he could make a successful automobile.

"Why don't you do it?" she urged.

He then explained that in order to experiment they would have to move to Detroit. He would have to sell virtually everything they possessed in order to raise enough money.

Now at this point in the lives of the Fords, Mrs. Ford did not chirp out, "You'll be the death of me yet!" She did not say, "I should have married that handsome piano salesman!"

She did not say either, "Here I have skimped and saved for years and haven't had a new dress for a whole year—and you have the *nerve* to suggest we sell the farm!"

Instead, she gripped his arm and whispered, "I am ready to go any time you are, Henry."

There is a little more to the story. Several years of hard work and failure—of sacrifice—of long experiments. Years when he kept her house cluttered up with all sorts of ungainly equipment and machines.

You know, of course, the important part of the story. Henry Ford became one of the most successful and one of the richest men in the country.

He was also one of the happiest—and this is *more* important!

He said on a number of occasions that his wife never nagged him during more than fifty years of married life.

She never fussed at him. She never destroyed his confidence in himself.

OTHER "HAPPY" MEN

Winston Churchill is another man whose success in life is partly due to a happy married life. Henry and Dana Lee Thomas* in their *Living Biographies of Famous Men* say of Churchill:

"With the accession of a loving and understanding wife, his ambitions and his achievements grew more rapidly than ever. A little too rapidly, perhaps, for his success tended to make him precipitate."

Justice Oliver Wendell Holmes was famous as a happily married man. In his youth he was brilliant but didn't get along very well with people.

He liked to use his great mind to "knock the props out" from under stuffy people, much as Joan Davis now does on her radio programs.

With his brilliant mind, his stinging wit and logical argument, he usually succeeded; but he wasn't very successful and he wasn't very famous.

Then he married—and became more agreeable and friendly. His wife didn't nag him out of his gruffness. She laughed and "teased" him out of it.

Out in company, she didn't always try to put her "ten-cents' worth" into the conversation. She let him "have the floor."

She didn't sit back like a wallflower, but she never tried to inject her personality continually into the circle of listeners, but was able when the time came to "speak her piece."

She made Holmes the *hero* in her life.

HOW TO BE HAPPY

If you want to become or to remain a happy wife, remember this:

If you want your husband to be able to buy you ermine—keep him out of the doghouse.

* Henry Thomas and Dana Lee Thomas, *Living Biographies of Famous Men* (Garden City: Garden City Publishing Co., 1944).

If you want to be a queen—help your husband be a king!

Build up his ego and self-confidence by letting him *know* you think he is a pretty swell person.

Nagging takes the "heart" out of a man. Praise is the most powerful vitamin for imbuing him with the *will to do* and *dare* and *achieve.*

Let your man be the *head* of the house.

You can be the neck that turns the head—but always turn the head toward success by making him happy at home.

The very foundation of a man's self-confidence is the opinion that his woman has of him. If she lets him know that she thinks he is a great guy, his self-confidence will overflow into his work.

If she makes him think he is *king*—he'll make sure she becomes his *queen!*

IS YOUR HUSBAND HAPPY?

Edison's happy home life is well known. He once said, "A good wife contributes very greatly—enormously, indeed, to the success of her husband."

A motto hangs over the desk of each executive of the White Motor Company. It says, MEN ARE JUDGED TO A LARGE DEGREE BY THEIR ABILITY TO WORK WITH OTHER MEN!

Where do they get this ability? Why *at home* of course from the little wifie.

If a man is unhappy at home—chances are he is unhappy at his work.

When accidents occurred in war plants during the war, personnel directors didn't bawl out the man—they investigated his home life.

Perhaps a better home, better transportation to work, something to make the wife happier so she would send her man off to work whistling, not grumbling himself into an accident.

Many a back-seat nagging wife has caused a motor accident. The police records show this only too often.

Nagging, you see, can be a very *expensive* habit!

Just a little bit of nagging could have kept many a famous man in history just a plain everyday nonentity!

We could fill books on famous men who were happily married.

There was Nathaniel Hawthorne. You might never have heard of him if he had been unhappily married.

Hawthorne wanted to write, but wasn't sure of his ability, until his wife encouraged him. One day when he lost his job at the customhouse, she didn't nag, but said:

"Now you will have time to write!"

Judge William C. Dodge of New York made it official when he said a short time ago, *"There is nothing worse in the world than a nagging person!"*

And, in conclusion, if you want me to summarize this whole chapter into one sizzling sentence, I would quote the wife of John Stuart Mill who with the wisdom of Cleopatra and Helen of Troy said:

> *"No man can help a woman—unless she helps him!"*

Don't Point Empty Guns of Threat at Husbands

CHAPTER 32

WHY DO MOST INVENTORS DIE POOR?

A Short Short Story Number 7

DID YOU KNOW that the majority of inventors die broke?

Clarence E. Birdseye, the famous inventor of frozen and dehydrated foods, tells me it is because they are *poor* salesmen.

"For some reason or other most individual inventors are habitually broke," he said, "and yet inventing should be a profitable profession. Certainly it is one that always catches the public interest."

He points out that generally speaking an inventor is just a one-man idea factory whose output has cash value only as raw material upon which many other people must spend a lot of time and money over an extended period to transform the ideas into something tangible people will buy.

This requires sizzlemanship!

SELLING YOUR IDEAS

There are millions of ideas and patents in Washington, but it takes somebody's energy, dreams, and selling ability to put them across.

That is why Birdseye says that if an inventor is to eat regularly he must be enough of a salesman to induce people to invest money, time and labor to develop and sell the idea.

Ideas are harder to sell than actual merchandise, because you can touch and see and feel most products, but ideas are often in the thinking of people.

Yet your ideas can be sold by *enthusiasm, persistency,* and *persuasiveness!*

Marconi invented the wireless, but "Ted" Husing recently signed a radio contract which in one week will perhaps pay him more than Marconi got all his life.

It isn't what you invent but *what you do* about what you invent that makes for financial success.

Many a "platter jockey," the announcers who play phonograph records on radio programs, makes thousands more than the inventors.

One, in particular, in New York for some three or four hours a day grosses $400,000 a year!

It isn't what you *invent*—but *what you do* about what you invent, that counts most!

Fit the Chair to the Person—not the Person to the Chair!

CHAPTER 33

HUSBANDS—TRY A LITTLE TENDERNESS

Eddie Cantor used to sing a song about "Try a little tenderness."

I DON'T REMEMBER quite who wrote that song, but whoever it was knew the secret of winning a woman's heart.

A man who didn't understand women might naturally think that the way to make a woman happy, who had been wearing a shabby dress, would be to buy her a new one.

This is all wrong. This song writer knew better, so he sang, "Try a little tenderness!"

You can stay out too late with the boys; you can forget to come home for dinner; you can do a lot of things, men; but if you try a little tenderness she'll forget all.

The old Irishman with his bouquet of flowers and box of candy soon made the little woman forget it was 3 A.M., and overlook his long breath.

Try a little *Irish* tenderness-tact!

WHY GIRLS MARRY OLDER MEN

Adela Rogers St. Johns in *American Weekly* Magazine, recently told her ideas of why girls like older men, and often marry them.

She said that most people have the idea that only gold diggers marry men over forty, but what about the rich Gloria Vanderbilt who at twenty-one married the sixty-three-year-old Leopold Stokowski?

Lauren Bacall married Humphrey Bogart about twice her age.

Miss St. Johns said she thought the secret was that the older men had something the youngsters didn't—*tenderness!*

In recounting what a movie heroine in a divorce case had told her in answer to the question, Miss St. Johns quoted this woman of the world as follows:

"I think if they would tell the truth, most women who are out of the adolescent stage at all, prefer tenderness in a man to any other quality."

She means that while young and beautiful women may admire the *tough guy,* the gay heartbreaker, the handsome lover, *in theory;* in actual practice they want a guarantee of tenderness.

That is the *big* secret, men!

THE TOUGH-GUY MYTH

The idea that women fall for the tough guy who slams them around and uses cave-man tactics, originated in fiction and then was dramatized in the movies.

Real-life Romeos never have been able to get away with it. They usually land in jail.

Casanova was handy with his sword—but when it came to women he was "oh so gentle."

François Villon, the half rascal, half genius, who captured the hearts of French women from chambermaids to duchesses, was a tough guy only when dealing with men.

With women he became gentle and tender.

Jimmy Cagney can throw a grapefruit in the face of his leading lady, and Clark Gable can sock 'em, and the women love it; but don't get the idea you could get away with it in real life.

When James Mason, the English movie star, arrived in Hollywood, several studios were fighting to get him. Mason gained this popularity by beating up his leading ladies—on the screen.

Mason has an international reputation as a wife beater, but does he try to be tough at home? Not according to his wife, Pamela who says, "At home he is as gentle as a lamb."

Then she adds, "Women like to see *another* woman beaten up occasionally!" But only the *other* woman! Not themselves!

So don't be fooled by the box-office popularity of the rough-and-tumble tactics of the jaw sockers and grapefruit throwers!

At home—be tender!

BETTER THAN MONEY

George Bernard Shaw has gained a world-wide reputation for being rude. He not only refused the Nobel Prize, but he insulted the committee which tried to give it to him.

He is famous for insulting people.

When he is invited out, people fully expect to be insulted by the Shavian wit, but Shaw is too smart a man to be rude at home.

He treated his wife with the utmost courtesy. A friend wrote of Shaw's behavior at home, "His wife comes before anything. He is the acme of tact and tenderness. Whatever betide, Mrs. Shaw must not be kept waiting ten minutes."

A scandal was created in a large Eastern city about twenty years ago when a banker's wife ran off with her chauffeur. Apparently her husband had everything a wife could desire in a husband.

He was the richest man in town. He loaded her down with expensive gifts. He put her in a palatial house and furnished it with servants.

She had money, social prestige, security.

What more could a woman want, you ask?

The most important things of all: thoughtfulness and tenderness!

In the divorce case which followed, her lawyer attempted to prove that she was temporarily insane. "No," she said, "I knew what I was doing.

"My husband gave me everything except the things that mattered. While the chauffeur was always telling me how pretty I was, and when he brought me some little something he always had a word to say that meant more than the gift itself."

One man knew that tenderness and thoughtfulness were more *precious* to a woman than money!

HITLER'S FAILURE AS A LOVER

If you need further proof that money and prestige are not the most important things to a woman, look at the love life of Adolph Hitler.

In his supreme egotism Adolph thought that the glamour and prestige of being courted by the most powerful man in Germany would be enough to turn any woman's heart.

In Eva Braun's diary she tells a different story. He never remembered her birthdays. He never sent her flowers or gave her little presents.

He never told her he loved her.

Once, when he gave her a large sum of money, she wrote in her diary, "If only he'd at least added a greeting or a kind word I'd have been so happy, but he never thinks of anything like that."

Which is how Adolph fizzled and failed to sizzle as a lover!

BIG BANK ROLLS UNNECESSARY

You better get the idea out of your head that women only go for the person with the big bank roll, the twelve-cyclinder limousine, and the handsome profile.

All these things help—but by themselves they have never made a woman happy.

When a married woman with two children ran away from home with Sonny Wisecarver, newspapers from coast to coast began speculating on what this young fellow had that other men didn't have.

Speculating on the Wisecarver technique became a national pastime, but when the woman herself was asked why, she said, "He's just so darned nice. He is always doing little things for me."

"Little things"—not big ones—little things, and one of them she said was bringing her a sandwich when she was hungry.

It's as easy as all that!

AN IMPORTANT SECRET

There have been all sorts of books written on, "How to Get Along with Women," "The Secret of Love," and related subjects, and men have tried every conceivable device.

During the middle ages they bought magic love charms to carry in their pockets. Later on they powdered their wigs.

Yet there is no occult formula for winning a woman. No magic hocus-pocus. You don't have to use a certain type of advertised haiı slick, nor a special scent or soap or razor or tooth paste.

You don't need a million dollars!

The real secret of how to win a woman's heart is as old as the human race, and wise men have used it, not secretly, but openly all through the ages.

Wise old King Solomon knew the secret and managed to keep over five hundred women happy.

Romeo knew it—Casanova knew it—all famous lovers in history knew it.

The most important thing to a woman is to *know* that her man loves her.

Just telling her one time isn't enough. When you join a club, are inducted, or elected President of the United States, you only need to take your oath and state your pledge one time.

When you get married you need to *keep telling your wife* you love her every day, and in a hundred different ways.

In marriage, more than in any other human relationship *actions speak louder than words!*

FLOWERS, CANDY, GIFTS

The old Irishman's stand-by of flowers and candy, an occasional evening out, are still as good as they ever were back in the days of Caesar and Cleopatra.

However, one warning: Don't make the mistake of using these things as a *substitute* for genuine affection!

If you do, these little things will no more satisfy than do the fine houses and servants.

Here again *sincerity* is the magic touchstone!

Women are too smart to be fooled by substitutes. A five-cent candy bar is enough if it symbolizes *giving yourself*, but the world with a blue ribbon around it isn't enough if it is given in lieu of yourself.

Candy won't "make up" for lack of attention, thoughtfulness, and tenderness!

The most flattering compliment you can pay your wife is to let her know she comes *first* in your life.

Women are jealous of everything else—your work included—even the morning or evening newspaper arouses their jealousy!

George Washington wrote his wife from Valley Forge that he would "much prefer" to be at home with her, and so she didn't get jealous of his job.

Robert E. Lee wrote his wife from the Mexico Campaign, "I pray that this shall be the last time I shall ever be absent from you in my life!"

Work—yes—but let the little lady know that it is secondary to her!

A man can be kind—he can be polite—he can buy fine gifts and still *not* give any part of himself.

With *tenderness* it is different!

He can't be tender and *not* be sincere—for when he gives tenderness, he gives what a woman prizes most—his heart!

So remember the woman in Eddie Cantor's song, the one with the "shabby dress."

She didn't want a new dress—just a little *tenderness!*

Fragile—Handle Wives with Great Care!

CHAPTER 34

MAKE YOUR "BOOK OF THE DAY" A "BEST SELLER" THIS WAY

The cigar-store Indian never sold a cigar because he lacked a human voice. Your voice advertises your personality! Put the voice in "neons."

RECENTLY I was in the offices of "Smoke" Ballew, nationally known sales executive, while he was interviewing applicants for a job.

Curious as to why he had selected the particular man he did, I asked him, "Why did you pick that man, Smoke, above all the others? His record is no better than the others, maybe not as good."

The reply was simply this: "I liked the way he talked!"

A big executive like Ballew choosing a man because he liked "the way" the man talked! This set me to thinking.

A great many times we do not quite know just what it is about a man that impresses us favorably, but if we analyze it, the chances are that we too "like the way he talks."

Each of us speaks an average of about 30,000 words per day, or the equivalent of a small book—and this "book of the day" is our best or worst advertisement to the world around us.

These little "books of the day" are constantly saying, "Here is an educated man—an illiterate man—an intolerant man—an egotist—a milk toast—a go-getter.

They are forever proclaiming that we are capable—or incapable, slovenly, neat, cultured, coarse—reliable, unreliable.

Unconsciously our hearers judge us more by our words and *our voice* than any other factor.

So make your "book of the day" a *best seller!*

IT'S THE WAY YOU SAY IT

Even more important than the words we use, is the *way* that we use them.

Our tone of voice tells as much as the words.

The words appeal to the brain of the listener, but the *tone* touches their heart!

After all, the heart is *closer* to the purse than the brain, in case you depend upon your words to make sales.

When Marc Antony delivered his famous, "Friends, Romans, Countrymen" speech which you read a few chapters ago, you read it with your mind. You didn't "hear" the tone of voice.

One day I heard an accomplished orator speak the lines, and I was enthralled. The message touched my heart this time.

One week later, by chance, I attended a high-school graduation and a lad whose voice was changing recited the same lines, and everybody laughed!

The same speech—but one voice sold it—the other voice failed to sell it!

Casper Milquetoast is still Casper Milquetoast even when he uses *courageous* words, because you just know his tone of voice gives him away. The artist makes sure of this.

I have tried yelling at my dog, *"Come here,"* and he would run away. I have said in soft tones, "Go away," and he would come to me. He understands *tone* of voice.

A woman can say "no" so that it means "maybe"!

MAE WEST'S "TONE"

When Mae West says, "Come up and see me sometime!" it is not what she says but the *tone* behind the words that have the real double meaning.

A man can call a woman a little devil so that it will be an insult, or become a sly compliment to her!

You can say, "This is a fine country!" or, "This is a *fine* country!" The words are the same—but the meaning changes!

There are three different ways to say, "What a man."

A woman goes to the movies and sighs, "What a *m-a-n!"*

On the way home, still enthralled with the hero, she looks at what is driving the car and sighs, *"W-h-a-t* a man!"

While the old maid looks under her bed and shouts, "*What?*—a man?"

It is all in how you say it!

PRACTICE "TONE"

You can call a twenty-one-year-old boy Mr. *Jones* and make him feel important, or call him *Mister* Jones and let him know you are making fun of him.

So practice "tone." Say things in various tones of voice, like the good movie people do when they rehearse a scene.

You will eliminate that tendency to let sarcasm creep into your voice, ruining your chances of impressing people, or winning them over.

"No one ever pays any attention to me when I talk," is a common complaint of people whose tone of voice is blank, saying nothing.

If you are this type of person, "listen" to your voice. Cup your hands behind your ears, like radio announcers do when they want to "hear themselves."

Put your voice on a recording machine. You won't like it, I can assure you. You will see a need to change your tone, until it commands attention from others.

The armed forces teach the right way to give orders, so that the men will react instantly when a command is given, because they *feel* the authority behind the command.

The way to eliminate sarcastic overtones, is to be sincere. Feel inside of you what you are saying, and your emotions will take care of the right tone of voice.

In all events, practice "tone."

IN POLICE WORK

Doug Walsh, assistant chief of the Dallas Police Department has often told me how his traffic department trains the men in the proper tone of voice to use in arresting people.

"The proper tone of voice in arresting a traffic violator is important," he says, "because if the officer is burly and sarcastic, trouble occurs at once. Tone of voice is as important in police work as in retail selling."

You have often heard a woman say, "Oh, I didn't mind getting that ticket at all—the officer was *such* a nice man. He was so polite!"

Indeed, you can arrest people "with dignity."

One of the most progressive police systems in America is that of the Michigan State Police, and while on a speaking program Oscar G. Olander, the commissioner, gave me his "police courtesy" booklet.

This booklet *must* be read by every state policeman before he gets his job.

Besides "teaching" the men how to eat in public—yes eat—because they can reflect good or bad manners in restaurants—Commissioner Olander teaches them "tone of voice."

Under the chapter on "Voice and Its Tone," he says:

"Every time you speak, you touch someone with your voice."

I like that. I like too:

"A low voice—low in pitch, not in range—is always more pleasing than one forced up against the ceiling and apparently let out through a steam-vent in the roof. Making yourself heard is chiefly a matter of enunciation."

The commissioner is more than a "policeman," he is a philosopher for he goes so far in his booklet as to say:

"According to Arnold Bennett whose stories are filled with reference to voice tone, 90 per cent of all the friction of daily life is caused by mere tone of voice. When a man speaks, his words convey his thought and his tone conveys his mood!"

In Michigan you are "arrested with the right tone!"

DON'T BE JOHNNY-ONE-NOTE

It is generally conceded by friends and enemies alike that the late President Franklin Roosevelt had one of the best radio voices of all time. If you will listen to a recording of his voice you will find that it possesses these qualities:

1. *Tonal Variation:*

The "tone" of his voice varied all the way up and down the scale. This made him easy to listen to. Speaking in a monotone is monotonous. It fatigues the sense of hearing.

The listener loses interest and thinks about other things if he isn't simply "rocked to sleep." Roosevelt's voice rose and fell in rhythmic pattern.

He would emphasize one word by dropping down a full octave.

A few sentences later he would achieve the same result by slightly raising the tone.

Practice this yourself. It will help your "popularity."

2. *He Talked In LOW Key:*

While the inflection of President Roosevelt's voice varied from low to high, he pitched his voice in a low key. Most people speak in too high a pitch.

This is especially true when we get excited.

There is nothing less charming or more irritating than a high, shrill voice. The low-pitched voice is *more convincing*. It is reassuring.

It is pleasant to the ear.

Try consciously pitching your voice just a little lower. It will not only create a better impression on your listener, but you will find that it will give you, yourself, a feeling of poise and charm you never knew was inside you.

3. *He Spoke Slowly and Distinctly:*

The nervous, ill-at-ease person, speaks in a flurry, as Billie Burke and Eddie Bracken love to affect over the radio in their programs.

The person who feels inferior—who lacks self-confidence nearly always talks fast. When we speak hurriedly and nervously, we are advertising to our listener that we lack confidence—that we are unsure of o-u-r-s-e-l-v-e-s!

Practice these three speaking traits of President Roosevelt for your own fireside chats with friends!

"MEAN" WHAT YOU SAY

A good rule to make sure your daily book of 30,000 words is a "best seller" is: *Say what you mean—AND MEAN WHAT YOU SAY!*

You may develop that right tone of voice, much like an actor, but people will soon catch on that you have practiced tone, but that it is all an "act."

You must be sincere—else you won't "go over."

The way that you *act* while speaking is also powerful in persuading people you are sincere.

I noticed this especially in that young man whom Smoke Ballew had hired because "I liked the way he talked."

Some of the other applicants kept their eyes on the floor while talking; one of them looked at his own hands, kept twisting them.

Another grinned self-consciously as he recited his background; as if ashamed of it.

Still another fixed my friend with "piercing eyes" and kept them "riveted" to Ballew, in a "stare battle," as though to convince Ballew "I am truthful."

The lad that got the job did none of these things. His expression told you that he *meant* what he was saying, because it came sincerely from inside.

It was neither belligerent nor apologetic.

Instead of staring into the eyes of Ballew and making him feel uncomfortable, he would look into his eyes for a moment, then shift to the man's lips, back to his desk, and so forth.

Most important of all, he was a good listener. He leaned slightly forward when Ballew talked. His expression showed he considered the future boss to be very important.

Summed up, remember you recite a "book full of 30,000 words" daily, and make sure your "book of the day" is a "best seller" by, first of all,

Watching the tone *of your voice!*

The Cigar-store Indian NEVER Sold a Cigar—He lacked a Human Voice!

CHAPTER 35

A VICE-PRESIDENT "IN CHARGE OF WINNING FRIENDS" TELLS SOME OF HIS "TRADE SECRETS"

A Short Short Story Number 8

A. F. Davis is vice-president of the Lincoln Electric Company of Cleveland, Ohio, the largest of its kind, and has endowed the A. F. Davis Welding Library at Ohio State University.

Many of these volumes "Charlie" wrote himself, and tells me he considers the *ability to get along with others* more important than technical knowledge.

Charlie doesn't discount the "know," for he edits the *Stabilizer,* a monthly magazine on welding technique, and as secretary of James F. Lincoln Arc Welding Foundation, has "brought know how" to over 25,000 people.

Both specialized *knowledge* and *personality* are important but of the two he claims *personality* is the most important, and explains it this way:

TRADE "SECRETS" REVEALED

"When I got out of school, I decided I had only average ability and intelligence, but that I *could* work hard to achieve the things which would make up for any lack of brilliance.

"By being a hard worker, I could *get the attention* of those who could help me. I did that—in fact, I overdid it!

"Nine years after I graduated I had a breakdown, and it seemed little payment for what little success I had achieved, but I soon learned that out of every hardship you gain something.

"During my enforced idleness I read—and thought—and soon decided no matter how smart or how hard an individual worked, he can't accomplish a great deal through his own efforts alone.

"It dawned on me that everything we get comes from *other people,* and that we must inspire this from others.

"If you go back in history you will find that it was Jesus who had the greatest effect on history through his ability to secure followers, to inspire them, and so he has lived on through the years.

WE DEPEND ON OTHERS

"So it is true of all lesser individuals. Going to the opposite extreme, take Napoleon. How much could he have done had he depended solely on his own efforts?

"While laid up I decided I had been negligent in not developing myself with my associates. I had not attempted to *make them thirsty* for me.

"I have since found that in order to do a good job of making friends, you have to like people. This makes them *thirsty* for your friendship.

"I found I had to be sincere in this. If people felt that I was making an effort, consciously or otherwise, to do so, they looked at me with suspicion and wondered what I was trying to sell them.

"As years went by I found that in *turning my interest to other people*—in thinking about other people—I had developed a genuine liking for others."

Did this pay off for Charlie, vice-president in charge of winning friends?

Well here is what his "boss," James F. Lincoln says:

"His ability to make friends is *worth more* to me than all of his technical knowledge—and if he knew nothing about welding, he would *still* be valuable to the firm!"

I guess that's the answer!

You Can't Wind Clocks—or People—BACKWARDS!

CHAPTER 36

"PLEASURE PAIN"—THE GOLDEN KEY TO INFLUENCING HUMAN BEHAVIOR

The playboy throws his money away; the miser hoards it—both do so for the same reason: PLEASURE!

DO YOU KNOW the *one basic reason* why anybody does anything at all?

Psychologists say that all our actions, every single thing we do without exception, is the result of following what they call the "pleasure-pain" principle.

It is inherent in human nature to seek whatever brings *pleasure* to one's self, and to avoid what brings *pain.*

Think a *long moment* about what I have just written!

It is a capsule formula for understanding the people around you, to know why they do what they are doing.

Because when they do anything, it is for *pleasure,* whether it is the fellow who invites you to lavish dinners—the hobo riding the rods—a man working on a disagreeable job.

They are all following the same basic formula!

You see "one man's meat is another man's poison."

The playboy is tossing his money away because that is *his* idea of pleasure. The miser is hoarding his money because a pile of it is more *pleasant* than a good meal or a decent suit.

WE FEAR PAIN

The hobo refuses to work because work is *painful* to him. More painful than the criticism and disapproval of society.

The work slave is working sixteen hours per day for the same reason the hobo is loafing!

In his case the *pain* of not being able to maintain a high standard of living would be much more *painful* than the long hours.

When I was writing the rough draft of this chapter, my friend

Tommy Luke, of Portland, began reading over my shoulder. "Just a minute, Elmer," he said, "you're going too far when you say *everything* anybody does is to seek pleasure and to avoid pain."

"All right," I said, "you tell me one thing that doesn't fit in."

"Well," he said, "you paid for my lunch today!"

"It was because of the pleasure of having you as my guest."

"You just paid me a compliment—why did you do it?"

"For the pleasure of having you like me!"

"What about the man who gives all his money to the poor?"

"Wouldn't he be the first to admit that he derived genuine pleasure from helping others—which is worth more than his money and the *pain* of thinking all the good it would not do in his vault?"

TOMMY LUKE CONTINUES

"What about the soldier in battle who marches forward in the face of enemy fire? Isn't he giving up the pleasure and accepting the painful?"

"The pain of admitting to himself that he is a coward," I replied, "or the pain of court-martial for desertion is much greater than the pain of physical danger involved."

"I knew an old lady who denied herself the necessities of life and sacrificed to educate her two boys in Portland," he said.

"But don't you think she got more genuine *pleasure* in the knowledge that her boys were starting out in life well prepared—than she would in anything else she could have bought with money?"

Tommy gave up! As past president of the Florists Telegraph Delivery Association, I think Tommy is now figuring the "pain-pleasure" principle for "Saying It with Flowers."

For stop yourself—think of any situation where people are not motivated by this *pleasure-pain* principle.

If you can, numerous psychologists would be glad to learn of it, for they know of no single situation where this principle isn't the deciding factor involved in what people do.

A TIP FROM THE ADS

Since this pleasure-pain principle is at the bottom of all human actions, what wonder rabble rousers, statesmen, politicians, debaters, salesmen, preachers, and big corporations make good use of it in attempting to persuade others to their views.

It is a perfectly legitimate device.

Without it, it would be impossible to influence human nature for the better.

Naturally, many use it to debase human nature. Hitler did this. He built up the Jew in Germany as the national menace. He painted vivid word pictures of how Jews were ruining Germany, stealing property and business.

This was the *"pain picture."*

Then he very graciously offered himself as the solution: "Follow me, and I will deliver you," he said.

This was the *"pleasure picture."*

The old-time preacher used the word *hell* as his "pain picture," and his own religion as the "pleasure picture" which would save them.

The politician tries to show you how his opponent will ruin the country—cause your business to fail. The "pain picture." You recoil from it; and then out of a hat he offers a "decent government—my style!" The "pleasure picture."

Indeed, take a tip from the advertisements!

Notice how many ads make use of this principle. "Do you suffer from body odor?" . . . "Do you have bad breath?" . . . "Do people laugh behind your back?"

You will see pictures of men and women who are social outcasts, the girl whose best beau won't call on her any more, the man who has lost his job. "Pain pictures" de luxe!

Then the solutions: Use the product and the skin will glow. The boy friend will return. The man becomes vice-president at thirty—"pleasure pictures" de luxe!

Indeed, take a tip from the advertisements!

WHAT ABOUT THE DENTIST?

Every time I pick up an advertisement and see those ads about products to hold false teeth in the mouth, I make an appointment with my dentist.

I know the fellow has a drill—and will poke and cause me pain, yet why do I run to this pain?

I do it because the pain of false teeth causes me to run off, for a little pain today may give me more pleasure tomorrow.

That is why we submit to operations. They are painful, uncomfortable, but the pleasure later on makes us go to the hospital.

Pain, you see, can be mental anguish, qualms of conscience, fear, guilt, remorse, as well as physical.

It is often better to suffer physical pain today—to save mental pain later on.

How much more effective would the advertising dentist be were he to say, "It will save you *more pain* later on!" than the old-fashioned banner, "Painless Dentist!"

That "later on" is more important to people than "painless!"

YOUR OWN SIZZLES

When you give a person the choice between something *pleasant* and something *painful,* he will usually accept the pleasant every time.

That is, until you point out that a little pain today may bring *more* pleasure tomorrow, then he will have the pain and choose it.

If you are in some business, sit back now and see how you can make profitable use of this chapter right away.

Figure out where you can point out some added pleasures to lure customers, point out, too, if that is your type of business, how a little pain now will be added pleasure on another day.

No one wants to "walk up one flight." It is painful, until we read "and save ten dollars," and that is a pleasure.

It is painful to drive to the suburbs to buy something, until we read, "No big overhead—you save the difference" and that savings is a pleasure.

It is "painful" to most men to shave—and so Barbasol advertises, "Just rub it on—no brush, no lather," and then shaving becomes *less* of a pain.

It is painful for women to sit for hours having their hair washed and dried under those huge heat devices that make them look like women from Mars, yet why do they submit to this torture?

They will get pleasure out of friends—husbands or sweetheart—liking them better!

Become pleasure-pain *conscious,* and you will find your own selling sizzles to enrich your life—and give *you* pleasure!

USE IT ON YOURSELF

This "capsule formula" can be used to influence your own behavior, as well as that of friends or customers.

When you make a resolution to break a bad habit, form a new one, or anything else—remember that you will do it if you can convince yourself that the new course is the more *pleasant* one.

Give yourself some *incentive.*

When you want to stick to a diet, or embark upon some plan for self-improvement—think about all the *pleasant* things that will result from following your plan, and all the *painful* results of not following it.

When you are tempted to reach for that extra piece of pie, that cigarette, that drink you are trying to stay away from—don't think of momentary pleasure, but of future pain.

Think that behind your back people will call you "Fatty," will say you are a "coffin smoker," that you are "drinking yourself to the grave."

Think of the *pain* that follows the *pleasure* and see if it is really worth-while—momentary pleasure for permanent pain!

"WILL POWER" NOT ESSENTIAL

A friend of mine tried for years to quit smoking. He tried using "will power," determination and just about everything else; all to no avail. When I saw him not long ago, I noticed he wasn't smoking any more and asked him how he had done it.

"I read everything I could find on the dangers of smoking," he said. "Then in my imagination I saw myself getting hardening of the arteries, heart trouble, and all sorts of other diseases. "I set out to give myself as big a deliberate scare as I could.

"Next I imagined all the pleasures that would result from *not* smoking. First of all would be a saving of at least one hundred dollars a year. I could buy that outboard motor.

"Then would come better health, more energy. I made up a list of these advantages and disadvantages and went over them each day—making my imagined pictures as *real* as possible."

He told then how the craving itself seemed to leave him. So you see nothing is impossible if you *sell* yourself on it, and the pleasure-pain principle will help.

WRITERS NEED IT

My good friend Arthur "Red" Motley, President of "Parade" magazine, uses this pleasure-pain idea in writing his numerous articles.

He tells me he detests sitting down daily to write. His mind rebels at the drudgery of batting out words on the typewriter.

He tells me that when he finds that he doesn't want to write any more, he stops dead, settles back, and relaxes.

He sees himself walking into stores and buying all sorts of gadgets—anything he wants—all as a result of having written so many words that day.

Usually, after about ten minutes of his daydreaming "treatments," he finds that his zest for writing has suddenly returned as if by magic!

If this doesn't work, he goes on a mental window-shopping

tour. He looks at all the most expensive clothes, fishing tackle, golf clubs, and other things.

He handles these things and deliberately arouses the desire for them. Then to be able to get them, he pounds and pounds on the typewriter—swapping pain now for later pleasure of owning the nice things he wants.

Try this "Red" Motley use of "pleasure pain"!

TO INFLUENCE OTHERS

When you want to influence others, try the principle.

Help people to get more pleasure—and avoid unpleasantness.

Offer them thrills instead of toothaches.

Don't *pain* people by boring them—by depressing them.

You give people pains when you gossip, toss wet blankets on parties, get overly "high," get belligerent, become noisy, get loud, and otherwise cause people pain.

Don't air your home feuds in public; don't gripe. Otherwise you will find that this pains people, and they will avoid you and seek people who give them pleasure.

You wouldn't cause physical pain by walking around a room and slapping people on the face, but you can slap them *mentally* and cause about as much pain by halitosis mannerisms.

The pleasure-pain principle is behind every social contact you make, as the psychologists have so ably pointed out.

This country was settled by people who came here to avoid the pain of prosecution and tyranny abroad. They came here seeking the *pleasures* of liberty and a better way of life.

They will leave a party—if they find it painful.

All history is just a delineation of the human race following this one principle—seeking pleasure—avoiding pain.

The Exodus—the founding of Salt Lake City—every big movement of people, every exodus, was to find more pleasure, less pain.

Moving out of a neighborhood—leaving your home—often is because of the pain there, and the pleasure elsewhere.

Take this principle and make it practical—right into your everyday life with others, and watch your friends increase.

"SELL" PLEASURE TO PEOPLE

Dr. Albert Edward Wiggam says:

"Real salesmanship either of yourself or your goods is talking someone—or a group or a nation—into doing something they don't want to do, *and then making them glad they did it!*

He says that the easiest way to make people happy—to bring them more pleasure—and thus influence them to do what you want done is to "add to their aggregate."

Offer them something that will *help them*—something that will make them more powerful—something that will make their life easier—or make them more money.

"When you apply for a job you must convince the employer that you will add to his aggregate," Dr. Wiggam says. "All your life you must be a salesman, and you will succeed just in proportion as you make other people feel you have brought something new into their lives."

So if you want to sell yourself to the neighbors—remember you must offer them *pleasure*.

When they can sincerely say, "It is a *pleasure* to know you," then you are in solid.

If you are selling goods and want people to trade with you, give them *pleasure*—trade this for what they may have to swap for more pleasure, such as money.

Keep this big, basic formula of human behavior foremost in your mind, and you will go far toward getting along with people, and selling yourself all through life.

Keep this *pleasure-pain* principle up front at all times when you are dealing with others.

For—it is the *only thing* that can really and truly influence human behavior to your way of thinking.

In a nutshell, to make a favorable impression,

Don't give people a pain in the neck!

People are Starved for Recognition

CHAPTER 37

HOW A SIZZLE SAVED A LIFE

A Short Short Story Number 9

PERHAPS YOU remember reading about the man in New York City who perched himself on a narrow ledge on the eighteenth floor of a New York hotel for eighty minutes, threatening to jump to his death.

Thousands gathered in the streets to watch the spectacle.

A rabbi, a priest, a doctor, and hundreds of firemen and policemen gathered in the streets to watch the spectacle, and to offer advice and suggestions.

On the roof tops of buildings all around, and from the windows of the Empire State Building, more thousands of eyes watched the "drama on the roof tops."

Appeals to self-preservation and religion failed to make the demented man move from his precarious position, and not jump.

Here are some of the appeals used as I heard them, being close to the man:

> Rabbi: "It is against your religion to take your own life."
> Priest: "Don't do anything you'll regret, my good man."
> Doctor: "You will seriously *injure* yourself if you jump!"
> Fireman: "Don't jump—get back—you'll injure someone."
> Police: "Get off that ledge—wanna get killed!"

You perhaps remember the headlines in all the daily newspapers that afternoon.

A NEW APPEAL USED

Finally in desperation the management of the hotel called on me, asking me to use some "word magic" to get the man not to jump.

With me, at the time, was Miss Diane Gregal, my vice president, and I figured a woman's appeal would be better than mine, so we worked out some "word magic" as the manager called it.

Sensing that these appeals to "self-preservation" and to "religion," physical pain, physical injury, and others were not working but failing, we thought fast.

The man was slowly moving closer to the ledge, preparing to jump the 18 stories to his death for what reason none of us knew, since he was recognized as a well-to-do Brooklyn manufacturer.

Then Miss Gregal had an idea and walked toward the man. Out on the roof top, in view of thousands, she said in a kind tone to the man:

"Shall I get you a cup of coffee?" He grunted negatively.

"Would you like a glass of wine?" Miss Gregal went on, and again received a no.

These appeals to his comfort failed.

THE ONE THAT WORKED

When these appeals to the man's personal comfort failed, and as he was about to jump, Miss Gregal took a great big chance. If it worked, she was the heroine of the day.

If he jumped, she might be accused of his death.

Being an alert woman, with a keen understanding of men, she took the chance and appealed to the man's *vanity*.

Here are the three sizzles that worked:

> "You look *silly* perched up on that ledge!"
> "Suppose your *wife* sees you in that *ridiculous* place!"
> "(Irene), your niece, is on the way over—better get down *at once* before she sees what a *fool* you are making of yourself."

Mad at the man, Miss Gregal stormed off the roof, and then, as if by a miracle, her words penetrated the blurred mind of the man perched 18 stories up on that ledge.

Slowly he brushed himself off, arranged his hat, and walked off the ledge back into the hotel!

His *vanity* had been pricked by three words: "silly," "ridiculous," "fool."

The anticipated *pain* of having people, especially his own family, think him a *fool* was too much for him.

Whatever it was in life that had proven painful enough to make him want to take his own life—took on a very pleasant hue when compared to making a fool of himself.

The man stepped down off the ledge to safety.

A Hobby is an endless amount of hard work that you would be ashamed to do for a living.—GILBERT NORWOOD

CHAPTER 38

THE GENTLE ART OF PASSING THE BUCK

It even makes the tax collector popular. It is a trait of leadership—the art of overruling objections, tactfully.

Most people seem to have the idea that "passing the buck" is a vice, and only for the Army.

This is a big mistake.

When we use the term to mean blaming others for our own mistakes, it is a good way to lose friends and prestige, but when used properly it is a sign of leadership.

Big men—successful men—are noted for taking full responsibility, accepting the blame of those under them, and nothing so wins popularity.

There is a time, however, when "passing the buck" becomes a real virtue instead of a vice.

While it is wrong to pass the buck of your own responsibility, it is just as foolish and stupid not to pass the buck when the responsibility belongs elsewhere.

When it is used right passing the buck can become a magic wand for smoothing out troubled waters, avoiding strife, and making people like you.

DON'T LOOK FOR TROUBLE

There is an old saying, "Don't go out looking for trouble even if you have to do without it!"

Suppose, for example, you are a room clerk and when somebody wants to cash a check you say, "Sorry—I don't *know* you!"

Trouble begins right then and there.

So the smart room clerk won't accept the responsibility, so cleverly says, "Mr. Jones, our credit manager, takes care of that."

Trouble—is side-stepped!

The buck is passed—but *where it belongs.* No one feels embarrassed. The incident passes unnoticed. No friends of the hotel are lost.

Next time somebody asks you for five dollars, don't blurt out that you haven't got it, or can't lend it, but try instead, "If I had it, Joe, it would be yours!"

The art of getting along with borrowers!

TAKE THE TAX COLLECTOR

Perhaps he is the most unpopular man in his circle of friends, yet he avoids such unpopularity by adroitly passing the buck and so doesn't lose friends.

The collector in Dallas where I lived once told me, "Most people want to argue and grouse about paying back taxes. But I refuse to argue with them. When they cuss out a law, I merely tell them I *agree* 100 per cent, but am as helpless as they are!"

He rightfully passes the buck to the state legislature which passed the law!

"When one man once told me the legislators were stupid," he went on, "I still did not argue, but told him that was still *not* my fault!"

Texas wit!

So the taxpayers around here feel that this man understands them. They feel that he wants to help but is not in a position to do so.

They feel he is on *their side* and so they are happy—with him!

OVERRULING OBJECTIONS

Try this art of passing the buck to overcome objections in handling the public, whether you are selling underwear, zebras, or your own personality.

The trick is to make the other fellow feel that you personally agree with him—but that some *third party* would object.

A smart auto salesman tells you that your old car will bring you only seventy-five dollars, and when you object he looks helpless and says, "I'm afraid the used-car department won't permit more!"

He has cleverly side-stepped an issue that might spoil a sale and lose a friend and prospect for a new car.

Another way he passes the buck is to show the Standard Rate Book for used cars, and then both he, *and* the used-car department pass the buck!

Detroit gets the blame then!

So by passing the buck to some *third party,* which doesn't have to be a person, you side-step the difficulty of placing the discussion upon a personal basis.

It is no longer a battle between *you* and the other person, but between him and the *third* person.

Often, then, you can take sides *with him* against the third party! Thus making a good friend out of him.

"I'll do all I can for you," is better than, "What—give you more than seventy-five dollars for that jalopy!"

"I'm afraid the home office would turn *me* down on that," is better than, "Are you crazy—asking for such terms!!"

When you leave a friend's home don't yawn in his face and say, "Boy, am I tired. Think I'll hit the hay!" The friend then says, "Huh—so we tire him out!"

Try, "I could stay all night—but I sure have a big day tomorrow!"

Pass the buck on tomorrow!

BUCK PASSING IN REVERSE

Passing the buck also works in reverse English. It is done this way:

Instead of "passing" blame to your co-workers or the boss, or on friends or neighbors, try passing *credit* to them!

If you want to be a leader of men, this one trait will do more to make people glad to follow you than any other.

Human relations expert J. C. Staehle, made a survey to find the principal causes of discontent among workers. Heading the list was failure to give employees credit for suggestions—failure to "pass the buck of credit" on down the line.

Give your men *credit* for what they do. Go a step further and give them *honors* that *you* win! Pass credit on down the line!

All the *E* Awards were given to the men at the machines.

Successful men like Henry Hazlitt, financial editor of *Newsweek,* and Bradford B. Smith, economist for the U. S. Steel Corporation, know the value of this philosophy of passing credit to others.

John S. Coleman, the youthful new president of the Burroughs Adding Machine Company believes in delegating authority to those men and women working with him.

This is one of the secrets of his amazing success. He doesn't try to hog the show. He isn't afraid someone else will show him up. He gives out responsibility to his assistants. They get full credit, too, when they come through for him.

General George Marshall, Secretary of State, knows the value of delegating authority, learned in the Army. To a greater degree than most Secretaries of State he delegates authority and frees himself for decision making at the very top level.

Justin Dart, president of United Drug, follows the same plan. "There's no need in giving a man a job if you are not going to give him the opportunity to be successful at it," he says.

Carl Ullman, president of the Dollar Savings and Trust Company of Youngstown, Ohio, takes his senior officers with him when he attends directors' meetings.

Instead of stealing their ideas as his own, he allows them to make their own reports to the directors and secure the credit for themselves.

Try this trait of big men.

THE SECRET OF LEADERSHIP

If you are a leader or want to become one—remember this one good rule. A man becomes successful only by raising those up around him—never pushing them down, hogging the credit.

Small men say, "None of my help is capable—I must carry the entire load!"

Nothing is further from the truth. One of the first marks of a *big* man or woman in business is the *ability to pick capable assistants.*

Real go-getters know this. They surround themselves with competency.

They try to make others *star* in the show.

Ed Stephens, president of Cinderella Foods, Inc., the world's largest manufacturer of peanut butter told me he owed his success to the ability of picking good men.

"This business became the largest of its kind in the world because of my assistants and workers," he said.

How people love to work for a man like that!

TRY IT AT HOME

Try this "big business" principle of getting along and selling others on yourself in the home.

Delegate authority in the home.

Let Wilbur wash the car, run it down for gas and oil changes. He'll love the responsibility you give him.

Let mother have the right to pick the stove, refrigerator, or washing machine she wants. Don't tell her she must have a certain one simply because you can get it wholesale, or know the salesman.

Let sister have a job in the house; let little brother have his work to do, and once they get their assignments, let them alone.

Maybe things aren't the way you would do them, but at least that is a big load of work off your shoulders.

If they make mistakes, don't be the first to shout at them, for they can always reply, "Then why didn't you do it yourself!"

Big men—in their office, and in their home—learn how to delegate authority, how to pass the buck, and how to give credit where it belongs.

When somebody comes to the door to sell you something, you can always pass the buck to the third party who isn't at home. Rather than slam the door with "We got all the magazines we need," say, "Mrs. Jones always buy the magazines. Please see her sometime."

Memorize these two rules for "PASSING THE BUCK":

1. *Use it STRAIGHT by* refusing to saddle yourself with responsibility that isn't rightfully yours. If you must object, let the objection come from the third person or thing —not from yourself.
2. *Use it in REVERSE by* passing the buck of *credit* to those around you. Pass the buck of authority down the line and give others an opportunity to make good and develop their own talents and abilities.

Talk—don't HONK!

CHAPTER 39

TO GET AHEAD FASTER PUT SOMETHING EXTRA IN YOUR BOX—BE UNDERPAID

Making sure you are "underpaid" is a hard pill to swallow, but here is what will happen to you if you are *underpaid!*

When I asked Harry White, executive secretary of the New York Sales Executives' Club, the secret of his rapid rise in that organization he surprised me by saying:

"What little success I have achieved I attribute to the following one simple rule which an old timer gave me when I was just starting out. I have always tried to make sure I was underpaid!"

Now that is a strange rule for getting ahead, especially for a young man who directs this club of 1,500 of the top sales executives, presidents, vice presidents and others of the leading corporations of America!

"Life is like a set of double-entry ledgers," Harry told me, sitting back in his offices in Hotel Roosevelt in New York. "What you enter on one side, Life enters on the other. You always get back just what you put in.

"When you always manage to do more than you are paid for, you keep Life in debt to *you!* You keep the world owing you something—and make no mistake, you'll get it!"

Harry White has got it—holding a job of running the world's foremost sales executives club with 1,500 "bosses," each a big man in industry!

THE URGE FOR "GETTING"

Inside all of us is a natural human weakness to want something for nothing—to be as lazy as we dare be, and get by. This is a normal instinct.

Yet people who put money in a bank don't expect to get much

more than they put in. They don't expect to get more water than the bucket will hold—but from Life, well, they seem to want more and more for doing less and less.

It doesn't work this way in Life though. Life's ledger books keep an accurate balance. You can't beat it. Like money in the bank you only get what you put in, plus a small interest.

If we follow the example of successful men and put our old reverse English to work and turn "something for nothing" into "do more than expected," we will compound our returns.

Joseph P. Day became the greatest real estate salesman of all times because of this principle. One day a big buyer came into the store where Day worked as a clerk and wanted certain samples next day, Fourth of July.

The boy who was asked to do the assignment complained on working on the Fourth of July, so Day volunteered, and his willingness to do more than was required, got him a promotion.

His whole business career was built then upon that same idea of giving more than expected. His "box" was not empty. In fact, it contained the baker's dozen, that thirteenth extra doughnut.

Give a baker's dozen yourself in Life!

THE SECOND MILE!

The idea of giving children free lollypops in grocery stores, a sliver of cheese from the butcher, base ball and bats from clothing merchants, all springs from this same desire to give more than expected.

A. W. Robertson, when he was Chairman of the Board at Westinghouse, said, "If a man does only what is required of him, he is a slave! The moment he does *more* he is a free man!"

It is doing a little more that leads to more happiness and contentment for ourselves, as Robertson knew so well.

J. C. Penney, writing in the *Rotarian,* said:

"Success in business does not depend upon genius. Any young man of ordinary intelligence who is morally sound and not afraid to work should succeed. . . ."

Roger Babson in his book, *Religion and Business,** says, "The secret of success is to do more than is demanded. . . . There is no power nor glory in doing only what we have to do. . . . The glory comes with the second mile!"

Incidentally, the Law of Equal Equation that Babson often refers to is Newton's Third Law in physics: "For every action there is an equal and opposite reaction."

If we throw a ball up it will come down with the *same* force. A falling body exerts a force equivalent to the power needed to raise it to its original height.

When we pull a bow string back with forty pounds pressure, it will send the arrow into flight with forty pounds pressure when we release it.

Mr. Babson points out that the very same principle works in human relations.

SOW AND YE SHALL REAP

In human relations when we do someone a good turn, we've earned a good turn for ourselves.

When we feed a hungry dog, he sits by our feet and guards us.

When we compliment the wife for a good meal, she comes up with a better one next time.

When we work a little harder for the boss, he will soon see our effort and reward us.

When we do someone a kindness, we have a kindness coming to us.

Extra benefits come to those that give a little extra, who put more in their "box of effort" than the other person expects.

When I sell a Doberman pinscher pup (I raise them), I always give a few pounds of dog feed and a collar, not part of the deal. A plus! It sells more dogs later on.

Practically every great philosopher, both ancient and modern, agrees with Mr. Babson. Jesus said, "With what measure ye mete,

* Roger Babson, *Religion and Businesss* (New York: The Macmillan Company, 1920).

it shall be measured unto you. . . . Judge not that yet be not judged."

Whatever a man sows, that shall he also reap!

DIVINE JUSTICE IN NATURE

Emerson wrote an essay on this principle of action and reaction. In it he says, "If you love and serve men, you cannot by any hiding or stratagem escape remuneration!

"Secret retributions are always restoring the level, when disturbed, of divine justice. It is impossible to tilt the beam.

"All tyrants and proprietors and monopolists of the world in vain set their shoulders to heave the bar. Settles for ever more the ponderous equator to its line, and man and mote, and star and sun, must range to it or be pulverized by its recoil!"

The Orientals call this "Divine Justice" in nature—or the law of action and reaction—by the name of "karma."

Their doctrine of karma is simply this: every deed that you do, every word that you say, every thought that you think—goes into the world, gathers others of its kind and returns to you.

You are a part of everybody you meet—a part of everything you read—a part of everything you hear!

If you think evil thoughts concerning others, these thoughts will go out from you and become boomerangs, returning to you in the form of like hatred and persecution.

If you do someone a kindness you have laid up that much kindness to your account in the karmic bank.

It is there registered in *your name* and you have it coming to you; and if you do more than is required, you are automatically making compound deposits in the karmic bank which will and must be repaid to you.

THE CRACKER JACK TECHNIQUE

A principle that has been endorsed by so many philosophers, scientists, industrialists, and businessmen, giving more than bargained for, must have something to commend it.

Henry Ford used the principle of giving more value than was expected to build his vast fortune. He was the first to offer an automobile at low price.

He voluntarily raised the wages of his workers before they asked for it—and just recently Ford's grandson, Henry III, made headlines by voluntarily cutting Ford prices while most others in the industry were going sky high.

The Cracker Jack people made a fortune on ordinary popcorn by putting a prize in the bottom of the box.

It was something extra—something not planned at first, until now we seek out this particular popcorn because we know we will get "more for our money."

E. M. Statler built his chain of hotels on the principle of putting "extras" in the box. Howard Dugan, vice president, once told me guests don't expect to find their home-town papers under their door—to have coffee served when they are called in the morning.

R. B. White, president of the Baltimore and Ohio, tells me he follows this great principle on his trains. Just as soon as you get into the dining room, a free demitasse of coffee is given the passenger—something he didn't bargain for.

Bill Patterson, president of United Air Lines, began giving his passengers free meals aloft, something for nothing, that has built his great air line and has been put into practice now by all others.

The Tampa Terrace Hotel in Tampa gives free orange juice just outside the elevators every morning, as a surprise plus to all guests in the hotel, who now travel extra miles just for this swell morning surprise.

Hilton, in his hotels, will take your laundry and forward it on to you, as a plus service, for the man who must be in a different hotel every night.

The New Yorker Hotel sends up flowers to women guests, and most big hotels today give free baskets of fruit to important guests to make them feel "at home."

It is these little "extras," not planned on, that make big businesses out of little or ordinary businesses.

THE PLUS THAT COUNTS

As Bill Wyatt, sales representative of the Columbia Mills, Inc., world's largest manufacturer of window shades, tells me, "Successful salesmanship requires a *plus attitude*—you have to give your customers all they are entitled to in the deal, *plus* just a little more—you must also give your company a little more than their deal with you called for."

How true this is.

In any phase of life that *plus attitude* is what will bring you success.

In the office, in the home, the club—how much smoother everything would be if we would adopt this *plus attitude.*

If we just forget about "doing my share" and do all we can—go that second mile, we will gain more happiness for ourselves.

Instead of regarding marriage as a "50-50 proposition," regard it as 100 per cent for me alone—and you will find more contentment in living.

You'll get 100 per cent in return!

DON'T RATION SERVICE

Sears, Roebuck and Company is another firm that built a very successful business on the principle of putting something extra into the box.

Charlie Kelstadt, merchandising manager of Sears, tells me when they are out of a certain article a customer orders, they ask his permission to put in a similar article, often a better one and more expensive, but at no extra price to that customer.

Sears concentrates upon giving their customers something extra—extra service—extra consideration. They follow the same rule in regard to the people who work for them.

Employees receive a share of the profits of the business in addition to salary. All employees are allowed to purchase merchandise at a discount, and bonuses are given yearly to those who responded with extra effort.

Nichols Field Wilson, editor of *Adventures in Business,* has written a series of stories on business careers. In studying the lives of these leaders, Nichols tells me, "Of the hundreds of men whose inspirational stories have appeared in *Adventures in Business,* I have noticed that every single one, without exception, followed the principle of rendering a service to their fellow human beings.

"And not only in merely rendering the ordinary type of service that is expected—but it seems to be a trademark of successful men that they go *all out* in giving *more service* than is either expected or required."

I once heard Babe Ruth remark to some sports writers, "There is only a very little difference between champions and ordinary players."

There are plenty of good prize fighters who have the strength and fighting heart, and have mastered the mechanics of fighting; yet these men will never be champions. They have all that is required, except that extra something that the champion must have.

It is the same in the game of Life.

It is not enough to be good. It is not enough to be able to cook, work, build a home, make friends—not enough to do just what is required of you.

The world is filled with people who can do what is required; but the leader, the champion, does more. He puts in an *extra* something that raises him above the level.

So, if you want to get ahead, don't be satisfied with merely doing a "good job."

Do a "better job"!

To keep this principle uppermost in your mind when dealing with others, remember this Wheelergram:

JUST ENOUGH TO GET BY ISN'T ENOUGH TO GET AHEAD!

He who stops being better, stops being good!—OLIVER CROMWELL

CHAPTER 40

TWO LITTLE WORDS THAT PAID OFF IN BIG DIVIDENDS

A Short Short Story Number 10

WHEN JESUS healed ten lepers, only one returned to thank him!

Those other nine probably were grateful, only just thoughtless, so busy thinking about themselves.

Only too many of us at times are thoughtless, playing radios too late at night, honking horns early in the morning, smoking cigars in planes.

We aren't mean—just thoughtless.

Yet nothing pays off better in the business, or social world, than "thoughtfulness."

While working with Johns-Manville on some "sizzle selling" for their salesmen, Lewis Brown, president, told me how after World War I he landed in this country without a job.

To kill a little time between trains he went on a "visitor's tour" through Montgomery Ward's plant in Chicago. Of the thousands of people who took the tour yearly, only Lew Brown had thought to thank the man who had arranged the tour.

This executive was so pleased with Brown's thoughtful "thank you," that he hired Brown on the spot as a sort of "human relations" man to keep up the morale of workers.

Later, this executive went to Johns-Manville—and took with him the man who said "thank you." From these two little words Lew Brown rose to become Chairman of the Board!

ORIGIN OF WALDORF-ASTORIA

It is the little things we do that push us forward, or that hold us back in life. We work on our big plans. We make sure of them —but the little things, well, they are just too little to bother with.

The late George C. Bolt got his chance because of a little thing he did—a little thoughtfulness on his part.

He was a night clerk in a hotel. One night a man and woman came in. She was ill. The hotel was filled with a convention.

On hearing the story of the man and the woman, George Bolt gave up part of his own suite. Next day the husband said, "A man of your ability should be in charge of a really big hotel and I've decided to build one for you."

He was William Waldorf Astor!

LOOK AROUND YOU

Don't be thoughtful just because there is a chance someone may reward you with fame and fortune, for if you do you won't get either.

If thoughtfulness is a *habit,* and you can make it a habit, then it springs from the heart, not the calculating mind, and will register sincerely with others.

It changes you into a nicer, more charming person.

It develops in you a sense of consideration for others, and this is a sure way to get ahead in life.

"Serving the needs of others," is the great secret upon which all great fortunes have been built.

Right now—why not resolve to be more thoughtful?

Ask yourself, how can I be more thoughtful of the newsboy, the streetcar conductor, the people at the office, or in the store?

What little something can I do for the elevator man, the automobile mechanic, the neighbor, the wife, hubby, the kids?

However trifling, these little things such as "thank you" will make a deep impression on someone, and make his day more pleasant—and yours in reflection will be nicer.

"Great oaks from little acorns grow," says the proverb, and you saw how two little words paid off for Lew Brown, and thoughtfulness started George Bolt off as head of the famous Waldorf-Astoria!

Thoughtfulness *does* pay big dividends!

Turn "NO" around and it spells "ON"

WHEELERGRAMS TO GET ALONG WITH PEOPLE

No one is interested until you *make* them interested.
You only hate people you don't know or understand.
Tell the truth—the truth is good enough.
Boil it down—before it boils you over.
Use "prophylactic" words not "therapeutic" words.
Don't let your words end up on a one-way street.
Don't use April Fool words on people.

* * *

C.O.D. words seldom find people at home.
Don't point empty guns of threat.
General delivery words end up in the dead-letter box.
Don't send your words "collect."
Suggest—don't shove.
Leave people smiling—not frowning.
Listen "a little closer" to people's conversation.

CHAPTER 41

HOW TO HELP THE OTHER FELLOW TO BE RIGHT

A correct way to correct people. Wrong criticism can curdle the milk of human kindness. Give him a chance to save his face.

DR. EDGAR LUCAS, a Christian minister, once told of visiting a man who was in jail for safecracking.

Dr. Lucas asked the professional safecracker if his conscience didn't bother him when he stole money out of bank vaults.

"Why?" asked the safeblower.

"Don't you ever think of the poor people you rob?"

"Poor people don't have money in bank vaults."

"Well, don't you ever think of the rich people you rob? They have to work for their money too."

"But they don't lose anything. The bank makes it good for them."

"All the same the bank loses the money!"

"No—the bank is covered by insurance!"

"Well," said Dr. Lucas, growing exasperated, "you're a robber just the same. It doesn't matter whether you are stealing from the bank or the insurance company. It hurts one as much as the other."

"Oh, no," said the safecracker. "I don't do the insurance company any harm. I keep them in business. If it wasn't for fellows like me banks wouldn't spend money for insurance premiums. The insurance companies would be forced out of business. The investors would lose their money—and millions of people would be unemployed!"

Here was a man who had been sent up four times for safecracking. He readily admitted taking the money; but did he for a moment admit, even to himself, that he had been *wrong*?

Certainly not! He had it figured out very nicely so that he was in reality a public benefactor.

CRITICISM CAN CURDLE KINDNESS

No matter how *wrong* a person is he can usually convince himself that he is *right!*

This is what psychologists call "rationalization."

"We do what we *want* to do—then think up *reasons* for it afterward," someone has wisely said.

The reason we *rationalize* is because it deflates our ego to be *wrong.*

We "lose face" when we have to admit we are wrong—even to ourselves.

So, even in the face of cold-blooded facts to the contrary, we manage to make up excuses to ourselves and convince ourselves that we did right.

Remember this trait of human nature when you find you must correct another.

"You are wrong!" are words that lose friends.

Even if the other person is in a corner where you have backed him to drag out the facts to prove your case—you still haven't come out the winner.

Instead of thanking you for setting him straight—he'll hate you.

If people can't stand to criticize themselves and admit to themselves they are wrong, you can be sure they won't tolerate this indignity from another person.

Do not correct people at all—unless it is necessary.

When a friend is telling a joke and makes a mistake, there is really no need to correct him. It doesn't matter.

If someone mispronounces a word, don't correct him unless he is paying you as a tutor.

If someone says, "Well, as it says in the Bible 'Cleanliness is next to Godliness,' don't jump in and flaunt your knowledge and tell him it isn't in the Bible!

The only reason for correcting a person is to make yourself feel good—at his expense. You assume the superior role and assign him the inferior role. You deflate his ego to make him lose face!

WHEN NECESSARY TO CORRECT

There are times, of course, when it is necessary to correct people. If someone in your office is doing a job wrong—he must be set right.

If you are a wise boss you won't say, "Look here, Smith, you are doing this wrong!"

You'll get better work and co-operation out of Smith if you "help him to be right."

Try these Tested Rules for correcting people to get more co-operation—to make people "thirsty" to do things *your* way:

1. *Apologize for Him.*

   Make an excuse for him so he can *save his face.*

   In calling a mistake to the attention of another make him feel that there was a good and understandable reason for his doing it the wrong way.

   "Any fool should have known better," is the worst possible approach. Instead *win* him to your side and *help him be right* by saying:

   "Anybody might have made the same error."
   "I've made the same mistake myself."
   "It is easy to make such a mistake."
   "It is natural for anybody to suppose your way was right."
   "I should have explained that to you first."

2. *Praise before Criticizing.*

   My old boss on the Baltimore *News,* Erwin Huber, would always pat me on the back before he sent out a "kick" where I sit. Here are some of his word tricks:

   "You are usually right about everything, but . . ."
   "Men of executive ability like you usually make such errors . . ."
   "You are so careful about other things, what happened on this?"
   "When I was your age, I made similar mistakes . . ."

3. *Leave Them with a Good Taste!*
   When you *must* correct someone, do it in such a way that you will leave him with his retreat protected! With his ego intact.
   That is General MacArthur's principle today in handling the delicate Japanese situation.
   Leave people feeling good—instead of "little."
   Do not play up the seriousness of the error. Make it appear as trifling as you can, say, "Everybody makes that type of mistake at one time or another."
   You don't have to magnify the importance of the mistake in order to impress it upon a person's mind.

Give people an incentive for doing things right the *next time,* by using these four little sizzling words:

"I'm counting on you!"

How those four little words gain co-operation! How they can make people *want* to work and sweat for you!

"I'm counting on you!"

When we feel that the boss is *on our side* and "betting on us," we will work harder than ever to keep from letting him down.

"I'm counting on you!"

We have a good incentive for working hard and being careful when someone has faith in our ability, for someone has sold us on the idea that he has a *high opinion* of us.

"I'm counting on you!"

Everybody likes other people to have high opinions of them, so being human, they will work out their hearts to keep others from changing their opinion.

So to insure better performance in the future, give the person a *reputation* to live up to, and the best way I know is with four little words:

"I'M COUNTING ON YOU!!"

Don't Correct—HELP!

CHAPTER 42

DREAMS, NEEDS, AND NIGHTMARES THAT MAKE UP YOUR DAILY LIFE

Each person in life is governed by dreams, needs, and nightmares, and here is how you can put them to successful use for you.

DO YOU REMEMBER that popular song, "I'll Buy That Dream"? Well people *do* buy dreams!

If you want to be a smart salesman with people, you will make a study of people's dreams, not the fortune-telling kind, but the fortune-getting kind.

If you know how to handle dreams of people, you *can* make a fortune! For there are three things that govern our daily lives, "dreams," "needs," and "nightmares."

A $1,000,000 DREAM "SOLD"

Napoleon Hill tells how a dream was sold for one million dollars in *How to Sell Your Way Through Life* (The Ralston Society, Cleveland). A midwestern university needed a new building. A $1,000,000 building. The board of trustees wanted to solicit donations over a long period of time, but the president asked them to let him try his hand.

He picked out three men who could afford to give a million dollars. When he went to see the first man, he didn't go in the role of a *beggar*. He didn't tell him how badly the university needed the building. He didn't tell him what a wonderful thing it would be for young boys and girls. He proved himself a good *salesman* by telling this businessman what giving a million dollars would *mean to him*. He worked on the *you* angle; and when he called at the man's office he had something inside his box.

What he had was a dream!

"I've always admired the wonderful work your company has done in serving the people of the Midwest," he said, "and I have often thought there should be some sort of public monument to attest to your contribution.

"Now at last," he went on, "I am happy to say that I have found an opportunity for just such a monument. We can name the new building at the university for you.

"It will stand as a monument of your greatness. Future generations will admire it and remember you."

The university president painted a wonderful dream. Then he used another one of the Tested Techniques by not trying to "force feed" the idea down the businessman's throat.

Instead, he offered it temptingly—like a skillful fly caster placing his lure just out of reach of the trout!

Like the chef who walks through a dining room once an evening with a sizzling steak, tempting the nostrils of the newcomers!

HOW THIS WAS DONE

There was just one drawback, he explained to the businessman. The board of trustees wanted to give this great honor to another man. He named the man who was the fellow's most bitter rival.

"But," he added, "should you accept first and I could present your check for the million dollars tomorrow night at our meeting, I believe I could get them to agree upon you."

Then he left. He left the man with something to think about—a dream to ponder upon!

To dream of the glory of a monument bearing his name—attesting to his greatness for future generations!

The businessman liked that dream.

He phoned the president the next day and told him a check for *one million dollars* was waiting for him.

A dream "bought"!

WOOLWORTH BOUGHT A DREAM

Woolworth once said that six months before construction began on the famous Woolworth Building, tallest in the world at the time, that the idea had never entered his head.

He was talking to an ambitious young architect one day and the fellow said, "Mr. Woolworth, do you see that plot of ground over there? That is where I am going to build you the *tallest* building in the world."

That started Woolworth to daydreaming, building Castles in Spain, only he was building the *tallest* building, not in Spain, but the world of reality.

Six months later the construction was begun!

* * *

Overstreet, in his book, *Influencing Human Behavior,** says that the ability to induce *imagined experiences* in the minds of others is one of the most potent means of persuasion.

So go to work on the imagination of your prospect. Give him some fuel for his *daydreams*—his Castles in Spain.

* * *

Brass Hats aren't the only people to buy and sell dreams, for it applies to you and me in buying a car, a new home, a trip far away; we dream about someone we want to marry, the things we hope to accomplish.

Our Castles in Spain—our will-o'-the-wisp thoughts that flutter through our mind from childhood on to the grave.

Our thoughts ruminate from a new electric range that will permit us to stay downtown until the very last minute—to a new car that puts the top up and down by pressing a mere button.

We dream of the luxury of a new electric blanket, to a cottage by a stream; from a farm in Penfield, New York, to a ranch outside of Lubbock, Texas.

Learn these dreams of people!

MAKE PEOPLE IMPORTANT

You may not be a little jinni that can say abracadabra and cause a dream to puff true—but you can fulfill many a dream with modern methods and up to date merchandise.

* Harry Allen Overstreet, *Influencing Human Behavior* (New York: People's Institute Publishing Co., 1925).

The bookkeeper, the accountant, the soldier, the doctor, the undertaker, the boy and his girl—young people, old people—everybody would like *you* to make their dreams come true.

Dreams on how to become another Caesar, an Alexander—a Ford, an Eric Johnston—*power!*

Show them how to gain this *power!*

Women love fancy hats; shoes with buckles; spangles—they love to show off famous husbands to make other women envious—they love flattery.

Show men how to gain *power*—women how to feel *important!*

Be a modern jinni!

THE THINGS WE NEED

Once you have mastered people's dreams, then you must make a study of their "needs."

Their everyday necessities that keep people going, food, clothing, shelter, transportation, amusement to give them the vitamins of effort and energy.

These *needs* aren't often romantic. They are bread and butter and milk and eggs and front rooms and bath rooms and roofs and garages and back yards.

We need medicine—we need long underwear—we need rubbers—and we don't dream about such practical things, for they are *requisites* to keep us alive.

They are just as important to keep people interested in you and to make them friendly, as their dreams.

The *needs* of people can make you rich in money and people!

FILL THESE NEEDS

Show a man how he can make his old car do another year; how she can have her furs cleaned for another season.

Show the couple how they can have an annuity for their old age, to make their *dreams* come true.

The man needs food. He goes into a restaurant. He has always dreamed of lobster thermidor, or a steak three inches thick, but a hamburger will fulfill the hunger need just as well and fit his purse better.

We all want a new car—but the old one will do, if we can get it going with new tires and an overhaul.

Along comes a salesman who understands dreams and needs, and we give in to his "word magic."

As if he were some Arabian jinni!

Remember the "pleasure-pain principle." It works in dreamland just as in real life.

People will buy pleasant dreams to gain pleasure, to avoid pain.

People will also buy *needs* to gain pleasure, to avoid pain!

THEN COMES "NIGHTMARES"

Once you have mastered the art of catering to the *dreams* of others and their *needs,* then you are ready for factor three in getting action out of others, in winning them over to your way of thinking.

This is to play upon their *nightmares!*

The things that make people jump up in bed at night; that make them fight their pillows; that puts cold sweat on their brow whenever they think of a nightmare.

Nightmares drive us to make purchases, to cultivate friends.

We fear losing our home—so we buy a fire extinguisher—we fear the financial loss, so fortify ourselves with insurance, and then once more we can sleep again in pleasure.

We are all victims of some nightmare in our lives.

Find these nightmares in your customers, prospects, and in your friends, and help them dissolve that horrible nightmare.

You will become a greater success in life!

DISSOLVE THEIR "FEARS"

Show the man who fears an automobile accident that your "dream car," that he "needs," has nonbreakable glass that will not injure him in case of accident.

Show another couple who fear the poorhouse how your pla

will dissolve their fear, and make their dream come true by your plan which they need.

Children fear toothaches; dogs fear dark shadows and cats; and cats fear thunderstorms and dogs.

We all have fears.

Every time you dissolve a fear you make somebody happy, and in turn they try to make you happy.

Dissolving fears is a great way to make friendships!

President Roosevelt said a lot when he told us that all that we feared was fear itself—and how true this is.

Fear is a strong motivator—to make us do things!

"DREAMLINE" YOUR LIFE

The modern merchandise manager streamlines his products—and the modern friendmaker "dreamlines" your life.

Study dreams of people but don't stop there.

The real "dream merchant prince" manufactures dreams and delivers them custom-tailored!

If he finds someone without dreams, he cultivates a ready-made dream. That is what the midwestern university president did.

It is what the architect did for Woolworth.

Stir up the other fellow's imagination. Give him something to dream about.

The secret of manufacturing tailor-made dreams is not just to talk about your merchandise. You must use vivid words to stir their dream depths.

You make it as "real" as possible. You show them that what they thought was an impossible dream is not so impossible after all by doing it your way.

Be a "dream merchant"!

THE PERFECT COMBINATION

Thus you behold how our "dreams" and "needs" and "nightmares" are all interwoven throughout our lives, and that the humblest clerk or shrewdest psychologist must draw upon *all three!*

The perfect combination!

The combination of giving needs to peoples wrapped up in their dreams, that will immediately banish a nightmare.

The perfect combination!

The combination that will win more friends for you, make you more influential in your club, or among your neighbors.

The perfect combination!

Put this infallible combination to work for you. It will add to your life, make you happier!

Be a "dream merchant"!

"TACT" is not spelled "TACKY"

CHAPTER 43

TO GET AHEAD FASTER—TAKE OFF THE BRAKES

You can't sell yourself to others, if you don't relax, and here are some ways to relax yourself, and others.

YOU CAN MAKE yourself sick by just thinking!

You can get your entire body mechanism out of gear, have bad dreams, indigestion, and colon troubles, among a few things, merely by what you think.

Dr. P. C. Talkington, a psychiatrist from Dallas, Texas, recently told a conference of the Southern Clinical Society that modern man makes himself sick with the same bodily mechanism that saved the life of the primitive man.

When faced with danger the cave man's stomach stopped digesting food; his blood pressure went up; his heart beat faster; his adrenals poured out adrenalin into the blood; his muscles tensed.

His whole body mobilized for fight or flight.

Thus, because he did engage in muscular activity in fighting or flight, he was left with no "nervous tension."

"Consider modern man," said Dr. Talkington, "who must put up with the same sort of involuntary reactions. He does not fear for his life but he worries through the stresses and strains of everyday living—he is anxious. . . .

"Anxious about his business, his home, his social life, his religion. So his stomach churns with anxiety and his intestinal tract clamps down and pretty soon he develops pains that are quite real and he goes to his doctor."

The doctor's report goes on: "I have a physician friend who tells me that every time he begins to brood over his financial troubles he looks down the street and smiles. 'I know,' he tells me, 'that next cotton season I'll be getting seventeen paying patients from the Cotton Exchange with peptic ulcer out of that building.' "

TENSENESS AN AMERICAN CUSTOM

William James once said that the great American characteristic was tenseness, hurry, bustle. We are a nation of "doers." We feel that we must be "up and doing" every minute of the day.

According to James, most of us become overambitious and work against ourselves. It is fine to work while you work, but we should also observe the second admonition of the old proverb and learn to "play while you play."

Dr. Donald A. Laird calls this national characteristic of tenseness "Americanitis" and blames many of our modern ills upon it.

"A salesman," said Richard Grant, "like the storage battery in your car, is constantly discharging energy. Unless he is recharged at frequent intervals he soon runs dry. This is one of the greatest responsibilities of sales leadership."

What Grant says of the salesman is true of us all.

We need to stop now and then and "unbend the elbow"—to relax.

James says our very ambition to get ahead may hold us back unless we learn to relax. We develop tension in our muscles. We feel hurried and then more hurried.

We become overly anxious of results, and these serve to hold us back—rather than let us go ahead.

When we develop tension in mind and body we are applying the *brakes* to our thinking and to our muscles as well.

Working with the body tense is like driving an automobile with the brakes on!

So—take off the brakes!

* * *

Way back in the fifteenth century Criticon wrote: "A sage once reduced all virtue to the golden mean. Push right to the extreme and it becomes wrong; press all the juice from an orange and it becomes bitter. Even in enjoyment never go to extremes.

Thought too subtle is dull. If you milk a cow too much you draw blood, not milk!"

Moral: Don't overdo anything!

* * *

Here is what *relaxation* can do for you:

Just "resting" isn't necessarily relaxing. Tests have shown that some tense individuals never achieve relaxation of muscles even in sleep.

Few of us are able to relax completely without a period of learning and some practice.

The benefits to be derived from learning complete muscular relaxation and practice it daily sounds almost like magic. Dr. George Humphrey, of Queens University, Kingston, Canada, says that relaxation is one of the best "beauty treatments" that women can take.

It smooths the brow, brings tone to the skin, lessens wrinkles, gives a woman a soft, gentle look.

A woman always looks more beautiful to her husband when she is rested and relaxed.

He also states that relaxation may be used as a "love charm." He recommends this for husbands and wives who are growing apart—relaxation before divorce!

Dr. Rudolph S. Fried of Katonah, New York, has used this method to turn naughty children, as he calls them, into good children. He says: "It is impossible for a thoroughly relaxed person to become angry."

Various researches have shown that relaxation helps in the cure of stomach ulcers, high blood pressure, nervousness, insomnia and a host of other diseases.

Other researches have shown that workers perform more and better work when taught to "take it easy and relax."

That is the principle behind canned factory music!

USE WORD MAGIC TO RELAX

You can use words to relax away tension. Let me explain how these "magic words" work.

In the early days of our "Tested Selling" I worked with psychologists Knight Dunlap and Roy Dorcus of Johns Hopkins University, using a quartz string galvanometer, an instrument similar to the lie detector. It measures the emotional response of words and phrases.

In these tests I proved conclusively that when subjects heard certain words there was a positive effect on the physical body. Certain words made the heart beat faster. Others caused the breathing rhythm to change. Others altered perspiration.

"Fear" words caused the blood vessels to contract—which is the reason a person turns pale when frightened.

"Thrill" words affect the liver. Words suggesting flight, "run words," or patriotic music affect the feet.

I found that practically any part of the body could be affected by using appropriate words. I also found that certain words could bring about muscular tension in the body.

SO TRY "WORD MAGIC" RELAXATION

In just the same way that words can bring about these other reactions in the human body, it has also been proved by psychological tests that *words* can cause your muscles to relax.

Learning to relax by "word magic" is both easy and effective. There are three rules for using this method which you should be careful to obey:

1. Repeat the words over and over, without effort or will power, or without any thought of trying to "make it work." Just let the words themselves do all the work—which they will do if you will let them.
2. Say the words over in a monotonous, sing-song tone of voice.
3. Select a comfortable position in bed or chair and select a time and place where you will be quiet and undisturbed.

When you are sitting quietly with eyes closed, fold your hands in your lap.

Keep both feet flat on the floor.

Let go as much as possible and give yourself up to the chair, or bed, until you can feel it supporting your weight.

Let your attention go in turn to your feet, your legs, your torso, your arms, your neck and your facial muscles.

As you think of each group, let them go as much as possible and repeat *several times:*

> "My feet are so *relaxed* and so *limp!*" . . . "My legs are *so* relaxed and *so-o-* limp!" . . . "My arms are so . . ." etc.

Imagine your entire body is just a sack of grain and let it be heavy and limp.

Feel the bed, or chair, pushing up against your arms—your legs—your body—holding them up!

Then repeat in a low, monotonous, sing-song voice the following:

> "I am so very *comfortable.* So *comfortable* and *relaxed.* My arms are so *relaxed* and so *heavy.* My legs are so *relaxed* and so *heavy.* My whole body is very *relaxed* and so very *comfortable.* I just want to *rest* and *relax.*
>
> "All my muscles are *letting go.* My muscles are becoming more and more *limp* and *relaxed.* Every worry and every care has *flown away.*
>
> "Everything is so *calm* and *peaceful* and I just want to *rest.* It is so wonderful just to *let go* and *give up* completely to rest and relaxation.
>
> "Nothing matters now except *rest* . . . just *rest* and relaxation . . . so heavy . . . and so relaxed . . . my whole body is *so-o-o* heavy and oh *so-o-o* relaxed. My whole body is so . . . so . . . so . . . *h-e-a-v-y* and *r-e-l-a-x-e-d.* . . .
>
> "I am relaxing more . . . and more . . . and more . . . and . . ."

THE FORMULA WORKS

Keep this up for at least five or ten minutes. In fact, fifteen to twenty minutes are better.

If you find it convenient, speak the words out loud . . . otherwise, just think them.

Repeat them in a low voice, mumbling them over and over to yourself. Make no attempt to "concentrate" or to use will power.

Just let your mind wander as it will. The more you practice this exercise the easier it will become and the more relaxed you will become. After a week or so of regular practice you should be able to relax completely within two or three minutes.

Try this "word magic" method to relax and see how much better you feel . . . how much easier you will do your work.

Learning to relax will also increase the "free flow" of ideas. Our mind works smoother when the brakes are off.

So do as successful people do—*take off the brakes!*

Edison relaxed by stretching out and taking frequent short naps during the day. He often played parcheesi.

Napoleon, when tired, would take a nap for half an hour, even in the midst of a battle.

Churchill recharges himself by laying bricks; and FDR read detective stories.

RELAXING THE CUSTOMER

Nothing is a greater drawback to a salesman, which most of us are in life, than a tense nervous attitude when approaching others, our "customers."

The "salesman's" tension causes the customer to become tense and freeze up, and a tense customer is the most difficult of all people to convince.

Relax your customers by approaching them in a relaxed condition; a wife can't sell the idea of a fur coat when hubby is tense and worried.

Laughter is one of the best safety valves for letting loose tension. It often saved lives during the war.

Restudy our chapter on telling jokes, and practice this psychology to relax.

Smile. Be cheerful, and soon you will have the customer cheerful.

Relax before you plan your sale. If you work with your hands for a living—take time off now and then to read a book—solve a puzzle.

If you are a so-called brain worker take time off periodically to work with your hands, in the garden, for example, or golf. Go swimming.

When you take that Holiday, don't make it a Postman's Holiday—do something different. You'll come back to your selling job more refreshed.

RELAXATION AND SALESMANSHIP

The clever housewife gets her husband's pipe and slippers, before she sells him on a new dress. She relaxes him.

Psychologists will tell you people are more receptive to suggestion and persuasion when they are relaxed in body and mind, and good wives know this.

So do good salesmen.

The most powerful form of *persuasion* known to man is *hypnotism,* and all hynotists know that hypnosis is impossible as long as the person is tense. So they relax him.

Approach people after the dinner—not before it, and you will find them in their best relaxed mood.

Big companies spend huge sums entertaining prospective customers who are wined and dined before they are asked to buy.

This is not bribery, because few men would "sellout" for a steak dinner. The dinner serves a far different purpose. It *relaxes* the customer—and the seller, and they get on equal friendly terms.

The buyer with a full stomach can unbend better mentally to a seller's proposition.

We never argue and fight with people we "understand." It has often been said we will never fight a war with England because we understand each other, we have broken bread together across too many plates.

If our people could get to know the Russians better, there would never be any quarrel. We send over men to speak with the Russians. A banquet is the result—and everybody is happy.

More Russians should eat with more Americans!

GOLF COURSE SIZZLEMANSHIP

It is often said that more insurance is sold on golf courses than in office buildings or in homes. Smart insurance men know this.

Smart husbands—smart wives—smart mayors—smart neighbors, all know when people are at play they are in the best relaxed mood to absorb a new idea, or be sold a fur coat.

Joseph P. Day, often called the world's greatest real estate salesman, once told how he sold Judge E. H. Gary, head of the United States Steel Corporation.

Day invited Judge Gary to attend a baseball game. They each told how they had "baseball fingers." They held up their "bum" fingers and wiggled them at each other, each insisting that his was the worse.

At the moment Charles M. Schwab walked in:

"We must have looked like a couple of nuts," said Joseph Day, "standing there wiggling our fingers, but just the same I sold Judge Gary a five-million-dollar office building next week."

Baseball games relax some people!

Getting to know each other relaxes people.

In a large Eastern city recently a group of men, all living on the same street, decided to know each other better so they gave a back-yard barbecue. At first everybody was tense—then as they ate they warmed up.

Jews, Greeks, Irishmen, Englishmen—all relaxed, and enjoyed the company of each other. They became real "neighbors."

Governments might take notice!

TAKE A TIP—AND RELAX

Remember our chapter on Marco Polo and don't be "all business." Get to know the person you would do business with. Learn his interests. This is a great Latin trait in business.

When you approach people all keyed up and "strictly business," the other person puts up his best tense guard.

Learn the hobbies of people and use that hobby as your "approach." The other person immediately relaxes from his work to enjoy the hobby mentally.

A trick of old-time salesmen was to approach women on doorsteps and say, "I am not selling anything!" They did this to relax the alert housewife.

"You'll get a rug cleaned free, madam," was the Hoover Company approach, so the woman could sit down and relax while the salesman did the "work."

"I don't care whether you buy or not," says another salesman, so that the prospect can relax.

In conclusion, remember:

> To feel better and do better—be *relaxed!*
> To relax the other person and increase his "buyability" of what you have to offer—be *relaxed!*
> To get along better with friends and neighbors—and your family—*be relaxed!!*

The bow that's always bent will quickly break;
But if unstrung will serve you at your need.
So let the mind some relaxation take,
To come back to its task with fresher heed.—PHAEDRUS.

CHAPTER 44

SELLING YOURSELF TO CHILDREN AND SELLING CHILDREN ON "LIFE"

If you can get along with children, you make friends. Children "rule the home." Ask the comics editor!

ALL CHILDREN are at first little savages!

Now mother and father—don't throw this book at me, until I have a chance to explain.

Children know nothing of the niceties of civilization. They have only their animal instincts to guide them—the instinct of self-preservation—desire for food—emotional satisfaction.

We are all naturally selfish and antisocial when we are born. Civilization and civilized ways are something that must be taught.

The old-fashioned way was dictatorship pure and simple.

Children were *forced* to do certain things—forbidden to do certain things.

They were ruled by decree, and swift and severe punishment meted out for infractions was the order of the day. Dictatorship, though, as a way of life is no more acceptable today in children than it is in adults.

The child rebels and breaks out of the prison of "don'ts" that enslave him. He "kicks over the traces" and becomes a "wild youth."

All the natural expression that was frustrated comes out like steam that is let off a boiler where the pressure is too high. Or else the child meekly submits, his will is broken, and he is deprived of the very factors—self-reliance—determination—self-determination—which would have stood him in good stead in his fight for success in life.

REBEL OR CASPER MILQUETOAST?

Whether the child becomes a rebel or a Casper Milquetoast as the result of dictatorship—one or the other is most certain.

It is a good bet that the child raised under dictator-type parents will grow into adult life laden down with guilt complexes, repressed desires, and ripe material for a neurosis.

When the child is grown he may, if he has the inclination and money, employ the services of a psychiatrist and "unlearn" all the neurotic traits which he would never have had if his parents had been a little more human and understanding.

The "new-fashioned" way to raise children is to use no discipline whatsoever. "Let them express themselves" . . . "Let them develop in their own way." When Junior bashes a toy on his little sister's head the "new-fashioned" parent says, "Don't scold him. We mustn't inhibit him."

So Junior becomes a first class candidate for a teenage juvenile delinquent.

What should parents do—be the dictator and kill the child's ambition and self-reliance—plant the seeds of a neurosis—or take off the brakes and get the child set for a juvenile problem?

THERE'S A THIRD WAY

There is a third and better way; and wise psychiatrists and child counselors have pointed out how the child's primitive instincts may be curbed and guided into civilized channels of expression without the dangers of either the dictator- or the "hands-off" type of parent.

Sell the child on Life!

The wise way to mold the behavior of the child is the same principle of influencing the behavior of the adult: "Don't try to make him drink—make him thirsty!!"

The parent who used to turn Junior over his knee and say, "This is for your own good," had somewhat the right idea. Only he wasn't salesman enough to put the idea across.

He wasn't very convincing. Especially when he proceeded to lick the daylights out of little Junior.

There are, however, many ways that children can be convinced that a certain course of behavior is "for their own good."

Say: "You must go to bed so that you can get up early to play tomorrow morning."

Not: "Come on—time for all kids to get to bed!"

Use the "pleasure-pain" principle and show the child something *pleasant* in the task that you want done—or in the behavior that you desire.

Almost any behavior can be sold as "pleasant" to the child unless you deliberately teach him differently.

The *big secret* is never let him get the idea that going to bed, for example, is something to be dreaded. Never threaten the child with, "If you keep that up I'll put you to bed!" or, "If you are naughty you'll have to go to bed."

This is definitely teaching the child that bed is something to be dreaded. A jail for naughty kids!

DON'T ASK CHILD "IF"

"If" is a weak word in selling yourself to children as it is in selling products.

When training the very young child never ask "if" he is ready to go to bed, or eat, or go out and play, or something else. To do that is to invite trouble and argument.

Many mothers make unnecessary trouble simply by asking, "Will you let mother put some iodine on the scratch?" or, "Are you ready to eat lunch now?"

All such questions *suggest* an alternative to the child—the alternative of not doing what is asked, and being human it is only natural for the child to stand up for himself when he finds he has a choice in the matter.

If the very young child is simply taken to the table when it is time to eat, taken outside when it is time to play, and to bed at the same time every night, he never knows that there is any alternative.

He learns to accept these things as a matter of course. There is no battle of wills. No argument. He is simply "sold" on doing the correct thing. Later, when the child is older, his opinion may be asked; but by this time wholesome habits will already have established themselves.

THREATS ARE A "DARE"

One of the best ways to influence people is by the challenge or dare. When we "dare" a person to do something we arouse a powerful urge within him to do that very thing.

"I dare you—!" shouts a boy, and the old boy takes off his coat and jumps into a swimming hole to challenge the person who dared him.

This "dare plan" can be of valuable use when we want to get more work or co-operation from a child—or an adult. However, daring a person to do something we *don't* want done isn't very good strategy; yet note how many parents do just that!

"If you do that *one more time* I'll spank you!" shouts the mother, and this invites little Wilbur to dare his mother, and he does do it once more out of challenge.

"If I have to tell you *one more time* I'll take the candy away from you," says a parent, and of course the child does it one more time—and often throws the candy away in spite before his parent can do so.

Not: "If you are naughty, I won't take you to the movies!"

But: "Help mother, dear, so we will finish up in time for the movies!"

Don't dare children to stop being bad; dare them to be good!

GIVE 'EM GOOD ROLES TO PLAY

Children are as susceptible to suggestion as adults.

In fact, they are even more susceptible. The same rules for influencing people in our chapter, "Be a Smart Casting Director" work quite as well with children as adults.

Don't give the child a bad name. Don't give him a bad reputation to live down to!

Dr. Harry R. Lipton, a psychiatrist who has made many studies of child behavior, tells me, "The attitude that many parents take of expecting undesirable conduct and of inability to cope with it has a strong influence on children.

"Children," he goes on, "like adults frequently live up to the role expected of them. A child is very suggestible and if you think he has a bad temper and tell him about it he will likely think he is expected to show off and have a bad temper."

Don't ever say in front of your child, "Johnny is beyond me. I can't do a thing with him. Nothing seems to do any good." If you do, the chances are that Johnny will continue to be difficult to manage just to keep from disappointing you.

Like a great many other doctors, Dr. Lipton thinks that parents are really more of a problem than the children.

"Very frequently a child's temper is a reflection of the parent's temper," he says, "and many parents not infrequently lose their temper when their child misbehaves. Shouting at a child only irritates the child and has no value except to relieve the feelings of the parent. The progressive development of the parent is of paramount value for the development of the character of the child. Children are imitators. Be what you want your child to be!"

WHEN TO SPANK

Whipping a child merely because he annoys us or "gets on our nerves" or because he is obstinate or wants to "show who is boss," is not only unwise and unsuccessful—it is downright cruel.

It has always been a mystery to me why we will heap indignities and cruelties upon children that we would not dare employ with a perfect stranger.

When a person disagrees with us in business we would not dare slap his face. Yet, how many parents whip their children because they "answer back" or are "disrespectful" or are "impudent."

Nine times out of ten what we mean by the term "disrespectful" and "impudent" is that we resent the child having a mind of his own. We cannot suffer our own opinion to be questioned—by anyone small enough so that we can whip them and get away with it.

We should encourage the child to use his own mind rather than discourage it. If we are right we should have no difficulty explaining the case to the child.

When children are four or five years old, we can secure their co-operation by explaining the reason for a command, instead of issuing blind decrees. Children are human beings which is a fact we too often forget.

Like an adult the child resents doing a task that "doesn't make sense." Explain to the child when you give a command.

This is sound psychology—and will make the child like you better, and in liking you better, the adult parents will like you better. For a good way to make friends is to like the children.

Every door-to-door salesman knows this.

* * *

Most parents have no system for discipline at all. If the child breaks a vase today and the parent is in good mood—there is apt not to be any punishment. Tomorrow, however, if the parent didn't sleep well or had indigestion and the child breaks a vase, that child is apt to be whipped.

"Whenever we handle a problem of childhood according to the impulse of the moment we are apt to do so in a way that is erratic, inconsistent, and destructive of the morale of the child," speaks Dr. Lipton.

"Whenever our idea of good or bad behavior is determined by what annoys us and gets on our nerves, we are uselessly training the child to conform to our own life pattern," he continues.

Whipping a child because he annoys you is always stupid and never justified; but as to whether whipping is ever justified or not authorities differ.

* * *

Dr. Fritz Redl, professor of group work at Wayne University, Detroit, is an authority on problem children who says that whipping is never justified. "Physical punishment may get revenge for scratched dignity out of the parent's system," Dr. Redl told a Chicago *Daily News* reporter, "but will it change the child? . . . Physical punishment produces aggression. If you get hit you get mad. You increase aggression in a child at the most inopportune moment, the moment when you want to teach."

Dr. Redl thinks that physical punishment encourages the child to be bad.

He feels that his wrong is atoned by the whipping. He has "paid for" his bad behavior and is free to do it again.

"But when they are forced to accept the fact that you really like them, they get scared," Dr. Redl points out, "because then they have to feel guilty for what they have done."

As a substitute for physical punishment Dr. Redl recommends love, kindness, and a serious attempt to understand the child and why he wants to misbehave.

PAIN—THE DANGER SIGNAL

Dr. George A. Humphrey of Queens College, Canada, is one of the psychologists who believes that corporal punishment does have a definite place in teaching children good behavior.

Dr. Humphrey does not believe that spankings should be given in moments of anger or haphazardly, but that certain acts should be predetermined which are "taboo" and whenever such acts are committed, swift punishment should follow.

You should read his book, *The Story of Man's Mind.**

Dr. Humphrey explains that nature is inevitable, and makes no exception.

Running into a wall hurts the child, just as putting a finger on a stove burns him; so the child learns from natural laws what is good for him and what is not.

If sometimes running into the wall didn't hurt and sometimes

* George A. Humphrey, *The Story of Man's Mind* (New York: Dodd, Mead & Co., 1932).

putting his finger on a hot stove didn't burn, the child wouldn't learn his lessons in life early.

Nature, however, has given us that priceless *danger signal!*

CERTAINTY OF PUNISHMENT

Every officer of the law and every judge will tell you that it isn't the amount of punishment that he may get that worries a prospective crook, but the *certainty* of punishment.

Certainty worries him.

The same with a child. If he thinks he can get away sometimes by doing a wrong, he will take the chance.

So nature makes sure her *danger signals* are always giving out pain to those who disregard, and so we get to respect nature.

This same psychology should apply to the child. Make punishment *certain,* not just "now and then."

J. EDGAR HOOVER AGREES

J. Edgar Hoover agrees with Dr. Humphrey's "swift and painful punishment" plan.

He recently said that he believed much of our present juvenile delinquency was due to the present-day method of "sparing the rod."

It is not cruel to spank the child for playing in the street, for that is not punishment but protection.

Nature won't see the possible automobile, or she would have warned the child some way as she does when the child touches a hot fire.

Soon the child begins to expect punishment every time he runs into the street. Certainty!

Punishment for punishment's sake is not good. There must be justification.

The enlightened parent never "punishes" but "teaches."

The wise parent will be respected by the child rather than disliked for his discipline.

Henry Ford's advice on teaching children was:

"You can help your son most by helping him to discover, not by trying to force him to learn—both teachers and parents are too much inclined merely to show off their own knowledge."

That is not teaching, says Mr. Ford, for a good teacher is merely a good sign post—to guide him down the right paths of Life.

EVERY OAK WAS ONCE AN ACORN!

CHAPTER 45

WHY YOU SHOULD LEARN THE ART OF REMEMBERING NAMES

People like to hear their names spoken—which is why they have loud speakers in hotel lobbies, movies, and restaurants these days for calling names of people.

INDEED, the sweetest music this side of Heaven is the sound of your own name.

I like to hear my name spoken—don't you?

It fills me with a sense of ego, self-importance, and like hundreds of others I am willing to "pay off" liberally to hear my name spoken.

"We have your special beef dish today, Mr. Wheeler," says the alert waiter, and I am most flattered.

"Good morning, Mr. Wheeler," says a ticket agent, retail salesperson, hotel employee, and I make a special effort to give them my business.

"Aren't you Elmer Wheeler?" asks a perfect stranger in a depot, lobby, or on the street, and I stop as if touched by a magic wand, ready to give my very best attention.

I am HIGHLY complimented!

One day in west Texas I went into a barbershop I hadn't been in in some ten years. "Why, hello, Mr. Wheeler," said the barber.

"How come you remembered my name?" I asked, surprised, and the barber replied, "Remembering names adds three-thousand dollars a year to my income!"

That set me thinking. Here was an easy way for sales people, housewives, bankers, lawyers—anybody—to add dollars to their yearly income simply by remembering names.

My friend, Clarence Draggert, once told a low-selling salesman, "You are this much (*showing two fingers*) between earning the one hundred dollars a week I now pay you, and fifteen thousand dollars a year!"

The salesman, you see, had a poor memory for names. It caused him constant embarrassment—and lost sales!

This is too bad because you can remember names easily with just a few simple rules, and thus add dollars and friends to your life.

For people do "pay off" just to hear their names!

THE MAGIC OF ONE'S NAME

Andrew Carnegie named one of his steel mills the "Edgar Thompson" Steel Works. After that Thompson, president of the Pennsylvania Railroad, insisted that all rails should be purchased from *this* mill.

Duke, the tobacco king, agreed to endow a small college at Durham, North Carolina, with a fabulous sum if it would change its name to Duke.

Just take a look as you drive down any highway—notice the names of businesses you pass: Bill's Place, Joe's Cafe, John Smith and Sons—for you see, everybody likes to hear his name or see it written.

That is the *magic* of using people's names.

Don't say you can't remember names. It has been proved time and again that everyone has a good memory—if it is trained and used correctly.

Bernard Zufall had a very poor memory as a young man. But one day he read a magazine story about memory training and it captured his imagination. He began to train his memory. He got so good—he made it his hobby.

He memorized 20,000 articles in a General Electric Catalogue.

He could memorize a complete copy of the *Saturday Evening Post* in one hour's time. He even memorized the entire Bronx Telephone Directory of 1,174 pages. All you had to do was call off any person's name and Zufall could give you his phone number.

I have seen Bob Nutt, world's foremost memory expert, call off

100 names at a luncheon club; then have seen his wife get up and do the same thing to prove it is easy for anyone to learn the secret. (Read Robert H. Nutt's book.)*

You may not want to memorize the telephone directory; but you can learn quickly the names of people you meet—and this will be worth money in the bank.

So, for an easy method of remembering names, study the next chapter.

* Robert H. Nutt, *How to Remember Names and Faces* (New York: Simon & Schuster, 1941).

THEY PUT PEOPLE'S NAMES ON PULLMAN CARS!

CHAPTER 46

HOW TO REMEMBER NAMES

Three Wheelerpoints that will help. Get It–Repeat It–Associate It–that's all there is to remembering names!

"FORGOTTEN" is the most cruel word in the language.

It's an insult to the other person when we forget his name. It means that we do not consider him worth remembering.

A jeweler once used an advertisement of a broken-hearted wife sitting at home looking at the calendar–and just the words "He forgot." To forget hurts more than most anything we can do to another person.

You say you cannot remember names. But suppose I introduced you to a man and told you he was going to give you a million dollars or buy a million dollars' worth of insurance from you. Would you forget his name. No sir-e-e-e.

Even if his name was "Pfstchzorkem" you would get it right the first time. You'd not only remember his name–you'd have his telephone number and his address indelibly engraved in your memory for all time.

Why? Simply because you'd be *interested* enough to take a little time and trouble to remember the name.

A worker never forgets the time to quit. A man who carries the batting averages of two ball leagues in his head may complain because he cannot remember what his wife told him to buy at the grocer's.

He wasn't interested in grocers, but ball games!

WE FORGET ON PURPOSE

Sigmund Freud said we forget on purpose. I forgot my brief case because unconsciously I didn't want to go to work anyway. Someone gives us a tie we don't want to wear so we mislay it and forget where we put it. Forgetfulness is often a trick that our unconscious mind plays on us.

Forgetfulness helps us do the thing we really want to do.

So, before going any further in learning to remember names—make it a rule to get interested in other people. *Want* to remember their names and you've already improved your memory.

It has often been said, for example, that Jim Farley's ability to call thousands of people by their first names was responsible for his political success.

Samuel Gompers, the famous labor man, used to brag that he knew all his "boys" by their first names. His ability to call the workers by their first names was no doubt partly responsible for his influence in labor circles.

Once you've taken the first step by giving yourself an *incentive* to remember, use these three tested Wheelerpoints to help remember names.

THREE TESTED WHEELERPOINTS

Wheelerpoint 1: "Get The Name RIGHT!"

Only too often you fail to "hear" the name, you do not bother to ask the other person to repeat his name.

You keep on fumbling with the name, sliding over it, or just merely do not bother trying to get it correctly.

If you get the name RIGHT from the start, it is a thousand to one that you will NEVER forget it!

You won't be calling him Mr. Folz when his real name is Foltz.

You won't be embarrassing yourself and the other person, by calling her Mrs. Davies when her real name is Mrs. Davis.

The trick to use to catch the proper pronunciation and name of the other person at the *start* is to give *full attention* to the other person when he is being introduced, or when he tells you his name.

Don't let the mind wander to something else; don't divert your eyes. Look 'em square in the face. Get the *full force* of their name right smack in your ears!

See them say the name as well as HEAR it said!

Concentrate on the person being introduced. Listen to the name. Hear it. Hear it *clearly*. Hear it the *way* it is pronounced.

If you still fail to get it, save yourself later embarrassment by asking, "Would you mind repeating your name? I am sorry, but I didn't quite hear it!"

The other person is highly flattered to think you really *want* to get his name correctly. That, therefore, is Tested Rule 1 to the secret of remembering names and how to pronounce them correctly:

Get the name *right*—Right off the bat

Wheelerpoint 2: "REPEAT the Name!!"

Once you hear the name correctly, don't immediately set it aside to forget it.

Repeat the name.

Repeat it *once*. Then *twice*, then for good measure, repeat it the *third* time—and it is yours to remember for a long, long time.

Repeat it tactfully. Say, "I am pleased to meet you, Mr. Pickeltwister." Not, "Glad to know you."

Impress the name on your memory by using the name *several times*. Say, "Won't you step this way please, Mr. Pickeltwister." Not, "Please step this way, sir."

Then you might say, "What is your opinion, Mr. Pickeltwister?"

Pretty soon that name "Pickeltwister," which is a tongue twister, will be firmly worked into your memory muscles.

When you leave Mr. Pickeltwister don't say, "Hope to see you again, sir." But, "Hope to see you again *Mister Pickeltwister!!!*"

Sink that name into your memory! Repetition will do it!

Remember this second Tested Rule: *Make excuses to REPEAT the other person's name at least THREE TIMES!*

Wheelerpoint 3: "ASSOCIATE the Name!"

If you will at once associate a new name with something, you will have an easy time recalling it.

This is the third secret to remembering names of people.

The more unusual, out of the ordinary, or incongruous thing you associate the name with, the *longer* you will remember it.

For example, the minute you hear Mr. Pickeltwister you at once say to yourself, "Pickel—twister—a pickel twister in a pickel factory!"

Zingo! the name is socked into your memory muscles!

Miss Daisey comes in. She introduces herself. You say to yourself, "Miss Daisey—she loves, she loves me not, daisy—Miss Daisey!!"

The name clings!!

Mr. Jacobs is introduced. You think, "Ah, Jacob's ladder!" And so you will remember Mr. Jacobs because of Jacob's ladder.

You meet Miss Henrietta. You think "—an old hen—a hen on a chicken coop—Miss Henrietta!"

You see the more incongruous the mental picture, the more exaggerated the association, the *easier* it will return to your memory when you try to recall the name.

You won't have to stammer and stutter, hem and haw, when you meet somebody the second time; nor struggle to remember the name of somebody you met last night at the park.

These Three TESTED RULES will help you to remember names, and summed up here they are:

1. Get the Name *right!*
2. *Repeat* the Name!
3. *Associate* the Name!

PEOPLE LIKE THEIR NAMES

Waiters and hotel employees have always known the magic of bigger tips by remembering names, so also salespeople out on the road, or in retail stores, in show rooms, on front porches—everywhere!

People "pay off" to hear their names spoken.

Both Plato and Aristotle wrote that we believe by associating the new with something else in the mind. Modern psychologists agree with them. Association is the key to memory. And a psychoanalyst can even make you remember forgotten events of childhood by reviving your memories by "free association."

Louis Dorn became nationally famous when he was an information clerk for the White Motor Company because of his ability to remember 10,000 people by their first names. Dorn stated he was able to do this by forming an association between the person's name and some *peculiarity*.

"It may be from an odd way of pronouncing a word, or an odd droop of a shoulder or a way of walking, yet all of us have these peculiarities that make us individuals," said Dorn. Take the pains to hunt them out and you won't easily forget a man thereafter." *

Associate the name with the personality sizzle of its owner.

Mr. Moore is short. He needs about four inches *more* height.

Mr. Bushnell has bushy eyebrows. Mr. Bushnell hides behind a bush in the knell—he looks out with his bush eyebrows showing.

Mr. Patrick has big hands. It would be bad for Mr. *Pa*trick to pat you.

Mr. Herlihy has big broad shoulders. Mr. *Herl*ihy could really *hurl* a discus with those shoulders of his.

Remember people by their sizzles.

MAKE IT VISUAL

In associating names with personality sizzles—don't just repeat the words in your mind—conjure up mental pictures. You meet Mr. Ellis. Say to yourself, Mr. Ellis has a trellis—then in your mind's eye see Mr. Ellis standing before a huge trellis with roses blooming all around him.

He has a red nose. So this means he has pricked his nose on one of the thorns. The next time you think of the man you'll immediately remember this picture. You see the trellis—that reminds you of "Ellis."

Another good "trick," known to famous psychologists, is called "negative practice." Try *not* to think of something. Then you will. For example:

Try *not* to think of the word "abracadabra" while you finish this chapter! Try it!

ONE LAST METHOD

This is the Mark Twain method. Once you meet the other person and he is out of sight, mark the name down.

When you do it, though, give it the Mark Twain touch. He would sketch a crazy picture opposite some name or thing he wanted to recall.

* W. S. Dutton in an article in *American Magazine,* October, 1927.

For instance, you meet Mr. Angel from Iowa. You mark his name down, then sketch a silly picture of an angel on a corn-stalk.

Silly?

No—just another way to *fix* the name in your memory muscles.

Marshall Field kept a small pocket notebook in which to jot down things he wished to remember.

Lloyd George's biographer* relates that the great man "always carried with him a small pocketbook, in which he jotted down ideas and suggestions as they came to him in thought or talk."

You don't need to be a cartoonist. But writing things down is a sure-fire way to *impress* something deeply in your mind.

Like these other rules and methods, this one will add dollars to your bank book—and friends to your social book.

People, you see, "pay off" to hear their names.

* Harold Spender, *David Lloyd George* translated from the French by Robert L. Crue, New York, Geo. H. Doran, 1920.

Put People's Names in "LIGHTS"

CHAPTER 47

HOW TO REMEMBER "THINGS"

You can improve your memory in five minutes, if you will put the following into practice. You may have to read this chapter several times—but it will be profitable if you do.

NAPOLEON, who had a prodigious memory, said that he remembered things by filing them away in mental filing drawers in his mind. When he wanted to remember something all he had to do was pull out the right drawer and there it was.

In speaking to over 1,000,000 people a year I couldn't afford to forget. Using 3x5 cards or written text, as some speakers do, never appealed to me.

To memorize a speech word for word sounds too stilted and "canned."

So I worked out for myself ten "mental filing drawers" which I can use as effectively as 3x5 cards held in the hand. Before you finish reading this chapter I want to show you how easy it is to make this mental filing cabinet your own. It only takes five minutes.

YOUR MENTAL FILING CABINET

The "drawers" we are going to use in this mental filing cabinet will be words. Here are ten key words which you can use as "drawers" in which you want to file things to remember. Memorize these ten words in order, from one to ten. Notice how we've made this easy for you by the association involved.

Code word No. 1 is . . . *WAND* (Wand reminds you of the sound of "one.")
No. 2 is . . . *TUBE* (Tube sounds like "two.")
No. 3 is . . . *TREE* (Tree sounds like "three.")
No. 4 is . . . *DOOR* ("Shut the door" rhymes with "four.")

No. 5 is . . . *FAT MAN* (Mr. Five by Five)
No. 6 is . . . *DOCTOR* (Looks after the "sick" —six.)
No. 7 is . . . *DICE* (Seven come eleven)
No. 8 is . . . *AUTOMOBILE* (V-8)
No. 9 is . . . *BASEBALL GLOVE* (Nine men to the team.)
No. 10 is . . . *WOODEN INDIAN* (Ten little Indians.)

Go over these code words until you have no trouble calling them off. Be able to tell, for example, that "Code word No. 5" is "Fat man"; No. 9 is "Baseball glove." About three minutes is all you need to memorize these code words so that you can call them off forward or backward.

Now let's see how you can file things you want to remember in these code words. All you need to do is to associate something you want to remember with one of the code words. And because the code words are always in the same sequence, you can memorize objects or pointers for a speech of sales talk, in sequence.

Suppose your wife tells you to go to the store and buy eggs, bread, coffee, a head of cabbage, and some black pepper. Take the first thing—"eggs" and file it in your first "file drawer" or code word. See a magician producing an egg out of thin air with his magic *wand.*

No. 2 is bread. Form a mental picture of a large tube which squirts out loaves of bread when squeezed instead of tooth paste.

No. 3 is coffee. Picture a *tree* with packages of coffee hanging from the limbs.

No. 4 is cabbage. See a *door* with a huge cabbage for a door-knob.

No. 5 is black pepper. Make a mental picture of a *fat man* who snuffs pepper up his nose and sneezes so hard he blows the walls down.

IT'S DONE WITH PICTURES

Notice how easy it is to remember when you use *mental pictures* to associate the thing you want to remember with one of your code words. Make these pictures as ridiculous as possible. It helps to remember them.

When you get to the store all you do is pull out your first file drawer or code word which is *wand*. What do you see? That picture of the magician producing an egg with his wand immediately comes to mind.

Next you take No. 2 word which is *tube* and right away you see those loaves of bread coming out of the tube. You see how easy it is.

What was the third thing you were to get at the store? Your third code word is *tree*. What picture did you make with *tree*?

Doesn't the picture of a tree with coffee hanging from the limbs immediately pop in your mind?

You see you have already learned this easy memory system—and in less than five minutes.

REMEMBERING SELLING POINTS

How often the salesperson has said, "Oh, if I had only thought to tell her so and so, I'd not have lost the sale!"

Of course you can write each "point" down on a 3x5 card and keep pulling cards out of your coat pocket. But this way you fizzle.

Instead of writing your various points down on cards—just file them away in your brain with the system of code words.

For example, suppose you're selling electric shavers and you want to remember to emphasize three points: (1) "It gets the whiskers under the chin." (2) "It fits the hand." (3) "It's easier, no blades to change, no lathering the face."

One simple way of remembering selling points when you have only three or four is simply to associate each of the three points together with mental pictures. Just form a picture of a man with his *chin* resting in a huge hamlike *hand*. This ties "chin" to "hand" in your mind. Then tie "hand" to "blade" by seeing a man cutting his hand with a razor blade.

If you have more than three points to remember, however, it's best to use your regular code words.

Take word No. 1—*wand* and make a picture of a fairy touching

Andy Gump on the chin, causing this "chinless wonder" to grow a chin.

Then take code word No. 2—*tube* and make a picture of a tube of shaving cream that is so large the man can't get it in his hand—it doesn't "fit the hand."

Then comes code word No. 3—*tree.* Form a picture of a man trying to prune a tree with razor blades.

ADDITIONAL TIPS FOR REMEMBERING

Here are three easy Tested Memory Methods to remember your selling sizzles in what you sell:

1. *Make the Talk Logical.* Start at the top, go to the bottom, in logical order. Begin with the engineer, go to the front seat, then back seat—then the luggage compartment.
   If you skip from one end to another, soon you have lost yourself; so proceed in logical one, two, three order. It helps you to remember *all* your selling points.
2. *Say, "Point 1, Point 2, Point 3."* In this way you will eliminate the mistake of going from point one to point five or nine. You will then always *know* where you are in your sale.
   It also helps the other person to remember the selling sizzles, and in logical order, too. This makes him buy faster.
3. *Tell BIG Benefits FIRST.* Start off with your best selling features, then proceed to the next biggest, and so on down to the smallest feature.
   Then if you left out anything, or the customer had to cut you short, at least the *big sizzles* were told; so start off with your best *exclusive* sizzles.

HOW TO REMEMBER TO REMEMBER

Some people complain that they still can't remember things to do, even after they learned a memory system.

They forget to use the system. The night before they want to remember to do something the next morning—take the car down and have it greased. So they form a picture of the car being greased with Code word No. 1—*wand.*

But the next morning they forget to use the code word! What are you to do in cases like this?

Try waving red flags—putting up signals that will *make* you remember.

1. Put a string around your finger. Simple kid stuff? Yes —but it is so fundamental it works.
2. Put a piece of paper under your ring. Keep it there annoying you until you have done what you wanted to remember.
3. Throw a book or package of cigarettes on the floor. Don't pick them up until you have done what you planned.

If you want to remember to do something first thing in the morning, put one shoe on the chest of drawers. Tomorrow morning when you go to get your shoe—you'll ask yourself—"What in the world is my shoe doing up there?" That will *force* you to remember.

You want to remember to take something to the office with you. What is the *last* thing you do before leaving the house? Putting on your hat? Then your hat is the logical signal to make you remember.

Put whatever you want to take *in your hat.* If it's too big to go in your hat—place your hat on the floor. Its being in a strange place will remind you.

You want to remember to get something on the way home from the office. So what is the *last* thing you do before leaving the office? Whatever it is, use it as a *signal* to make you remember.

These are just a few "short-order tricks" to help jog your memory. They're silly, but they do work. And if you use them you need never face a friend, a customer, or a client with a red face and have to say, "I'm sorry—I just forgot."

"Remembering" Is Money in the Bank

CHAPTER 48

HOW TO "DRESS UP" YOUR PERSONALITY

All you have learned thus far will be of no avail in your life—selling yourself—unless you read this chapter, and put it into immediate effect!

IT IS AS important to know the art of dress to add to your personality, as it is to learn "personality tricks."

Your personality can be buried behind a wet blanket of slovenness—hidden by improper style—blacked out by a loud necktie!

If your clothes hit the eye of the other person before your personality, your chances of a success are nil!

When you enter a gathering, when you approach a group, when you make that first appearance, others should not "see" your clothes—but rather "feel" your taste.

When somebody asks, "What did she wear?" the other person should never say, "Wear—why she had a yellow dress and costume jewelry and shoes—why—!"

Much better to have that person's clothes described as, "Well, I didn't quite notice her dress—but it seemed rather expensive-looking—she . . . well . . . I believe she had a pin that looked rather—well she was nicely dressed."

Don't give people a chance to talk about you as a "clothes horse"!

If they saw the horse, chances are they didn't see *you!*

THE COVER OF BOOKS

Proper dress is important. You are as out of place mowing the lawn with a high-topped hat, as you are wearing a sweat shirt at the opera!

It is as important to know *when* to wear what—as it is to know *what* to wear!

The answer may lie in Lord Chesterfield's comment, *"Dress fine where others are fine, and plain, where others are plain."*

Your "appearance" is important—whether you are to "sell" yourself to a prospective employer or husband or friend or customer.

For, unfortunately, people form snap judgments of you based on "how you look."

People *do* form opinions by the cover of books! This is the reason smart publishers "dress up" the practical cover with an outside "jacket."

So the person who studies his "jacket" will have a better chance of immediate success at "first glance," than the person who fails to catch the eye of others at first introduction.

Study your "selling look"!

"KILLER" MILLER'S STORY

Manufacturers of canned goods know the value of "first impressions," the value of their "cover," their "outside look."

Tests have shown that the best made mousetraps won't sell wrapped up, for example, in brown paper—but when dolled up in colorful cellophane, they do sell.

Take the real-life story of "Killer" Miller, the man who has the reputation of "taking the bug out of Congress" after DDT was supposed to have failed.

His product was so effective it worked magic—that is, after it caught the eye of the public, but you will see it didn't go over for a long time due to the "cover."

When Killer first discovered his magic roach killer, he put the stuff up in fruit jars and pasted on homemade labels, and no one would buy the amateurish-looking killer.

He even offered $1,000 reward if it failed—still no sales for people had no confidence in the "homemade look" of the bug killer.

One day Killer met "Goldie," a charming and brainy woman and they were married. Shortly afterward she gave the product the name of "Jay-Gol," composed of the first three letters of their first names.

They hired a professional package man who redesigned the bug killer, and gave it a "look."

It sold—and as I said, Congress then invited Killer to try out "Jay-Gol" and it did a job that DDT didn't quite do!

So take a tip from Killer Miller's story. Watch *your* first impressions you make on others.

MAKE YOUR CLOTHES "YOU"

A suit hangs on a rack in a store. It lacks character—until it has been worn by you and has taken on your "look."

Then people will see it and remark, "Sure looks like John!"

You see it begins to form on your frame, take on your ways of wearing it, and soon becomes as much you, almost, as your personality.

That is why so many folks when their sons went to war hid the clothes of their soldier family, for to look at them was to "see" their son or husband.

Your clothes soon become you.

That is why it is so important to choose them right in the first place, so that you make your clothes adapt their "personalities" to you, rather than have them adapt you to their personality.

You lose your hat check. You tell the hat-check girl. She comes up with a hat and says, "This looks like it might be yours."

Instinctively, she has seen in the stray hat a "look" about it that reminds her of you.

Your clothes, you see, tell others you are rude, kind, unpolished, disorderly, sloven, bold, quiet, aggressive, prudish, a braggard, or a prim or cultured person.

So be sure to dress well—but not conspicuously!

MORAL EFFECT OF CLOTHES

Did you know your clothes can change your morale?

They can entirely change your feelings. For example, put on slacks and you will put your leg over the arm of a chair.

Put on a Tuxedo, and you want to sit straight!

"Give me a red handbag and a red hat," says the girl, "and I'll catch the eye of every man I meet."

Put on a ten-gallon hat and cowboy boots and by gosh you catch yourself saying, "Pardner" and "Howdy."

You go to a lodge meeting and don the fez and cape of your order, and suddenly the humdrum John Doe that you are vanishes!

You are now a mystic knight—and doggone, if you don't feel "mystic."

You can change your entire personality many times a day by merely changing your outfit.

Armies are dressed alike—to make them think and act alike—so are prisoners of war dressed alike.

If armies and prisoners were permitted to dress individually, they would act individually and cease to become a co-ordinated unit that could be easily directed and controlled.

Clothes do have a direct moral effect on your soul.

Careless in dress—careless in manners. That is why we let our "back hair down" when we want to relax and take things easy.

Careful in dress—careful in manners and thinking!

A HAT "CURES" NERVES

Did you know that clothes can cure many ailments?

Many a doctor has cured simple ailments of the body by merely recommending a change of locale.

In fact, I know one clever doctor, Dr. F. R. Copeland of the Medical Arts Building in Dallas who has cured many a so-called case of "nerves" in women by hats.

He simply recommends they go out and buy a new hat!

This simple solution to their problems, of course, isn't very remunerative to the doctor, but it certainly works miracles on nerves.

If you want to give yourself a quick uplift, a new tone of self-confidence, a moral shot in the arm—buy a new hat, necktie, suit.

Nothing helps dress up your ego as much as new clothes.

Right away your step becomes livelier, you want to go places and do things—for the garments are as vitamins; only they work faster!

Your whole attitude in life changes when you put on a new outfit, hats, shirts, neckties, dress, suit, or merely an accessory or two.

A new style in hair do, a fresh shave, just a new shoeshine—and away you go!

That is why the armed forces, in all countries, insist on so many inspections. Somehow a soldier gets a "lift" every time he steps out with shoes shined, suit brushed, and buttons polished.

He may not like doing it—but he likes the results.

So millions of hours are spent by the armies of the world on personal appearance.

How many hours—or minutes, maybe—do you spend?

TIPS ON DRESSING

Walter Hickey, of Hickey Freeman Company, has a few good pointers on how to dress, and to maintain your dress.

In a lecture before the Rochester Sales Manager's Club he once said:

1. Don't leave heavy or bulky objects in the pockets when hanging up your clothes.
2. Brush often—because dirt and grit reduces wearing qualities if allowed to penetrate the fabric.
3. Remove stains promptly—to defeat moths.
4. Patronize *only* reliable dry cleaners—as they add years to the life of garments.
5. Build a wardrobe to take care of all your needs—have many changes—to give a good impression and because clothes allowed to hang for a few days give the weave a chance to reset and this cuts down on ironing or pressing continually.
6. When not in use, keep your clothes neatly centered on a hanger—preferably a shaped or slightly curved hanger made of substantial material. This will aid the garment in regaining its shape from wearing.

TRICKS IN BUYING CLOTHES

Before writing this near-the-last chapter, I asked a number of leaders in the field of women and men's clothing on pointers in proper dressing to accentuate personality and help sell yourself. The replies—all the way from the Tobé Coburn Fashion School in New York to the makers of shoe polish—are too numerous to enclose here, but for a quick summary:

> A man selling movie productions can be less restrained than a salesman in New England selling investments.
>
> For longest wear, get gabardines, sturdy worsteds, or twisted cloths.
>
> Flannels, soft tweeds, fleeces are fine luxury materials, short-lived but fine-wearing as to "feel."
>
> Pick dress and suit materials to match your hair, eyes, or complexion.
>
> Padded shoulders give height; belts divide the height.
>
> Up-and-down stripes slenderize—cross stripes, of course, cut height.
>
> Long pointed collars are best for broad faces; wide points for slender faces.
>
> Full faces take a pointed, thin bow tie; thin faces can take the square-end wide bow tie.
>
> Dark colors are always less a gamble in footwear than lighter colors or tones.

Harry Rolnick, hat designer and manufacturer of Resistol wear, in speaking on hats advises:

> A tall slender man should choose a hat with a medium-low crown.
>
> A short slender man will look best with a tapered crown pinched high in front.
>
> Tall stout men need a full-crown hat with no taper, although a full-snapped brim.

> The short stout person needs a hat tapered to add slenderness—with an up-roll brim such as a Homburg.

This same "styling," points out Mr. Rolnick, applies, of course, to women's hats.

Short women need hats that flare upwards—tall women can wear them either way but both should avoid extremes in brim and crown proportions.

YOUR FOOTWEAR AND NECKTIES

The shoe manufacturers and stylists advise conservatism in shoes, and shoes that "fit the occasion."

Wing tips for dress; brogues for travel or work; moccasin lasts for comfort and sports.

Bright "yaller" is out in shoes—subdued tones of browns or blacks blend with your outfit best of all.

But—*Be sure your shoes are always shined!*

Shoes unshined seem to dim your cheerfulness—subdue your personality.

As the shoe manufacturers and polish men point out: a bright shine brightens a dull soul!

Arrow Shirts has an interesting booklet on how to make your ties last longer. In part it reads:

1. Don't yank a tie off—untie it by reversing the tying process.
2. Change neckware daily to give your tie—and your friends—a chance to relax.
3. Hang ties so they can drape back into shape.
4. Remove spots before they get a chance to sink into the material.

A LAST WORD OF ADVICE

As I explained you have read the boiled-down ideas of the best stylists and manufacturers in the women and men's wear business.

One warning they all give: *Don't overdress!*

Don't be a clothes horse.

As Bulwer put it, "A gentleman (or gentle woman's) taste in dress is, upon principle, the avoidance of all things extravagant."

Socrates said it another way: "Nothing in excess!"

Fancy, loud, outlandish clothes advertise you as a person who isn't quite sure of himself.

Loud clothes are naturals for adolescents—but only those with inferiority complexes try to make up for their feeling of inadequacy *inside* them by piling on plenty of adornment on the *outside!*

By this I don't mean dress in serges and white shirts and dark ties—or dresses that are overly plain and drab—but don't go the other extreme and be a clothes horse.

Dressing properly consists in a quiet simplicity of neatness—but the neatness of good tailoring well-executed.

Don't skimp on clothes. One expensively tailored item once a year is worth five mediocre outfits.

And in conclusion let me remind you of what William Shakespeare said which proved him a keen student of human nature, an outstanding salesman as Walter Hickey calls him.

In *Hamlet* we find Polonius advises his son, Laertes:

> *Costly thy habit, as thy purse can buy*
> *But not express'd in fancy; rich, not gaudy;*
> *For the apparel oft proclaims the man!*

Fancy Clothes Like Fancy Words Self-Attract!

CHAPTER 49

WHEN TO THROW THIS BOOK OUT THE WINDOW

The time to "stand up for yourself." Often the breaking of the rules serves a good purpose. Anger has its place.

DOUBTLESS MANY PEOPLE will regard this chapter as "heresy" because I am going to tell you "how to get mad," in a book on "how to get along with people."

There are exceptions to the rules, of course, and times when legitimate anger is justifiable in getting along with people.

Most of the time when you get hot under the collar you are merely putting yourself into the other person's hands. The good lawyer knows, "Whom the gods would destroy they first make mad."

As a rule the person who remains calm and poised is the person who commands the situation.

There are times, though, when controlled anger can be a most powerful and ethical instrument for influencing people to your way of thinking.

FAMOUS "ANGRY" MEN

Abraham Lincoln, for example, was known for his forebearance and patience, yet once threw a visitor bodily from his office.

General George C. Marshall is known for his "best dispositioned" mannerisms by diplomats, but in an article in *Look* Magazine his wife stated he could unleash a temper which would make strong men quake in their boots.

Jesus, the world's greatest teacher of brotherly love and getting along with others by doing good, drove the money-changers out of the temple at the point of a whip.

Eddie Rickenbacker, of the "sunny disposition," when he is

convinced someone is deliberately and maliciously trying to put something over on him, knows "how to get mad."

There are, you see, times to "get mad." On occasions "righteous wrath" is one of the most powerful instruments for influencing human behavior.

HOW TO "GET ANGRY"

The first lesson to be learned in using anger is to use it sparingly.

A recent survey showed that you cannot bluff successfully more than 6 per cent of the time in poker.

Bluffing oftener than that becomes useless. The percentage for effectively using anger is much less, probably in neighborhood of ½ of one per cent.

The person who "continually blows his top" has no power in influencing others—except to his own disadvantage.

When you point your gun at somebody, make sure it is loaded. Don't aim empty guns—too often!

A second rule for using anger is to be sure that the occasion is one which cannot be solved by other means.

We are not justified in "getting mad" just because the other fellow loses his temper; but we are justified in getting angry when someone is obviously out to impose upon our good nature.

FRANK DAVIS'S STORY

It is reported that General Pershing once lit a cigarette at night near the front lines only to have a private tell him to douse "that damn light."

When the private saw whom he had spoken to, he tried to mumble an apology but Pershing stopped him, "Just be glad I'm not a second lieutenant," he said.

Yet this same General Pershing, who was too big to become offended by the rebuff of a private, had no inhibitions at all about "laying low" anyone, regardless of rank or station, who he felt was deliberately in the wrong or who was trying to impose upon him.

Webb and Morgan, the noted authors of *Strategy in Handling People,** tell how Frank Davis, an insurance salesman, used anger effectively.

"I can't talk standing up," said Davis of an executive who had kept him waiting too long. "I have a definite appointment with you."

The executive blinked a moment, then lost his "front," held out his hand and invited Davis inside to talk things over. Davis made a sale three minutes later.

Anger here was justifiable. Davis used it sparingly, and made it work for him—not against him.

ANGER A POWERFUL MOTIVATOR

The strongest men quail before genuine "righteous wrath." It puts us on the defensive. It takes the fight out of us.

I saw a flashy car drive quietly up to a woman, the other day, and let out a blast on the horn, scaring the poor woman half to death.

A small, gray-haired man in his seventies walked up to the motorist, a huge 240-pounder, and laid the fellow low in strong language.

The big fellow wilted and made no move to "answer back." He was overpowered by the legitimate wrath of the old man—a most striking example of the power of anger in putting an overbearing person on the defensive.

Anger is a big motivator—but so is dynamite. Both must be used with caution. Sometimes, however, the most effective method of cutting through apathy, red tape, laziness, or just plain cussedness is to *get damn mad!*

Use anger sparingly—use it *wisely*—make sure that no other way can be used to solve the problem before you.

* Erving T. Webb and John B. Morgan, *Strategy in Handling People* (Garden City: Garden City Publishing Company, 1930).

FIRE CHIEF BROSNAN

Fire Chief Dennis Brosnan of Albany, Georgia, is known as the "World's Champion Fire Chief" because of his perfect 37-year record in not having a person killed or injured in a fire—and because the fire loss per capita in Albany is the lowest in the United States.

To accomplish this Brosnan had to know when "to get tough" as well as when to make friends. He is known for his patience and tolerance. He never bullies his men.

Once a city politician told Chief Brosnan it would cost too much to install a sprinkler system in his business. "Overlook it just this once," he asked of the chief.

"If you know which side your political bread is buttered on you'll learn to overlook it," the politician shot back when Brosnan shook his head "No."

Now the chief could compromise with the politician, or "get tough." The time to get tough was here. "In that case," he said, "I suppose I'll have to arrest you for wilful violation of the building code."

The politician saw Brosnan meant business, and quickly assented to install the necessary fire-prevention equipment. Brosnan, incidentally, didn't lose his job.

BEST WAYS TO USE ANGER

General Allenby, the famous World War I general, failed to get his supplies because his superiors felt he was asking for too much.

Did the general continue to plead for supplies? No—he was beyond further pleading so wired his superior that he had pitched camp and did not intend to move "one damn inch" until his supplies arrived. They did.

James O'Donnell Bennett in *Liberty* Magazine tells how when young Lieutenant Colonel Dawes was asked, in all British military mightiness where General Pershing was, and why he wasn't on hand in person, how Dawes flung back:

"I am here to represent General Pershing—and here with all his power, God damn you!!"

When you meet with an overbearing, pompous person who is obviously bent upon imposing upon you, don't lie down. If you do, he will make a door mat of you.

You cannot afford to offer a compromise for he will consider it a sign of weakness and will attempt to impose upon you all the more.

There is just one thing left to do: *Get mad!*

USE ANGER ON YOURSELF

The best way to use anger is not on others, but on yourself. Just as it is the most powerful motivator in influencing others' behavior, you can harness it and make it a powerful influence in getting things done yourself.

Many a man has risen to the heights spurred on by anger.

Clarence Darrow might have remained a small-town lawyer if he had not "got mad" at the remark of his landlady. Darrow wanted to buy the house, pay $500 down and sign notes for $3,500.

"I doubt if you'll ever make $3,500 in your whole life," scoffed the landlady.

This remark so stung Darrow that he determined he would "show her," and it so spurred his energy and ambition that he became the successful lawyer that he was.

I doubt very much if I would ever have become a public speaker had not a college professor told me that I was "too dumb" to ever speak in public.

This made me mad. It made me forget my fears of an audience. "I would show that professor," I said, and I did.

John D. Murphy, the writer, once had an article of his read out loud in a schoolroom, then torn up in front of his eyes by the teacher who said, "You'd better spend your time studying something worth-while—what makes you think you could ever write?"

Murphy tells me that up to then he never really wanted to write, but that he became so enraged he determined to write for publications or bust; and his articles since have appeared in over forty national magazines.

Make anger work for, not against, you!

ANGER OFTEN PAYS OFF

Then there is Howard Hughes who got mad and talked back to a Senate committee investigating him, and won out.

Dawes also put a Senate investigating committee on the defensive when he was called upon to testify regarding expenditures during World War I.

"Sure we paid," he shouted. "We didn't dicker. Why man alive, we had to win the war. We would have paid horse prices for sheep if sheep could have pulled the artillery to the front. . . . Hell and Maria, we weren't trying to keep a set of books, we were trying to win the war!!"

A plain, unqualified and firm "NO" at the outset can keep down much unnecessary argument when you cannot afford to compromise!

Nuisance can be a powerful factor, too, in getting what you want providing you don't overwork it—and have tried all other means first.

The baby gets what he wants by making a nuisance of himself. The office worker who "raises cain" is apt to get a new desk quicker than one who won't stand up for her rights.

Many people give in to others for fear they will raise their voice, kick up a fuss, or go into a tantrum.

Hitler used this nuisance technique to perfection. He would storm and rant, stamp his feet on the floor, pound the desk, pull his hair, and go into a wild rage when anyone opposed him.

So few people wanted to oppose him, and start him off.

Napoleon also used this same technique time and time again to get his way at conferences.

Personally, I don't think too much of this system, any more

than I like the idea of using a baseball bat on people—yet both methods *do* work!

There are salesmen who actually sell things by making a complete nuisance of themselves. You buy often to keep them from pestering you any further.

This is not good sizzlemanship—yet, it, too, works!

Labor unions use the nuisance technique—strikes!

So you see there are times to throw this book out of the window; when anger serves its full purpose.

It is not well to use this technique continually as did Hitler and Napoleon, for the good reason—see what happened to them!

However, when people are really taking advantage of you; when they are strutting pomp all around you—then it is often effective to "let off steam."

First, though, use anger sparingly—and make sure no other way will work.

If you do this, then I say anger has its place and then is the time to win people over by tossing this book out of the window.

A LEADER IS ONE WHO HAS FOLLOWERS

CHAPTER 50

THE SECRET INGREDIENT

Editor's Note: *This chapter was written for* Kiwanis Magazine *in September of 1946. It has been reprinted so many times it is almost classical. Wisely, Elmer Wheeler concludes his book with this timely advice.*

ALL OF US authors and lecturers have magic formulas to help you make friends or sales; but just try to use them yourself!

What happens?

You say, "Guess I can't do what that fellow advises. He made it sound so easy, too!"

You read a book on how to cook, build a sailboat, write a play, sell an automobile, play golf—get along with people—but you never seem to be quite as successful as the three-colored picture in the book.

You learn someone's tested formula on public speaking; on making people like you; on being the "life of any party"; yet, you find the stuff doesn't work when you try it as the book said.

WHAT'S WRONG?

It is like the farmer who bought the book on growing tomatoes, and wrote the publisher, "The man who writ the ad shoulda writ the book."

What is wrong with all these formulas, from winning a wife to growing tomatoes; from reducing to getting a raise from the boss?

Nothing is wrong with the formulas!

They just lacked one secret ingredient—*proper timing!*

That is the *secret ingredient* of getting a job, a promotion, a sweetheart, or baking a cake and planting a garden, or making someone propose.

Proper timing—without which nothing succeeds!

SMILE—BUT TIME IT!

"Smile when you first meet people," says the formula on how to win friends.

"Keep your eye on the ball," says the golf pro.

"Add a soupçon of garlic," advises the cooking expert from New Orleans.

(Elmer Wheeler says: "Don't Sell the Steak—Sell the Sizzle," in his advice to salespeople.)

All are sound formulas, many times tested. All are proven, and the creators or inventors back up their formulas with many testimonials!

But if you don't *time their use,* they won't work!

The book says "smile" but you timed it wrong, and somebody thought, "What's that fellow grinning about like a cat filled with gold fish?"

Improper timing makes you look silly!

THE CHOCOLATE BAR

A little boy one Sunday wanted a chocolate bar. Pop was smoking in his easy chair, reading the comics.

The boy, from experience, knew that if he asked his pop for a chocolate bar, the father would avoid having to disrupt his reading and walk to the corner store, but would reply:

"Son, not before dinner!"

So the tactful son said, "Pop, mind putting my bicycle out on the porch?"

It wasn't far from the chair to the porch, so pop obliged, and no sooner was the bike on the porch when son said:

"Pop, mind putting it on the sidewalk—the sun is so nice?"

The sidewalk now wasn't too far from the porch, so pop again obliged.

Immediately, the son jumped on his bike and said, "Pop, push me to the corner—and get yourself a Sunday cigar!"

Swell idea! Pop and son went to the corner store, and *after* the father had purchased himself a cigar, sonny said:

"Mind buying me a chocolate bar, pop!"

I ask you, could pop refuse!

WORKS ON EVERYBODY

Try proper timing on wife, on husband, on the boss, on the prospect. Time what you have to say.

Time the favors you are asking.

Time your requests for a new fur coat, a raise, a trip to New York.

It works on everybody, from the mayor down to the plumber; from the police down to the street's bad boy.

Proper timing works magic on them all!

The *secret ingredient,* you see, of making rules and formulas work for you is: *proper timing!*

To everything there is a season, and a time to every purpose under heaven. ECCLESIASTES, 3:11.